Future

Anterior

Future Anterior
Volume XVIII, Number 1
Summer 2021

Retrofit: Energy Crises and
Climate Exigencies from
Preservation's Perspective

Designing the Future of Preservation

Although "'Reduce, Reuse, Recycle" has served as a catchy public education tool for American environmental activists in the recent past, adaptation of the built environment to the challenges of climate change has deeper, broader roots. Even recent efforts to reduce new construction, reuse existing building stock, and recycle materials follow decades of considering the environmental stressors and material metabolism of the built environment. As conceptualized and practiced globally in accordance with diverse disciplines, politics, cultures, and resources, "retrofit" registers historical and contemporary responsiveness to unsustainable building conventions and endangered built environments. "Retrofit," however, can carry many meanings: to mitigate weathering, abate decay, reduce waste, limit emissions, extend livability, redress inefficiency, and even to contest colonialism, claw-back indigeneity, and materialize local ingenuity. This issue of *Future Anterior* offers research on the pluriverse of adaptive practices, conservation theories, and mitigation methods that have transformed the pedagogies and praxis of preservation.

Only a few decades ago, preservation's leading academic, cultural, philanthropic, and governmental sponsors treated environmental design and hazard mitigation as marginal to their mandate to redesign built environments for the future. Today, research of *retrofits* sprawls across preservation's fields of inquiry and intervention—architecture, planning, and engineering as well as history, archaeology, anthropology, geography, and the material sciences.[1] Such expansiveness yields discontinuity, disconnectedness, and dissonance between critical discourses on building form and performance, land use and utilization, infrastructure integrity, and investment. Nonetheless, scholars, educators, and practitioners have organized and ordained responses to energy and climate crises.[2] Revised building regulations, design pedagogies, construction specifications plus planning prescriptions, policy recommendations, and legal briefs in multiple spoken and spatial languages reflect investigation and collaboration at multiple scales (i.e., interior spaces, singular structures, building complexes, planned unit developments, neighborhoods, and cities) by a multitude of actors.[3] Who, currently and historically, convenes such collective thought and action on energy and climate exigencies? What is the value of knowledge and networks built?

Future Anterior
Volume XVIII, Number 1
Summer 2021

Where and how can or has the value been measured, seen, and demonstrated?

Contributors to this issue, who hail from a half-dozen disciplines and conduct research on three different continents, reflected on these questions, researched relevant cases, and reviewed instructive publications. Each engages with ongoing research that treats retrofitting the built environment as a professional exercise, an industry practice, an investment thesis, a public policy, a social enterprise, a tactic of activists, and/or a subaltern intervention. Together, they explore what it means for jurors of the world's foremost honor for architects to award the 2021 Pritzker Prize to Anne Lacaton and Jean-Phillipe Vassal, French architects committed to making existing structures — single-family dwellings to social housing — livable, longer. The takeaway of these explorations is generative not conclusive: adaptation of venerated and vernacular architecture to current and future environmental conditions renders designers of change vital. What's a preservationist's place in a future of change to buildings, landscapes, and artifacts that make up World Heritage sites, national registers of historic places, cultural heritage trusts, and local historic districts? Explained further below, recent reports and reporting on retrofitting practices and practitioners suggest a viable if not venerable path forward for preservationists' inquiries and interventions in climate change and energy transitions.

The mere fact that centuries-old heritage still stands, serves communities, and showcases culture across the globe suggests somebody — or rather some bodies of governance, finance, or resources management — long ago considered how to retain and reuse them for profit if not posterity. Although diverse individuals and institutions have made material changes to tangible heritage, periodicals and pedagogies concerning the built environment primarily chronicle how designers optimize buildings and landscapes for changing ecology, energy, and economics. In these forums, architects of resilience largely envision and evaluate adaptation and mitigation even though engineers, planners, scientists, and archivists also design systems and structures that preserve the integrity and authenticity of historic structures and infrastructure undergoing reuse and reconfiguration.[4] Moreover, first-person narratives of retrofit and dialogue on reclamation that appear in architectural media, syllabi, webinars, and reports tend to elevate the built works of well-known predecessors and peers known to the authors, and in many cases, erase the work of subcontractors, laborers, and even the local architect of record.[5] Thus, written histories and forward-looking plans abound for residences and housing designed by once-esteemed modernists (e.g., Le Corbusier), still-revered colonialists (e.g., Daniel Burnham), and often-forgotten socialists.[6] Meanwhile, designers underrepresented in architectural media and education—such as licensed architects of color who meet the U.S. Secretary of the Interior's Qualifications for a "historic architect"—apply for and await monetary awards to fund documentation, publication, and dissemination of their rehabilitation research and its applications.[7]

Three sets of stakeholders in preservation support learning from and research about a wider range of retrofit adherents and a longer history of redesigning the built environment for present crises and future risks. Since the 1960s, those looking for technical as well as financial support to save places of historical and cultural significance from "all hazards" turned to the Getty Conservation Institute, J. M. Kaplan Institute, their state's or country's National Trust, or local historical societies. With their aid, the stewards of UNESCO World Heritage sites, national parks, state landmarks, and local historic districts have undertaken research on how their organizations have managed and could manage to protect their heritage from destruction, disrepair and disuse.[8] Still, from Africa's World Heritage sites to Asia's vernacular architecture to America's national parks, resources and research have fallen short of the tasks at hand: reorientation of institutions and reeducation of individuals in preservation practices that drive sustainability of the artifacts and site, the systems and infrastructure they rely on, and the people and institutions that maintain them.[9] Righting a ship, Getty and Kaplan leadership have recently acknowledged, takes not only more capital investment by endowed institutions in diverse preservation stakeholders, but also more diversity of leadership in the research endeavors and education efforts of these institutions.[10]

The types of inquiry and intervention explored in this issue—from LEED-certified reconstructions to reengineered wastewater infrastructure—call for wholesale interrogation of the financial means and fiscal limits on where and how retrofit takes place. The dearth of academic scholarship and professional discourse on the funding frameworks for retrofit practices—and rehabilitation more broadly—warrant further examination than the primary documents of the enclosed case studies afford.[11] Yet, our contributors draw from the archive and examine the language of grant, tax, and loan documents that shape the scope, scale, and specifications of retrofits; for example, the tax code that compensates real estate developers for the costs of adapting commercial buildings. Such reflections prefigure, perhaps, the efforts of conservation advocates and heritage stewards to include preservation sponsors in discussions of next steps. This issue of *Future Anterior*, in other words, is an introduction to and, hopefully, instigation for further research—not only in terms of episodes to be described but also in terms of archives, funding, and pedagogies that can be reanimated.

Two alternative sources of adaptation knowledge — both encompassing histories, theories, and criticism — have emerged in recent years. The first is an international community of preservation practitioners, now largely affiliated with the Climate Heritage Network. Foundational to this effort, a series of UNESCO, ICOMOS, Docomomo, and INTBAU publications on the state of the field set the terms of critical debate about climate and heritage in the early 2000s.[12] In the years since, these groups have disseminated their research findings through practitioner convenings, policy summits, design awards, and in the teaching and research of numerous architecture and planning faculty. Between 2005 and 2015 alone, UNESCO, under the guidance of its World Heritage Committee, prepared numerous reports on how to predict, identify and manage climate change effects, and issued a more practical guide to the research for site managers dealing with the technicalities of climate change firsthand.[13] According to Susan Ross, who reviews two volumes published by UNESCO for this issue, these international bodies and their research not only inform local conservation practices and policies, such as regulations responding to pending climate impacts and precarious energy. They also indicate who counts as respondents to these crises, which responses are worth teaching and learning, and whose methodologies, technologies and epistemologies need to change so that practitioners and theorists of adaptation and mitigation can think and act most effectively.

Ironically, the U.S. Building Council relies on this wider set of building, real estate, and heritage professionals to assign LEED certifications to architecture designed for carbon sequestration, stormwater reuse, renewable energy markets, et cetera. Without their knowledge, awards and accreditation would elude architects of "innovation" and "excellence" in adaptive reuse, reconstruction of building envelopes and foundations, reconsideration of conventional material specifications, reconfiguration of spaces, redesign of structural elements and infrastructural components, and relocation of the entire structure vis-à-vis the sun, wind, stormwater, and vegetation prone to conflagration.

Architects' engagement in climate and energy discourse has enabled academics interested in the agency of architectural thought, practice, and media to examine their impact on the sustainability of local landmarks and global heritage. Iconic urban form and monumental landscapes — such as Fallingwater, the Industrial City of Tema, Ghana and the Panama Canal — have been subject to contextual analysis and critique from environmental historians, ecological theorists and planners of climate adaptation and energy transition, as well as planning and architectural historians versed in these adjacent discussions.[14] Furthermore, architects' preservation pedagogy, not just their design projects and discourse, are receiving new attention as historians assess the impact of climate actions and actors around the world. For instance, the editorial projects and pedagogical initiatives of James Marston Fitch and other Western advisors on preservation education in the Global South reflect little of the cross-cultural and cross-continental exchanges underwriting emergent epistemologies of the Anthropocene.[15] These and other forthcoming studies raise questions about preservationists' relative inclusion and possible role in architecture's environmental movements and moments.

Arguably, the same playbook guides climate knowledge production today. Too much of contemporary retrofit practice is content to operate at the superficial level of sustainability-speak accepted as engagement amongst many designers. Many such projects to reduce hydrocarbon fuels and petro-chemical-fueled injustice—from the *After Oil* publication of the Petrocultures research group, hand-drawn speculations and open-access coursework on the future of Arab port cities, to the Energy Justice Lab's engineering metrics for measuring progress toward promises of the Green New Deal—offer rich opportunities for equitably realigning mechanical systems, renovating fenestrations and regulating land use with emissions reduction goals.[16] On the other hand, as discussed in the roundtable, buildings of the past offer complex and varied examples of how the structure of buildings, their program, and the urban fabric in which they sit can all be attended to in such a way that they reduce or eliminate dependence on fossil-fueled mechanical systems. Such attentive approaches to the history, context, and energetic position of a building offers a compelling horizon for preservation and for architectural research more generally.[17]

Researchers of ancient, modern and contemporary architecture increasingly question the ability of iconic artifacts of globalist architects and lesser known contemporaries to "remain with us" in physical form or in preservation curricula without reinforcement of the extractive processes and exploitative practices that have produced and sustained them. Preservation planners Jennifer Minner and Erica Avrami contest restoration in accordance with "original plans" and consider retrofits of building envelopes and systems as corrective of harmful building narratives as well as toxic building performance.[18] In this issue Priya Jain's study of architectural renovations in partnership with India's first air conditioning vendors and Juliana (Yat Shun) Kei's analysis of building system upgrades in Britain's business landmarks highlight the need for interdisciplinary and international inquiries into the colonialist and universalist claims of climate knowledge among architecture practitioners, educators, editors, and accreditors. In other words, case studies of singular works of architecture in the West and its colonies serve as a caution to architects, academics, and advocates, demonstrating that building for energy transitions can involve rebuilding colonial systems, reinvesting in extractive economies, and reaffirming wasteful means and Western metrics of adaptation.

Research on retrofits may generate new conceptual touchstones and collective frameworks as it reckons with the concepts of "integrity," "authenticity," and "appropriateness" that have long functioned as connective tissue among preservation and conservation stakeholders worldwide. Publications on adaptation to a particular locale, specific site, set of resources or steward of the built environment afford researchers of retrofit to learn of distinct points of views, including that of "the field" and "the academy." An uptick in commercial, academic, government, and nonprofit publications underwrote collaborative intervention in a piecemeal fashion, albeit in ebbs and flows akin to the resources and reach of network builders. Hosted by the Climate Heritage Network, APT, and other organizations, dialogues built between 2019 and 2021 amidst a pandemic created a shared understanding of methodologies, technologies and epistemologies that shape this volume. The online discussions — illustrated with Google Earth images, hosted on cloud servers, and dependent on high-bandwidth internet — also revealed the challenges ahead for preservationists committed to decarbonization, decolonization and bridging the digital divide within and beyond our field. Thus, for preservationists, reckoning with unsustainable ecologies and unjust economies of architecture must include reevaluation — and research — of our pedestrian, roving, and orbital gazes.[19]

This issue of *Future Anterior,* an international journal for historic preservation history, theory, and criticism, assesses where and how architectural heritage stands amidst international heritage organizations and preservation schools thinking anew about how to present our knowledge to each other, to stakeholders and to the public. "Upgrades" to historic buildings — solar panels, most notably, but also the installation of flood gates, raised foundations, hardy siding, and newly-fabricated windows — changes the aesthetics of intervention and the affordability of taking action.[20] Retrofits visible to passersby, recorded via Google StreetView or noticeable via satellite imagery can raise property values — as Stafania De Medici finds across Italy — or reduce them, counterbalancing the value historic designation reportedly affords in the United States.[21] Even when the US government undertakes renovations—such as the replacement of high-rise buildings' reflexive cladding, a significant contributor to the heat island effect of city neighborhoods—its actions can conflict with local design guidelines and federal standards for "contributing" to local historic districts and national historic landmarks.[22] Contributors to this volume revisit some of these debates over how to situate architectures of fuel-efficiency and embodied energy within localized understanding and local politics of climate adaptation and energy transformation, not just international models of reconstruction and reform.[23] Still, far more research, analysis and exchange on the standardization, bureaucratization and accreditation of building adaptation is needed to further account for, let alone address, the relational power of governmental bodies, nongovernmental organizations, Indigenous nations, and grassroots and legislative movements (e.g., the Green New Deal) in placing preservation's response to the acute impacts of our chronic energy and climate crises.

At stake, then, in the context of retrofit and reuse, is remaining attentive to the value that disparity, discontinuity and disaggregation between designers of the Global South and Colonial North can bring to the movement for decarbonization of the world's monuments, national historic sites and other tangible heritage. Decolonization movements throughout Asia, Africa, the Indian Subcontinent, and South America have made space for subaltern theories of being in the world as a means to reexamine the ethical dimensions of hydrocarbon fuel-efficient practices in the design of the built environment. The situatedness of building knowledge and practices call into question a model of knowledge building and movement building dependent on the migration of starchitects or sustainability experts between World Monument sites and UNESCO summits. Noted in our roundtable discussion, opposition to LEED building in the North reflects a different spatial epistemology of energy and ecology than the organization's global standards promote. To achieve its benchmarks, designers across Europe and America have prescribed (via architectural specifications) the extraction of rare earth minerals from the Global South for measurable change in building performance up north. Likewise, research exchanges that expend energy and emit carbon are not only ironic for retrofit scholars and practitioners, but also reinscribe colonial knowledge building practices. Shaped by a call for contributions amidst the COVID-19 pandemic and a convening of contributors amidst an acute energy crisis in Gulf South states of Texas, Alabama, and Louisiana, this volume of research on retrofit demonstrates too few knowledge exchanges in the field of preservation take place virtually, inclusively, and equitably.

In this issue of *Future Anterior*, scholars and practitioners reexamine historical or contemporary retrofitting practices and theories in relation to climate crises and energy challenges. Contributions—essays, reviews, artwork, primary texts, and even Twitter threads—focus on three topics of conversation across disciplines, geography, and time. Each of these topics— retrofit's roots, how "other" retrofits measure up, and retrofitting conservation—represents an intersection of disaggregated and discontinuous discourses on energy and climate impacts on historic preservation, conservation, architecture, landscape architecture, urban and regional planning, real estate development, and community/economic development. The authors illuminate the ideas and projects of both underrepresented and canonical practitioners by exploring how and why certain works of design and development have become sites of disciplinary adoration and/or discursive attention. Together, these case studies of retrofit shed light on the archive of preservation that motivates and mobilizes individuals, institutions, and industries to invest, both financially and culturally, in smart growth and degrowth.

Biographies
Dr. Fallon Samuels Aidoo is Jean B. Boebel Assistant Professor of Historic Preservation in the University of New Orleans's Planning and Urban Studies Department. She researches and advises preservation of cultural heritage and cultural economies. Latin and African American heritage endangered by disasters, disinvestment, and development are the focus of her public scholarship, service, and consulting. Currently, she is contributing to the African American Heritage Trail of Martha's Vineyard and its counterparts in Los Angeles, New Orleans, and Tulsa. Recently she's served on federal, state, and local commissions responsible for renaming, revitalizing, and retrofitting historic streetscapes. Dr. Aidoo's research collaborations with community organizations and governmental authorities yield historical designations and preservation plans as well as public writing and academic publications in *Preservation & Social Inclusion, Platform, Future Anterior, Spatializing Politics,* and the *Journal of Environmental Studies & Science.* At the University of New Orleans, she teaches planning studios and seminars, directs the Historic & Cultural Preservation program, advises the PhD in Justice Studies and leads digital, public, and community initiatives of the Urban Entrepreneurship & Policy Institute. Previously she taught architecture and urbanism at Northeastern University, Harvard, and MIT, while researching hazards to historic structures for VREF, AECOM, DMJM, and the Smithsonian. Dr. Aidoo holds a PhD in urban planning (Harvard), MS in architectural history (MIT), BS in civil engineering (Columbia University), and a GIS Certificate (Harvard).

Daniel A. Barber is Professor of Architecture at the University of Technology Sydney (UTS). His research and teaching narrate environmental histories of architecture and explore pathways into the post-hydrocarbon future. His most recent book is *Modern Architecture and Climate: Design before Air Conditioning* (Princeton UP, 2020), following on *A House in the Sun: Modern Architecture and Solar Energy in the Cold War* (Oxford UP, 2016). Daniel edits the *Accumulation* series on e-flux architecture (https://www.e-flux.com/architecture/accumulation/) and is co-founder of Current: Collective on Environment and Architectural History. He has held fellowships at Harvard and Princeton universities and the Alexander von Humboldt Foundation. Daniel is currently a Senior Fellow at the Käte Hamburger Centre for Apocalyptic and Post-Apocalyptic Studies at Universität Heidelberg. He is a recipient of the 2022–23 Guggenheim Fellowship

Notes
[1] S. Fatorić and E. Seekamp, "Are Cultural Heritage and Resources Threatened by Climate Change? A Systematic Literature Review," *Climatic Change* 142 (2017): 227–54, https://doi.org/10.1007/s10584-017-1929-9.
[2] A testament to such diversity and what it can yield, an audit of monuments in the

United States by the nonprofit Monument Lab (based in Philadelphia, PA, USA) may produce a national record of climate change impacts as it assesses how monuments are historicized and contextualized after their creation and installation. https://monumentlab.com/projects/national-monument-audit, accessed April 29, 2021.

[3] See, for example, the term's use in: M. Beniston, "Sustainability of the Landscape of a UNESCO World Heritage Site in the Lake Geneva Region (Switzerland) in a Greenhouse Climate," *International Journal of Climatololgy* 28 (2008): 1519–24; E. Brabec, E. Chilton, "Toward an Ecology of Cultural Heritage," *Change Over Time: International Journal of Conservation of the Built Environment* 5, no. 2 (2015): 266–85; M. Gomez-Heras, S. Mccabe, "Weathering of Stone-built Heritage: A Lens Through Which to Read the Anthropocene," *Anthropocene* 11 (2015): 1–13; A. J. Howard, "Managing Global Heritage in the Face of Future Climate Change: The Importance of Understanding Geological and Geomorphological Processes and Hazards," *International Journal of Heritage Studies* 19, no. 7 (2013): 632–58; H. Phillips, "Adaptation to Climate Change at UK World Heritage Sites: Progress and Challenges," *History of Environ Policy Practice* 5, no. 3 (2014): 288–99. Monuments and other historic structures not classified as buildings also undergo retrofit, but their transformation is increasingly framed as conservation.

[4] Within the past five years, interdisciplinary alternatives have been developed by the McHarg Center at the University of Pennsylvania and the Buell Center for the Study of American Architecture, contributors to the Black Landscape Symposium Speaker Series, www.blacklanetwork.com/symposium.

[5] Notable exceptions in the US context identify labor as critical to achieving preservation goals of inclusivity as well as sustainability. See Terremoto, "Landscape Architecture Has a Labor Acknowledgement Problem," *Metropolis*, April 14, 2021, https://www.metropolismag.com/architecture/landscape/landscape-architecture-labor-terremoto/, accessed April 16, 2021; Anjulie Rao, "Keep the Commons," *Landscape Architecture Magazine*, April 2021, https://landscapearchitecturemagazine.org/2021/04/22/keep-the-commons/, accessed April 30, 2021.

[6] The latter consisted of modernists and colonialists as well, see Christina E. Crawford, "The Case to Save Socialist Space," in *Routledge Research Companion to Landscape Architecture*, ed. Ellen Braae and Henriette Steiner (London: Routledge, 2019), 260–73; Łukasz Stanek, "Architects from Socialist Countries in Ghana (1957–67): Modern Architecture and Mondialisation," *Journal of the Society of Architectural Historians* 74, no. 4 (2015): 416–42.

[7] National Trust for Historic Preservation's African American Cultural Heritage Action Fund, *Annual Report* (2021), https://nthp-savingplaces.s3.amazonaws.com/2021/12/07/15/29/08/18/NTHP_AR2021_lo-res_spreads.pdf.

[8] Some research pre-dating the 1990s can be found in the archives of only some sponsors such as the Getty Conservation Institute. Others, with fewer resources, prioritized preservation of "brick-and-mortar" sites, so to speak, over preservation of site documentation and other research conducted.

[9] Colin Breen, "Advocacy, International Development and World Heritage Sites in Sub-Saharan Africa," *World Archaeology* 39, no. 3 (2007): 355–70, DOI: 10.1080/00438240701464772; Kou, Huaiyun, Manish Chalana, and Jian Zhou, "Diverse Approaches to the Preservation of Built Vernacular Heritage: Case Study of Post-disaster Reconstruction of the Xijie Historic District in Dujiangyan City, China," *Journal of Architectural Conservation* 26, no. 1 (2020): 71–86. Casey, Alanna, and Austin Becker, "Institutional and Conceptual Barriers to Climate Change Adaptation for Coastal Cultural Heritage," *Coastal Management* 47, no. 2 (2019): 169–88; Erica Avrami, "Making Historic Preservation Sustainable," *Journal of the American Planning Association* 82, no. 2 (2016): 104–12, https://doi.org/10.1080/01944363.2015.1126196.

[10] Kwesi Daniels, Amy Frietag, Brent Leggs, Randall Mason, "Understanding Civil Rights Heritage: Center for Civil Rights Heritage," Philadelphia, University of Pennsylvania, October 27, 2020, https://vimeo.com/474767631.

[11] Notable exceptions include: Christian A. L. Hilber, Charles Palmer, and Edward W. Pinchbeck, "The Energy Costs of Historic Preservation," *Journal of Urban Economics* 114 (2019): 103–97; Fallon Aidoo, "The 'Community Foundations' of Allyship in Preservation: Lessons from West Mount Airy, Philadelphia," *Preservation and Social Inclusion* (Columbia Books on Architecture and the City, 2020); Fallon Aidoo, "More than Meets the Eye: Institutional Philanthropy behind Façade Revitalization Post-Disaster," *8th National Forum on Historic Preservation Policy* (National Preservation Institute, 2021); John Royall Warman, "Incentivizing Historic rehabilitation and Adaptive Reuse in the United States and the United Kingdom," PhD diss., Massachusetts Institute of Technology, 2020.

[12] United Nations Educational, Scientific and Cultural Organization (UNESCO), International Council on Monuments and Cities (ICOMOS), Docomomo (International

Committee for Documentation and Conservation of Buildings, Sites and Neighbor-hoods of the Modern Movement), INTBAU (International Network for Traditional Building, Architecture & Urbanism).

[13] *Predicting and Managing the Effects of Climate Change on World Heritage* (2007), followed by the compilation *Case Studies on Climate Change and World Heritage*, and a *Policy Document on the Impacts of Climate Change on World Heritage Proper-ties* (2008) and *Managing Disaster Risks for World Heritage Guidelines* (ICOMOS, 2010).

[14] See, for example, Daniel A. Barber, *Modern Architecture and Climate: Design be-fore Air Conditioning* (Princeton: Princeton University Press, 2020); Joaquín Medina Warmburg, and Claudia Shnidt, eds., *The Construction of Modern Architectural Climate (1920–1980)* (Madrid: Lampreave, 2015); J. Ferng, J. H. Chang, E. L'Heureux, D. J. Ryan, "Climatic Design and its Others: 'Southern' Perspectives in the age of the Anthropocene," *Journal of Architectural Education* 74, no. 2 (2020): 250–62.

Daniel J. Ryan, "Thermal Nationalism: The Climate and House Design Program in Australia (1944–1960)," *ABE Journal: Architecture beyond Europe* 18 (2021). In turn, architectural and landscape studies are, in many cases, reviewed and read by their environmental scholars. See, for instance, Fallon Aidoo, "Architectures of Mis/Managed Retreat: Black Land Loss to Green Housing Gains," *Journal of Envi-ronmental Studies and Science* (2021): DOI: 10.1007/s13412-021-00684-3; Claire Antone Payton, "Chapter 4. Concrete Kleptocracy and Haiti's Culture of Building: Toward a New Temporality of Disaster," *Critical Disaster Studies,* ed. James Remes and Andy Horowitz, 71–84 (Philadelphia: University of Pennsylvania Press, 2021); Brenda Chaflin, "Wastelandia: Infrastructure and the Commonwealth of Waste in Ur-ban Ghana," *Ethos: Journal of Anthropology* 82, no. 4 (2017): 648–71; Ashley Carse, "Nature as Infrastructure: Making and Managing the Panama Canal Watershed," *Social Studies of Science* 42, no. 4 (2012): 539–63. Other impactful scholarship is available in the proceedings of heritage and preservation convenings and university archives of dissertations and theses, as is the case for: Stephen J. Sparks, "Apart-heid Modern: "South Africa's Oil from Coal Project and the History of a Company Town," PhD diss., The University of Michigan, 2012; Nicole A. Ambrose, "Building a Better Future on the Foundations of the Past: Incorporating Historic Districts into Ecocities," PhD diss., Columbia University, 2013.

[15] James Douet, *The Heritage of the Oil Industry: TICCIH Thematic Study,* The Inter-national Committee on the Conservation of the Industrial Heritage (2020), https://ticcih.org/wp-content/uploads/2020/07/Oil-industry-thematic-report.pdf; Rania Ghosn, After Oil (New York: MOMA, Coursera, 2016).

[16] Ghosn, *After Oil*; Urban Energy Justice Lab (Tony Reames, University of Michigan), *Interactive Energy Efficiency Equity Baseline Map:* https://umich.maps.arcgis.com/apps/Cascade/index.html?appid=28f6792ea2134ffba888413e70647c0c, accessed May 1, 2021.

[17] See Giuseppe Amoruso, ed., *Putting Tradition Into Practice: Heritage, Place and Design: Proceedings of 5th INTBAU International Annual Event,* vol. 3 (New York: Springer, 2017).

[18] Erica Avrami, "Creative Destruction and the Social (Re) Construction of Heritage," *International Journal of Cultural Property* 27, no. 2 (2020): 215–37; *The Preserva-tion Fallacy in the Mediterranean Medina* (Cambridge: Harvard University Graduate School of Design, 2013); Jennifer Minner and Martin Abbott, "How Urban Spaces Remember: Memory and Transformation at Two Expo Sites," *International Planning History Society Proceedings* 18, no. 1 (2018): 1063–74.

[19] New Orleans, for instance, has very recently settled on a threshold of change after which "retrofit" yields demolition. Whether beloved or recognized historical features "remain intact" after interventions is not the measure, but a discernible physical and visual record of the past is.

[20] Amalia Leifeste and Barry L. Stiefel, *Sustainable Heritage: Merging Environmental Conservation and Historic Preservation* (London: Routledge, 2018); Alessia Buda, Ernst Jan de Place Hansen, Alexander Rieser, Emanuela Giancola, Valeria Natalina Pracchi, Sara Mauri, Valentina Marincioni et al., "Conservation-compatible Retrofit Solutions in Historic Buildings: An Integrated Approach," *Sustainability* 13, no. 5 (2021): 2927; Sharon C. Park, "Sustaining Historic Properties in an Era of Climate Change," *APT Bulletin: The Journal of Preservation Technology* 49, nos. 2–3 (2018): 35–44; Luisa F. Cabeza, Alvaro de Gracia, and Anna Laura Pisello, "Integration of Renewable Technologies in Historical and Heritage Buildings: A Review," *Energy and Buildings* 177 (2018): 96–111; Masayuki Ichinose, Takashi Inoue, and Tsutomu Nagahama, "Effect of Retro-reflecting Transparent Window on Anthropogenic Urban Heat Balance," *Energy and Buildings* 157 (2017): 157–65.

[21] Stefania De Medici, "Italian Architectural Heritage and Photovoltaic Systems. Matching Style with Sustainability," *Sustainability* 13, no. 4 (2021): 2108; Andrew Stein, "Greening Historic DC: Challenges and Opportunities to Incorporate Historic

Preservation into the District's Drive for Sustainable Development," *Georgetown Law Historic Preservation Series* 32 (2009), https://scholarship.law.georgetown .edu/hpps_papers/32.

[22] R. Chang, S. Hayter, E. Hotchkiss, S. Pless, J. Sielcken, and C. Smith-Larney, "Aspinall Courthouse: GSA's Historic Preservation and Net-Zero Renovation Case Study," No. DOE/GO-102014-4462, National Renewable Energy Lab (NREL), Golden, CO (United States), 2014. See also Chenghao Wang, Zhi-Hua Wang, Kamil E. Kaloush, and Joseph Shacat, "Perceptions of Urban Heat Island Mitigation and Implementation Strategies: Survey and Gap Analysis," *Sustainable Cities and Society* 66 (2021): 102687.

[23] Kathryn Rogers Merlino, *Building Reuse: Sustainability, Preservation and the Value of Design* (Seattle: University of Washington Press, 2018); A. Moschella, A. Salemi, G. Sanfilippo, M. Detommaso, and A. Privitera, "Historic Buildings in Mediterranean Area and Solar Thermal Technologies: Architectural Integration vs Preservation Criteria," *Energy Procedia* 42 (2013): 416–25; Chuhan Zheng, "Redesigning Historic Districts: A Study of Preservation Plans for Historic Districts of Jingzhou Ancient City in Hubei, China" (Master's thesis, University of Pennsylvania, 2017).

In This Issue

Superfund to EcoDistrict: Progressive Preservation for a Net-Zero Neighborhood
Jessica L. Morris

Social cohesion at the heart of neighborhoods can be a powerful catalyst for change. It can steward the development of governance that supports balanced approaches to achieving and maintaining progressive social, cultural and environmental goals. As a cultural development strategy, the district scale can carry systems-level benefits of advancing infrastructure strategies and may offer a scale of governance capable of overcoming municipal, state and regional bureaucratic hampers. Coupling a prototypical net-zero district, a measured smart growth methodology, with the idea of retrofit understood as a practice of progressive preservation the two parallel approaches, one looking forward and one looking back offer an alliance capable of optimizing outcomes as they relate to quality of life, health and well-being, community economics and climate mitigation. Illustrated through a case study on the Gowanus Canal, designated a Superfund site in 2010, the methodology of a 2050 Net Zero Neighborhood is considered in parallel with the potential of climate mitigation and preservation co-benefits setting up a new paradigm; a comprehensive built-environment strategy working within limits to growth. Though the aesthetics of comfort and convenience alongside balanced and integrated systems are not in themselves drivers of development, when considered as design priorities by way of sensitive and responsive measures for energy accounting including life-cycle analyses, these priorities can yield highly desirable characteristics within alternative development scenarios, inclusive of community centered bottom-line balances. In meeting a 2050 Net Zero goal, both preservation practice and smart growth strategy stand to gain when aligned. Regulatory flexibility and broad community support are needed to achieve these integrated models of reinvestment as we move toward balanced and equitable neighborhoods replete with power to leverage technical and cultural strategies augmenting their authentic histories of place.

Preservation Themes in Mass Housing's Retrofit: Climate and Energy in Tor Bella Monaca, Rome
Francesco Cianfarani and Michele Morganti

Future Anterior
Volume XVIII, Number 1
Summer 2021

Nowadays, urban climate change and energy efficiency of the built environment are major challenges worldwide. Mitigating the main anthropogenic factors at the base of climate change and adapting to the inevitable consequences become urgent. In a climate-responsive and energy retrofit perspective, we focus on contemporary debates, best practices and design strategies regarding the preservation of Italian postwar mass-housing complexes. Specifically, we discuss the case of Tor Bella Monaca (TBM) in Rome, a vast self-sufficient public-housing complex completed at the beginning of the 1980s. Today, TBM is subject to a series of public debates, pilot projects, and research proposals by public and private institutions focused on retrofit as an alternative to demolition. We approach the issue through an interdisciplinary perspective, addressing the contribution of climate-responsive and energy efficient design strategies for the preservation of modern mass housing complexes. In addition, we propose a critical framework on cross-scale approach useful both for building and open space quality and comfort. Finally, we present the most discussed design strategies in literature and practice in the case of TBM and how they intend to support social, historical, and urban values of the neighborhood.

Graves's Portland Building, 2020: Preservation as Transformation
Joseph Siry

The Portland Public Services Building, designed by Michael Graves from 1979 and opened in 1982, is central to Postmodern Classicism in the United States. Although historically recent, the building's mechanical and material systems have been superseded in the ensuing decades. Meticulous, comprehensive assessments led to the phased renewal completed in 2020. Interiors were notorious for their darkness, in part because the 4 x 4-foot-square windows on upper floors had been filled not with the clear glass as envisioned, but with a tinted glass, now being replaced with clear glass. For a seismic upgrade, 110,000 pounds of steel reinforcing bars per floor were added to the structural core and exterior columns. For sustainability, both heating and cooling are supplied by heat pump/air conditioning units on the roof to minimize consumption of fossil fuels. After decades of repairs, deteriorated painted concrete surfaces and affixed ceramic tiles were overlaid with an exterior rainscreen of metal panels at upper levels and terra-cotta at lower levels. Controversy has surrounded this unusual approach to preservation, but the city and architects DLR Group strove to have transformed Graves's canonical monument to meet today's environmental and material criteria while respecting original intent.

Retrofitting the Monument of Commerce: Unilever House, London
Juliana Kei

When Unilever House London was completed in 1931 it was celebrated, in *The Times* newspaper, as "The Monument of Commerce." This paper examines its two large-scale retrofitting exercises: first by the multi-disciplinary design practice Pentagram (1980–83) and then by the international architectural office Kohn Pederson Fox (KPF) (2005–2008). I examine the different approaches taken by Pentagram and KPF to inject more value into Unilever House: the former sought to accentuate the building's artistic and historical value while the latter focused on reducing, recycle, and reuse. Drawing upon these two different attitudes toward Unilever House's monumentality, particular attention is paid to how the Lever Brothers' troubled history in colonial exploitation was treated in these two retrofitting projects. Writing around Unilever House's twice retrofitting, this research seeks to parse out more about the "values" in architecture and retrofitting.

Mies à jour: Nuns' Island Gas Station as a Transitional Object
Kai Woolner-Pratt

How might we contend with the cast-off (infra)structures of a petroculture that has an uncertain future? Just off the shore of the Island of Montreal, the community of Nuns' Island was urbanized by Chicago-based Metropolitan Structures in the 1960s. As part of the petroculturalization of what had up to that point been a pastoral landscape, Imperial Oil commissioned the Office of Mies van der Rohe to produce an Esso gas station. Renovated in 2011 by Les architectes fabg as an intergenerational community center La Station's heating and cooling is accomplished by means of geothermal wells in a design that materially and symbolically reclaims gas pumps as ventilation structures.

Borrowing a concept from psychoanalyst Donald Winnicott by way of art historian Caroline van Eck, this article interprets La Station as a *transitional object* that is oriented toward degrowth even while it remains inscribed within an urban landscape that is still utterly dependent upon the automobile. By reconfiguring the structure of La Station, another kind of infrastructure is implied, or even demanded, which would revise the Nuns' Island territory as a whole. But what would this revision be? The gas station is a transitional object that begins to make present a fully post-carbon—albeit subjunctive—future that is rooted in a different past.

**Selling Comfort: Volkart Brothers and Origins of
Air Conditioning in India (1923–1954)**
Priya Jain

This article offers an analysis of the development of air conditioning in India in the mid-twentieth century, from the vantage
point of one of its largest trading firms, the Swiss merchant
house of Volkart Brothers. It reveals that the marketing strategies and air conditioning installations by the firm extended and
intensified exclusionary colonial notions about race, climate
and civilization. The article analyzes the practice of "retrofit" — retroactive installation of air conditioning in existing
buildings in India, and "future-fit" — design of new buildings
for later accommodation of air conditioning, within the context
of the inequitable sociocultural framing mentioned above.
The analysis is supported by a juxtaposition of the firm's
external and in-house literature, which allows a rare insight
into publicly advertised and privately-held notions about air
conditioning. Such an investigation is deeply instructive in understanding subsequent and current architectural approaches
to thermal comfort, not only in India but at a broader global
level, where alternative transcultural approaches are receiving
increased attention in the Anthropocene era.

**Roundtable Discussion: Retrofitting Research: A Global
Conversation on Challenges and Opportunities**

Book Review: *Perceptions of Sustainability in Heritage Studies,*
**edited by Marie-Theres Albert, Berlin: De Gruyter, 2015;
and** *Going Beyond: Perceptions of Sustainability in Heritage
Studies,* **No. 2, edited by Albert, Marie-Theres, Francesco
Bandarin, and Ana Pereira Roders, Berlin: Springer, 2017**
Susan Ross

Book Review: *Case Studies in Retrofitting Suburbia: Urban
Design Strategies for Urgent Challenges,* **by June Williamson
and Ellen Dunham-Jones, John Wiley & Sons, Inc., 2021**
Douglas R. Appler

Art Submission
Creator: David Hartt

Figure 1. Clockwise from top left: Beton-Coignet's restored façade, next to Whole Foods housing Gotham Greens on its roof; BRT (Brooklyn Rapid Transit) home to Power House Arts, currently undergoing renovation, showing recent development at 360 Bond Street across the canal; Red Hook Community Farm Compost Operation; South Third Street, looking West toward the canal. Photos: Author.

Jessica L. Morris

Superfund to EcoDistrict
Progressive Preservation for a Net-Zero Neighborhood

Social cohesion at the heart of neighborhoods can be a powerful catalyst for change. Cohesion can steward the development of governance that supports balanced approaches to achieving and maintaining progressive social, cultural and environmental goals. In terms of bridging cultural paradigms, balancing ecosystems and energy expenditures over time, the identification of parallel, cross-disciplinary methods to quantify the relationship of growth to resources alongside net effects of coordinated investment presents an alternative mode of community economics achievable through preservation, retrofit and a progressive net-zero framework for revitalization.

At once authentic, yet also prospective, this model requires visionary leadership to identify and bridge gaps across practice to steer investment toward realizable, shared cultural values that underlie comprehensive sustainable built-environment strategies. Through consideration of methods at the intersection of empirical research and social infrastructure, embedded in places that are inherently reflective of authentic history, leveraging district-scale environmental reinvestment to bolster aspirational goals of carbon-neutral lifestyles presents a series of long practical challenges. To meet those challenges, the *district* is an operative tool that extends beyond discrete limits of property and ownership and carries with it the collective power drawn from harnessing the creative potential of a community. The district, as a sustainable development tool, carries systems-level benefits of advanced infrastructural strategies while it may also offer a scale and style of governance able to overcome jurisdictional constraints of the bureaucratic status quo.

Change is felt locally, in collective places larger than a building and smaller than the city. As places are more tangible and familiar at the district scale, impacts are also potentially more measurable. The *neighborhood* as vehicle for this shift toward a balanced future centers responsive, integrated strategies for decision-making and investment.

Consider: broadly and most simply defined, *net-zero* is a system with an equal measure of carbon expended as is sequestered or offset.[1] Working within existing context, not tabula rasa, a carbon neutral development strategy must necessarily approach aspects of preservation as a component in the equation. Preserved assets are not only indicative of an

Future Anterior
Volume XVIII, Number 1
Summer 2021

historical authenticity but become place-based value statements that anchor change, especially when both things that stay the same and those that change reach a critical mass. Preservation points to retrofit as functional improvement, not only for buildings but also for infrastructure, enabling more livable, endearing and affective places for the communities that steward them. While discrete research exists among a range of disciplinary stakeholders, synergies in preservation, planning, and other associated disciplines that may address parallel gaps in a targeted approach to sustainable development, such as through EcoDistricts, Net Zero Neighborhoods, or Smart Growth have not been made explicit.[2]

The case study of a 2050 Net Zero Neighborhood in Gowanus, Brooklyn highlights an opportunity to explore the potential for a preservation-planning retrofit smart growth alliance. In approaching the Gowanus case, one measure of the organizational model for achieving environmental progress will be by virtue of rehabilitation. The case also illustrates that the regulatory environment is not yet nimble enough to guide redevelopment to encourage and support this type of progressive model for investment across public and private sectors while achieving balanced, pro-social carbon-neutral priorities.

Civic History of Gowanus
Together, the ecological, civic, and industrial histories of Gowanus set forth a vehicle for arriving at the neighborhood's sustainable future. From native salt marshes to millponds and grist mills, the Gowanus Canal has long been a progenitor of growth. Eventually epitomizing the unintended consequences of churning industrial development, the area of Gowanus has always been charged with harnessing natural systems in service to energy systems, as a factor of growth-dependent infrastructure.[3]

Prior to the start of modern industrial development along the canal, the 1850s brought a rapidly diminishing absorptive ground surface in comparison to the pastoral capacity of the Gowanus Lowlands.[4] Ease of movement for goods along the canal rendered the banks a site of prime real estate for heavy industry such as coal and manufactured gas operations, the residue of which significantly contributed to the present day state of the canal. The changing ground coupled with the exponential population growth and rapid development of downtown Brooklyn would contribute to and be indicative of a prolonged trajectory of lagging infrastructure services and increasingly foul conditions along the canal.[5] Significant investment was critical for Gowanus to avoid land-based assets served by the canal being rendered valueless. Through the late 1800s into the early 1900s, the Gowanus Canal made good on its mission; the area emerged as a catalyst for growth. However, with profit from investment came industrial hazards, environmental degradation, and mismanagement of public infrastructure. In 1859, Citizens Gas Light Company was established as the first industrial business along the modern canal. Though the company held contracts for lighting public space that enabled the advancement of the public realm and supported civic life in Gowanus, Citizens Gas Light and other manufactured gas plants along the canal had operational practices that resulted in extreme industrial pollution, and marked what would become a century of environmental decline for Gowanus.

While Citizens Gas Light et al. were seeding the banks of the Canal with toxic deposits of coal tar, there were significant public and private investments being made in built assets nearby. Exemplary of the era of industrial advancement and prosperity, Long Island Stone Company constructed the Beton-Coignet building in 1872 at the southwest corner of the intersection of 3rd Street and 3rd Avenue. The jewel-box of a building was a showcase for the innovative stone-like material used for its concrete façade.[6] On the opposite corner of 3rd Avenue, Somers Brothers Tinware Factory built out a multi-building complex in 1884. Both Beton-Coignet's and Somers Brothers' buildings are now landmarks, and relics of advancing industry buoyed by infrastructure investment. With the nineteenth-century investments in the canal and improvements to the combined sewer system in the area alongside the build out of surrounding streetscape and energy systems to support rapidly advancing transportation futures, the identity of Gowanus was cemented — as industrial engine in service to Brooklyn, and as a place where urban dwelling occurred proximate to industry.

Following trends of private investment, Brooklyn Rapid Transit (BRT) Central Power Station, built in 1903 (and landmarked in 2019), was sited along the canal west of 3rd Avenue, across from Beton-Coignet and diagonally across from the Somers Brothers complex.[7] BRT was monumental in scale and at the time it was erected it served as the centralized infrastructure that powered all of Brooklyn's integrated mass-transit system. With both public and private investments flowing to the area, the Canal's rapidly deteriorating environmental quality could no longer be ignored.

In 1911, the Gowanus Canal Flushing Tunnel Pumping Station and Gate House, both public works, were completed. The Flushing Tunnel at the head of the canal pumped millions of gallons of New York Harbor water from Buttermilk Channel into refresh the canal each day. It greatly improved the canal's water quality, local air quality and consequently, the entire area's quality of life.[8]

By mid-century, the advent of modern transportation and arrival of the Robert Moses-era Gowanus Expressway had all but ensured the Canal's obsolescence, though with decades of decay yet to ensue. A broken propeller at the pumping station in the 1960s brought waters to a halt leaving a stagnant, festering admix of effluent and century-old seepage of toxic industrial waste. Meanwhile, the BRT Central Power Station endured, powering mass transit in Brooklyn for another decade until the mid-1970s when municipal bankruptcy descended upon New York City, amplifying effects of disinvestment along nearby commercial corridors and in the deteriorating public realm.

Nonetheless, the quasi-apocalyptic postindustrial landscape was not entirely inhospitable. Gowanus fostered ingénue artists, and residents who found the fringe of urban industrial wasteland to be cheap, charming and full of potential. In Gowanus—or places with a similar authentic historical mix of civic, industrial and artistic culture—*energy* is as much an atmospheric quality as it is measurable resource, or power to be leveraged by community-based coalitions.[9]

After decades of neglect, the Flushing Tunnel was brought back into service in 1999 coinciding with increased public awareness of the toxic conditions of the canal. The Flushing Tunnel reinvestment, along with municipal grants that repaired sidewalks, etc., represented a major turning point for the neighborhood and indicated a renewed interest in an inhabitable Gowanus. Indicative of what was on the horizon, a plan requesting a zoning variance for a significant residential redevelopment on the site of the Green Building was stymied in 2004 by community opposition on the grounds that the development would "alter the essential character of the neighborhood."[10]

Whether essential character is fixed or fluid is debatable, but what is certain for Gowanus is that legacies of industrial innovation and civic engagement are central to maintaining place-based identity while also stimulating investment and development. Alongside managing the pace of change through reuse and reinvestment, preservation has the capacity to prioritize authentic futures built on the past, placate evolving public opinion, and contribute to comprehensive district-scale sustainable planning.

Superfund to Ecodistrict
In Gowanus, the commitment to preserving neighborhood character came alongside healthy opposition to brownfield redevelopment strategies that were proposed across New York City as a panacea post-9/11. The tipping point toward a future Gowanus was perhaps not triggered by traditional preservation processes, such as landmarking, but rather with the building

of community support for a Superfund designation. Geographer Hamil Pearsall describes the broad local alliance as being composed of "long-term low-income residents, as well as newer middle-class professional residents," and frames the counterintuitive value proposition that was supportive of being deemed a high priority hazard, where for those stakeholders designation would effectively "reduce the exchange value (i.e., property value) of their land in hopes of increasing use value (i.e., community integrity)."[11] Steadily over a short period of time, support for a place on the National Priorities List and federal management of the cleanup grew. It was a debatable strategy: Rather than stigma, would listing bestow a storied type of privilege on Gowanus? While at the same time also deterring, or at least slowing the pace of developer driven investment?

The Superfund designation guaranteed comprehensive remediation on a federal timeline. Community-based support accompanied a growing awareness of the pitfalls of remediation tied to market-based investment, i.e., exclusion or total obsolescence of public participation in the process, and absence of public accountability in assuring the completeness of, and limiting residual effect from the clean-up.[12] Pearsall posits a position in which "the redevelopment of the Gowanus Canal under Superfund protocols provides an alternative to neoliberal urbanism by enabling community participation in the revitalization of the waterway," setting up an unprecedented opportunity to foster and deploy a suite of strategies.[13] Identified by Isabelle Anguelovski, these strategies unfold over time, are long term, and are concerned with how community-based coalitions work in support of improving environmental quality and neighborhood livability.[14] They include the building of strategic relationships with officials during periods of neglect, as well as engaging "broad and flexible coalitions" among professionals with interdisciplinary expertise and significant interests in the community. These coalitions include "local experts" who leverage *spatial* and *social* capital—harnessing trusted relationships of community leaders to anchor the work of technical experts and professionals to serve the needs of the neighborhood.

The Gowanus Canal was designated a Superfund site in 2010 and a phased clean-up of the canal began in 2020. The social cohesion resulting from the Superfund designation and the community's civic engagement throughout the process reinforced a resilient ground across groups with different social, cultural, and environmental goals throughout the Gowanus neighborhood. To consider the cleanup a *retrofit* of the canal may be a misnomer, but the plan includes remediating legacy pollution in the canal's waters and along its banks, dredging and capping the canal, and alleviating the

Figure 2. Gowanus Dredgers celebrating the start of clean-up in front of the Landmarked Brooklyn Rapid Transit Building, home to Powerhouse Arts, currently ongoing renovation. Photo: Gowanus Dredgers Canoe Club.

combined sewer overflow with underground retention tanks. As a strategic process, the Superfund designation delayed the start of remediation and rapid redevelopment in the area while effectively enabling coalitions to mature amidst the shoring up of "bottom-to-bottom" networks, alongside visioning and strategic planning with opportunity and cause.[15]

Toward a Net-Zero Future

In 2019, a team of professionals convened a series of workshops and discussions on Net Zero Neighborhoods through AIA New York that culminated in a public panel discussion at the Green Building in Gowanus.[16] The applied research initiative identified a solutions-oriented framework for achieving net-carbon neutrality by coupling city-scale sustainability benchmarks and occupant-scale behavioral shifts with integrated built environment interventions calibrated through a set of metrics that aided translation into this prototype for low-carbon urban lifestyles. The framework intended to align with existing local and global climate mitigation policies and to function as a conceptual tool that would advance a smart growth agenda.

To increase applicability of the study, scope definition was aligned with existing municipal benchmarking data as well as with internationally accepted greenhouse gas reporting protocols.[17] Three categories of sector specific emissions—Energy, Mobility, and Waste—were used alongside three emissions scope classifications in order to develop a framework based on carbon equivalency, CO_2e.[18] The research model aspired to be comprehensive, though it was necessarily limited to an acme frame of anywhere place, i.e. "Sunawog" ("Gowanus" in reverse). The engagement component of the research did

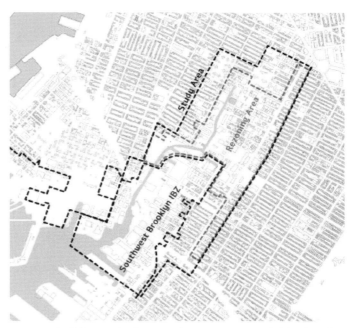

Figure 3. The area identified for the Net Zero Neighborhood Prototype consists of approximately one square mile of land surrounding the Gowanus Canal. NYIT Graduate Urban Design Climate Lab.

serve to build capacity in regard to a net-zero neighborhood concept, but by design the study did not account for historical elements, i.e., valuation of existing assets, cultural heritage, or preservation strategies such as adaptive reuse and building life-cycle analyses.

With any energy systems analysis, the determination of a boundary is a critical definition. The area of the Net Zero Gowanus district encompassed the entire area concurrently being rezoned, included a segment of the Southwest Brooklyn Industrial Business Zone, and also included the Gowanus Houses, a public housing development located two blocks north of the head of the canal.

The research used a 2020 baseline, projecting two 2050 scenarios: Business as Usual (BAU) and a Net Zero 2050 District. A growth target was established using the Reasonable Worst Case Development Scenario (RWCDS) defined in the Gowanus rezoning's Environmental Impact Statement (EIS) to estimate the population projection for a full build-out scenario, with the same projection used for both the BAU and the 2050 Net Zero scenario.[19] Parameters and assumptions were identified and defined as means to account for balancing CO_2e while responding to the spatial implications of growth. The *district* served the purpose of a boundary for accounting to meet the net-zero target, and also in theory as a definitive area within which social capital could be leveraged.[20]

"Stationary Energy" or energy use from buildings produces approximately 70 percent of citywide carbon emissions. Improved efficiency and building performance achieved through local policy initiatives relies on retrofit as an important strategy

7

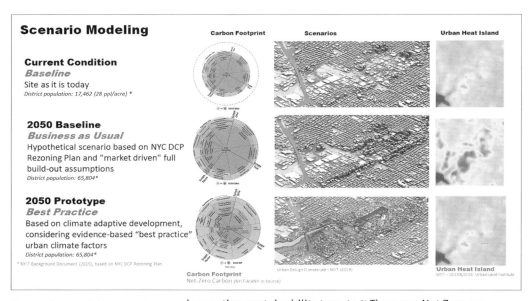

Scenario Modeling

Carbon Footprint   Scenarios   Urban Heat Island

Current Condition
Baseline
Site as it is today
District population: 17,462 (28 ppl/acre) *

2050 Baseline
Business as Usual
Hypothetical scenario based on NYC DCP Rezoning Plan and "market driven" full build-out assumptions
District population: 65,804*

2050 Prototype
Best Practice
Based on climate adaptive development, considering evidence-based "best practice" urban climate factors
District population: 65,804*
* NYIT Background Document (2019), based on NYC DCP Rezoning Plan

Carbon Footprint   Urban Design Climate Lab—NYIT (2019)   **Urban Heat Island**
Net-Zero Carbon (NYIT-AIANY-In Source)   NYIT – UCCRN/GISS- Urban Land Institute

Figure 4. The 2050 Net Zero premise identifies three scenarios with a hybrid definition of scope. Boundary and associated assumptions include scenarios for: 1. Current Condition; 2. 2050 Baseline—Business as Usual; and, 3. 2050 Prototype—Best Practice. NYIT Urban Design Climate Lab (2020) and UCCRN/GISS (2019).

in meeting sustainability targets.[21] The 2050 Net Zero scenario calculated floor area in accordance with growth targets, represented by building mass and aggregated form that was optimized for solar energy generation and natural ventilation strategies based on area prevailing wind. Through increased density and optimized urban form the Net Zero scenario yielded a significant increase in open space when compared to the BAU full build-out scenario. These increased open-space assets would support managed retreat (where appropriate), green infrastructure and increased coastal resilience while also reducing heating and cooling demand and providing ample opportunity for district energy schemes; e.g., combined heat and power, distributed storage, community solar.

While overall energy demand in the net-zero scenario remains relatively constant when compared with BAU, increased efficiencies are central to emissions reduction strategies. Solar energy can be estimated to meet approximately 60 percent of demand by utilizing rooftop areas and viable façades. Though, this strategy would require a distributed storage network, it would defer a need to increase traditional grid capacity while also managing the solar duck curve through micro-balance of energy-use intensities within the district.[22] The remaining gap to meeting net-zero goals could be met with offshore wind and solar field development nearby and supplemented by further reduction in demand through shifts in behavior and increases in supply with waste to energy technologies and alternative fuels.

Small-scale locally owned utilities and distributed infrastructure, such as community-based micro-grids have become increasingly viable economically, though the regulatory environment is still prohibitive. When ownership is shared, returns can be reinvested locally. Once the "buy it and burn it" model has been supplanted, resilience increases — for both the energy "grid" and for social infrastructure. The value of these systems, in terms of CO_2e and for the communities that deploy them exemplify the potentials of alternative governance of utilities in reshaping the regulatory environment of our urban energy landscapes.

Defined in terms of mobility, the "Transportation" emissions sector of the Net Zero model constitutes a middle ground of convenience that is the public realm, and where the experience of infrastructure is anchored. It is where we move around. It encompasses our coming and going. It is defined by a shared aesthetic that represents the very *places* where people ultimately want to be.

How we use our public realm comprises approximately 25 percent of citywide emissions, and 80 percent of that results from the use of private vehicles.[23] In a 2050 Net Zero Neighborhood, private vehicles have been supplanted by electric vehicle car share, markedly improved bus service and experience, and micro-mobility options that support seamless mode transfer options, alongside cycling and pedestrian priorities throughout the district. Dynamically routed mobility, including block-level last-mile freight distribution and micro-hauling have space needs met at integrated nodes throughout the district. As with the proven co-benefits of better building performance, mobility futures impact not only a draw-down of emissions but also through the encouragement of and support for lifestyles that improve health and wellness, promote communal, public activity that results in increased social cohesion.[24]

The last set of considerations in the 2050 Net Zero scenario quantified emissions and solutions for waste, including water, material, industry, and food systems. "Waste" is the smallest sector-based contributor in terms of the Global Protocol method of accounting and serves as a catch-all for consumption-based emissions that are difficult to count but often closest to behavior and deeply embedded in daily lifestyle choices.[25] The impact of waste emissions grows significantly if instead considered through consumption-based methods of carbon accounting, e.g., with upstream and downstream activities and embodied energy quantifications, as opposed to emissions-based carbon accounting. Reduced consumption such as with prioritization of maintenance, support for hyper-local industrial symbiotic exchange, and retrofit strategies that consider building life cycles reflect change in consumptive and stewardship behaviors that align with net-zero goals through a circular economy approach.[26] In acknowledging these Scope 3 behavioral-based challenges and given the absence of a historical context in the research framework, an opportunity to consider questions of life-cycle analysis within the framework of a net-zero district presents with consequence.

Net Energy and Life-Cycle Analyses

Even with rigorous scoping definitions, such as those illustrated by the Net Zero Gowanus case study, existing Net Energy Analysis (NEA) methodologies face place-based inconsistencies with emissions accounting. Whereas the Life Cycle Analysis (LCA) methodology has adopted ISO (International Organization for Standardization) standards. Counter to Murphy, who suggests that NEA should be considered a subset of LCA, inverting these scalar relationships between the analytical frame when considering the boundary as a district and not a building would be beneficial, once of course there is a standard practice established for NEA.[27] At the district scale, nesting LCA within NEA would set up systemically to integrate and compound.

Research suggests that strong relationships between Net Energy Analysis (NEA) and Life Cycle Analysis (LCA) serves to identify a "Preservation-Sustainability Nexus," which is aligned with a functional model for preservation as it relates to economic, social and cultural components of the urban ecosystem.[28] While market forces are drivers of development that contribute to the deployment of green market tools, *regulation* may stifle markets abilities to meet sustainability benchmarks. Alternatively, if considered part of a localized public-private investment strategy incentives, and increased flexibility building on a *preservation-sustainability nexus* is a catalytic frame, not only in terms of systems integration, but also as it relates to cultural, and aesthetic benefits affecting Health Related Quality of Life (HRQOL) measures to support human-centered environmental goals.

Theoretically, in a sustainability district, nexus points are the location where systems and *architectural program* meet, rendering these *places* as potentially iconic among existing assets, and when taken together can be proponents of equitable, community-based development scenarios. Further reconciliation of these intersections and work to define a methodology for achieving authentic, preservation-friendly sustainable development tied to models of twenty-first-century industry and culture, including measure of impacts on occupant health, e.g., through circular economy, and net-zero lifestyle frameworks, is needed. As operative tools, freedoms are as powerful as limits.

Co-Benefits

Together, the timing of the Superfund designation and a long-term community-driven culture of advocacy in Gowanus parallel a trajectory of increasing awareness and shift toward Environmental, Social and Corporate Governance (ESG) valuation and yield an opportunity for scenario-based prototyping of place-based sustainable, equitable economic development.[29] Gowanus by Design, a local nonprofit organization, partnered

Figure 5. Gowanus Atlas Interface, consisting of community-based narratives and geospatial data as an advocacy tool and portal of information. Showing Southwest Brooklyn IBZ and Gowanus Rezoning boundary, NYCHA Campuses, manufacturing land use, projected sea-level rise, and phased clean-up plan. © Gowanus Urban Design Advocacy, Inc. d/b/a Gowanus by Design. All rights reserved.

with the 2050 Net Zero research team to develop a Net Zero version of the Gowanus Atlas. The Atlas is a public facing engagement tool that combines narrative storytelling with geospatial mapping toward accessible, data-driven rendering of neighborhood challenges and opportunities. The Atlas represents Gowanus' culture of civic action and provides a platform for visualizing environmental progress relative to remediation and a neighborhood-scale rezoning.

While the municipal rezoning processes require community input, planning departments have not historically been equipped to be as nimble as may be desired in response to community input on sustainability practices and progressive preservation. In contrast to de facto engagement, which often results in predetermined outcomes, scenario planning may enable a collectively defined future by way of a more flexible, responsive, and integrated process.[30] The current zoning ordinance allows for *special purpose districts,* though the limits of such can be narrow. To consider a special purpose district grounded in performance metrics constitutes a significant departure from the status quo.

A Net Zero special district would operate through an energy theory of value, methodologically different from being centered on an energy master plan. Where energy master plans are typically engineering-centric plans focused on optimizing building systems for institutional ownership with top-down governance among a portfolio of proximate buildings, only more recently have these types of plans begun to extend beyond singular ownership, to include public private partnerships and incorporate accounting of occupant behavior. Unlike energy master planning, the district scale Net Zero framework sought to dissolve operational silos that characterize the

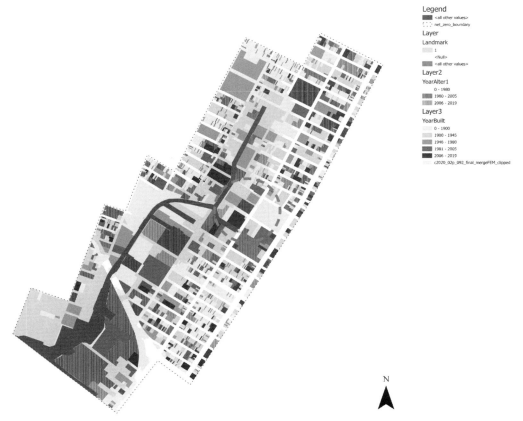

N
▲

Figure 6. Map showing building age, with alteration indicated after 1980 and after 2004. Landmarked sites show proximity and focus area of preservation activities. Photo: Author.

existing energy grid and replace with building systems and modified occupant behaviors toward a democratization of the system.

In parallel with the Gowanus rezoning process, five buildings in the area were designated landmarks, three of which are concentrated at one intersection. While landmark designation is a rigorous process with regard to architectural significance, the expanding retrofit toolkit and embodied carbon value of bricks and mortar lends older buildings new potential toward authentic representation of place-based histories. Yet, the economics of preservation and reinvestment, as strategies that anchor cultural identity, remain difficult to quantify. In terms of performance, a district frame shifts the function of landmark status away from the individual building and toward the aggregate effects of preservation. Paralleling a HRQOL frame of co-benefit, "economics once removed . . . preservation's *catalytic* effect on other economic development activities leads to the conclusion that historic preservation can have net positive effects on a regional or local economy."[31] Generational benefits of preservation described as "process" benefits, such as "community cohesion and social capital," are understood as secondary among more direct links between preservation and sustainability, e.g., "landfill impact, embodied energy, reuse of infrastructure, and lifecycle costing."[32] Preservation rarely has one single beneficiary. When overlaid on the context of a Net Zero scenario, the function of preservation, "organized primarily to sustain and create cultural values," enables the district, as *neighborhood,* to be a malleable, effective smart growth vehicle.[33]

Within this framework of *economics-once-removed,* consider the trajectory of Superfund to ecodistrict: EcoDistricts Protocol is a ground-up governance framework and flexible tool intended to guide place-based community and economic development by way of collectively established local sustainability goals.[34] The protocol proscribes a layer of governance, but also engages municipal partners to address allowances that fall outside of standard partnership models. Like a net-zero neighborhood, the EcoDistricts Protocol requires a boundary definition, which in the case of the EcoDistrict becomes an area for investment in its civic infrastructure.[35] Yet, even with organizations like C40s' Rocky Mountain Institute, et al., expounding the economic benefits of Deep Energy Retrofits and Net Zero Energy Districts, and with Civic Infrastructure a proven reinvestment strategy, awareness of relationships to ecosystem services resulting in increased social capital considered "a major correlate of community health and well-being," the values of preservation and creative place-making that define EcoDistricts and "green flag communities" had historically landed well outside status quo lending practices among banks and CDFIs (Community Development Financing Institutions) for those working to secure project-based underwriting.[36] There are perhaps widespread opportunities for pairing programs that have comprehensive environmental and social agendas with ongoing, successful preservation strategies, such as through a hybrid of an EcoDistrict with foundations of Main Street America.[37] Evidence shows where "environmental aesthetics may be closely associated with place attachment, or emotional bonds to a location," the power of programs to incite behavior change is well understood in the social sciences, "from behavioral scientists working on prevention . . . to the behavioral aspects of environmental psychology that are ultimately necessary for curbing consumption and building consensus."[38] These practices stand in contrast to the "buy-it-and-burn-it" model of resource consumption and development,[39] as an entirely smarter model and holistic system inclusive of energy analysis and preservation strategy designed to produce returns in support of its owners, operators, and occupants.

Scenario Planning

Where the pathway to clean energy gradually replaces older stock with newer cleaner technologically advanced assets,

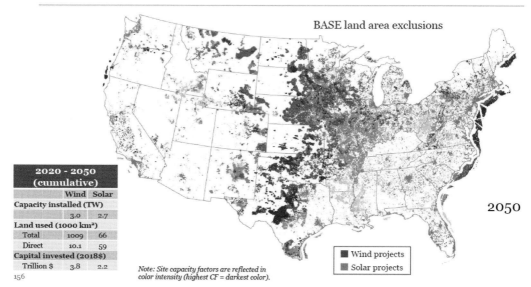

BASE land area exclusions

2020 - 2050 (cumulative)		
	Wind	Solar
Capacity installed (TW)		
	3.0	2.7
Land used (1000 km²)		
Total	1009	66
Direct	10.1	59
Capital invested (2018$)		
Trillion $	3.8	2.2

156

Note: Site capacity factors are reflected in color intensity (highest CF = darkest color).

2050

■ Wind projects
■ Solar projects

Figure 7. Land impacted by wind and solar in the Net Zero America scenario having the highest use of these resources. Credit: E. Larson, C. Greig, J. Jenkins et al. Net-Zero America: Potential Pathways, Infrastructure, and Impacts, interim report. Princeton University, Princeton, NJ. December 15, 2020.

selective reinvestment in retrofitting is a large part of this comprehensive long-term approach. A Net Zero Neighborhood humanizes the thirty-year national climate project outlined in the 2020 report *Net-Zero America,* while framing necessary and opportunistic disciplinary partnerships. At different scales, both Net Zero Neighborhoods and Net-Zero America are examples of *scenario planning,* "long term strategic planning that creates representation of multiple, plausible futures of a system of interest."[40] Scenario planning incorporates complex adaptive systems based in science and collaborative planning practices that emerged from social sciences and the critical social tradition. Scenario planning together with cross-functional interdisciplinary design practice that drives project governance and outcomes with sustainability benchmarking, early goal formation, multidisciplinary teams and process-based tools such as charrettes and engagement mechanisms involving community leadership and broad stakeholder groups can position architects as essential facilitators of these complex processes.

Achievement of long-term sustainability goals is contingent on widespread consensus-building that will require robust stakeholder engagement. As a priority in the next decade, major campaigns to shift behaviors, institutions, and markets toward the "acceptance, management and mitigation of impacts on landscapes and communities associated with the transition" will be needed.[41] It seems that the targeted sensitivity with which we maintain the past, i.e., by necessarily protecting and preserving in the present, is a vital contribution to the future. By retrofitting and maintaining the buildings and places that are determined to be of value to communities and society-at-large, the changes that will occur in support of that which should remain will at least be palatable and at best provide equitable amenity and far-reaching co-benefits.

Cultural Activism

The model for sustainable development posed by a Net Zero Neighborhood aligns with Hamil Pearsall's observation that the canal's Superfund listing sets up Gowanus to be an authentic place for investment in "green industry," not the next casualty of an urban postindustrial land grab. Such a net-zero future will require proactive community-based work to balance process and outcomes while taking caution to avoid inequitable trappings of "environmental gentrification."[42] Benefits paralleling the cultural shift to balance inherent to a net-zero framework that account for performance are inclusive of public good, incorporate both use and non-use value, where communities are also considered "investors" would signal increased status of "occupants" including their health and behaviors.

Retrofitting Value

Moving away from the dollar as a primary benchmark of return, toward a model that considers people and resources differently: "Economics are traditionally concerned with capital and labor, and more recently with technical innovation. . . . Energy use should be the primary standard of value by which all things and actions are judged."[43] Valuation methods change when accounting is conducted in terms of efficiency, reduction and carbon costs, similar to preservation analyses that identify dollars saved, rather than dollars gained.[44] There are widely used and accepted economic modeling systems within the historic preservation field, but they do not account for the gaps identified here such as with measuring public good, process benefits, or health related co-benefits.[45] While these types of fundamental shifts are possible and cause adjustment to widely accepted methods, change does not happen unless the status quo is disrupted. A shift in accounting principles for planning and preservation amounts to more than just semantics. A targeted practice to address this elusive accounting within transdisciplinary research practices throughout systemic built-environment relations, i.e., cultural and ecological, for public-health, HRQOL, social cohesion and social capital—all of which are dimensions of co-benefit—is needed.[46]

The common challenges of evaluating the economic benefits of climate change mitigation and historic preservation are predicated on differentiating between direct and indirect effects of investment, i.e., use and non-use value, private cost and public good. "Co-benefits are significantly more context, location, and case specific than direct climate or energy benefits" and "because most co-benefits, unlike the primary benefit, are enjoyed typically at regional or local scales, are closer to the agents bearing the mitigation costs, and have more immediate welfare effects, they provide incentives for decision makers to engage in more resolute climate action."[47] Co-benefits of building retrofits have been found to represent anywhere from 75 percent to 97 percent of direct energy-saving benefits.[48] Gowanus, in particular and a net-zero neighborhood, in general, would suggest that methodologies to assess and account for the co-benefits of climate mitigation and preservation may be similar, and may not be mutually exclusive.

Conclusion
In calling for a pre-engineered "retrofit" to achieve a carbon neutral future, sustainability planning must be balanced with preservation's humanist appeal. Scenario planning alone cannot achieve net-zero. *Cultural activism,* a tool and tenant of Cultural Infrastructure, is deeply embedded in the multidisciplinary strategies described here, from EcoDistricts and Net-Zero pathways to retrofits and historic preservation, all vehicles for stewardship. Cultural activism establishes shared goals, as "the range of collective and public practices and strategies that people use to alter dominant perceptions, ideas, and understandings for the sake of social change . . . must navigate complicated relationships with common public discourses and legal, political, and economic institutions."[49] In leveraging specific ecology to drive the local tenor of future development, "it is only through *collective* social action that resistance develops the potential for political transformation."[50] Counter intuitively, preservation and sustainable development are perhaps allied. Preservation is the agent of the *soft,* cultural work of social science, driven by the machine of planning, and forged from the *hard* science embedded in climate change. The places that compel action must at once remain and enhance the authenticity of that which is at stake.

The process of achieving net-zero is as much a social project as it is a techno-scientific accounting exercise. Engaging the tools, tactics and practices of historic preservation while acknowledging the evolving societal goals the toolkit must serve is an ongoing opportunity to appreciate and valorize our immediate past while collectively moving toward futures unknown. The National Park Service defines historic preservation as "a conversation with our past about our future" and similarly, identifying humanist pathways for sustainable growth should be considered: Defining today what matters thirty years from now is a truly radical act.[51]

Biography

Jessica L. Morris is an independent practitioner working at the intersection of environment and cultural sustainability. Driving the strategic advancement of client-side goals toward building healthy atmospheres in public and private realms, Jessica engages in research and practice with a focus on innovative, integrated thinking across disciplines. She holds a Bachelor of Fine Art from the Rhode Island School of Design and a Master of Architecture from the University of Pennsylvania. She serves on Manhattan Community Board 11 in East Harlem and as Co-Chair of the AIA New York Planning & Urban Design Committee.

Notes

[1] Nancy Carlisle, Otto Van Greet, Shanti Pless, *Definition of a "Zero Net Energy" Community* (National Renewable Energy Lab, 2009), https://www.nrel.gov/docs/fy100sti/46065.pdf.

[2] This range of stakeholders include, for example, geographers, cultural anthropologists, climate scientists, urban designers, planners, artists, architects, and community activists.

[3] For a narrative history of the canal, see Joseph Alexiou, *Gowanus: Brooklyn's Curious Canal* (New York: New York University, 2015).

[4] "Gowanus Lowlands" is a term used for the low-lying area surrounding the canal, and also the name of a masterplan released by the Gowanus Canal Conservancy in 2019.

[5] Foul conditions resulted from sewage overflow along the canal.

[6] City of New York, Landmarks Preservation Commission, "New York and Long Island Coignet Stone Company Building" (New York, June 26, 2006), http://www.nyc.gov/html/records/pdf/govpub/2469ny_li_coignet_stone_co.pdf.

[7] City of New York, Landmarks Preservation Commission, "Brooklyn Rapid Transit Company (BRT) Central Power Station Engine House," Designation Report (New York, October 29, 2019), http://s-media.nyc.gov/agencies/lpc/lp/.2639.pdf.

[8] The Flushing Tunnel Pumping Station was also landmarked in 2019. City of New York, Landmarks Preservation Commission, "Gowanus Canal Flushing Tunnel Pumping Station and Gate House," Designation Report (New York, October 29, 2019), http://s-media.nyc.gov/agencies/lpc/lp/2638.pdf.

[9] Power being the rate at which energy is transmitted; the rate at which work is performed.

[10] The Green Building is an architecturally insignificant but locally endeared venue. New York City Zoning Resolution, Section 72–21, https://zr.planning.nyc.gov/article-vii/chapter-2/72-21.

[11] Hamil Pearsall, "Superfund Me: A Study of Resistance to Gentrification in New York City," *Urban Studies* 50, no. 11 (2013): 2295, accessed on December 20, 2020, http://www.jstor.org/stable/26145582.

[12] See Melissa Checker, "Green Is the New Brown: 'Old School Toxics' and Environmental Gentrification on a New York City Waterfront," *Sustainability in the Global City: Myth and Practice,* ed. Cindy Isenhour, Gary McDonogh, and Melissa Checker (Cambridge: Cambridge University Press, 2015), 160.

[13] Pearsall, "Superfund Me," 2294.

[14] Isabelle Anguelovski, "Tactical Developments for Achieving Just and Sustainable Neighborhoods: The Role of Community-Based Coalitions and Bottom-to-Bottom Networks in Street, Technical, and Funder Activism," *Environment and Planning C: Government and Policy* 33, no. 4 (August 2015): 703–25, https://doi.org/10.1068/c12347.

[15] Anguelovski, "Tactical Developments for Achieving Just and Sustainable Neighborhoods."

[16] Net Zero Neighborhoods included partnerships between AIANY Planning & Urban Design Committee, AIANY Committee on the Environment, New York Institute of Technology's Urban Design Climate Lab, NSF supported InSource research consortium, and Gowanus by Design. The preparation for and program at the Green Building was underwritten by the Swiss Consulate General in New York, and included sector specific sustainability experts from ETH Zurich and the Future Cities Lab in Singapore.

[17] Net Zero Neighborhoods takes into consideration citywide benchmarking goals: 80 × 50, in 2014 calls for a citywide goal of 80 percent reduction of GhG emissions by 2050. For local benchmarking data see New York City, Mayor's Office of Sustainability, "Inventory of New York City Greenhouse Gas Emissions in 2017," December 2017, . For sector and scope definitions see: Greenhouse Gas Protocol, "Global Protocol for Community-Scale Greenhouse Gas Emission Inventories: An Accounting and Reporting Standard for Cities" (World Resources Institute, ICLEI, C40, 2014), http://c40-production-images.s3.amazonaws.com/other_uploads/images/143_GHGP_GPC_1.0.original.pdf?1426866613.

[18] The Global Protocol defines scopes 1, 2, and 3 as a method of classifying the source of emissions.

[19] The study accounts for 65,804 people living in the district in 2050, a 180 percent increase on today's population. See: New York City Department of City Planning, "Gowanus Neighborhood Rezoning and Related Actions: Final Environmental Impact Statement," Appendix A, September 10, 2021, https://www1.nyc.gov/site/planning/applicants/env-review/gowanus.page.

[20] See: Madeleine Steinmetz-Wood et al., "Is Gentrification All Bad? Positive Association Between Gentrification and Individual's Perceived Neighborhood Collective Efficacy in Montreal, Canada," *International Journal of Health Geographics* 16, no. 24 (2017); Robert J. Sampson, Jeffrey D. Morenoff, and Thomas Gannon-Rowley, "Assessing 'Neighborhood Effects': Social Processes and New Directions in Research," *Annual Review of Sociology* 28 (2002): 443–78, https://www.annualreviews.org/doi/10.1146/annurev.soc.28.110601.141114, accessed on June 15, 2020.

[21] In 2019, the Climate Mobilization Act, a suite of bills including Local Law 97, supports clean energy and building energy performance compliance, requiring retrofit for the poorest performers, and establishing financing mechanisms for renewable and efficiency investments to be made by owners.

[22] See U.S. Department of Energy, Office of Energy Efficiency and Renewable Energy, "Confronting the Duck Curve: How to Address Over-Generation of Solar Energy," October 12, 2017, https://www.energy.gov/eere/articles/confronting-duck-curve-how-address-over-generation-solar-energy, accessed February 18, 2021.

[23] Mayor's Office of Sustainability, "Inventory of New York City Greenhouse Gas Emissions in 2016," New York City, December 2017, https://www1.nyc.gov/assets/sustainability/downloads/pdf/publications/GHG%20Inventory%20Report%20Emission%20Year%202016.pdf.

[24] Viniece Jennings, Lincoln Larson, and Jessica Yun, "Advancing Sustainability through Urban Green Space: Cultural Ecosystem Services, Equity, and Social Determinants of Health," *International Journal of Environmental Research and Public Health* 13, no. 2 (2016): 196. While Jennings is looking specifically at the impacts of urban green space, however the research more broadly applicable to include impacts of improved environmental quality.

[25] Arup, and C40 Cities, "Consumption-Based GHG Emissions of C40 Cities," March 2018, https://www.c40knowledgehub.org/s/article/Consumption-based-GHG-emissions-of-C40-cities?language=en_US. Though, it is well understood that this behavior-based accounting is extraordinarily difficult for municipalities to accurately track.

[26] Greywater treatment and thermal energy storage at the building level, waste-to-energy systems, and more robust, integrated green infrastructure are all necessary strategies in the Net Zero scenario, as they contribute to drawing down overall emissions. Thorton Tomasetti, "Resilience and Circular Economy: Cities Reimagined," Roundtable Discussion, May 20, 2020, https://www.thorntontomasetti.com/news/resilience-circular-economy-cities-reimagined, accessed on May 26, 2020.

[27] David J. Murphy, Michael Carbajales-Dale, Devin Moeller, "Comparing Apples to Apples: Why the Net Energy Analysis Community Needs to Adopt the Life-Cycle Analysis Framework," *Energies* 9, no. 11 (2016): 917. My position is counter to Murphy's.

[28] Maria Karoglou, Stella S. Kyvelou, Christos Boukouvalas, Chryssa Theofani, Asterios Bakolas, Magdalini Krokida, Antonia Moropoulou, "Towards a Preservation–Sustainability Nexus: Applying LCA to Reduce the Environmental Footprint of Modern Built Heritage," *Sustainability* 11, no. 21 (2019): 6147.

[29] Checker, "Green Is the New Brown," 165. See also James S. Coleman, "Social Capital in the Creation of Human Capital," *American Journal of Sociology* 94 (1988): S95–S120. *JSTOR,* www.jstor.org/stable/2780243, accessed on May 29, 2021.

[30] See Checker, "Green Is the New Brown," 174. However, in December 2020 New York City Council introduced legislation to redesign the citywide planning process, intending to incorporate long-term scenario planning, increased accountability and community input. "Planning Together: A New Comprehensive Planning Framework for New York City," New York City Council, December 16, 2020, https://council.nyc.gov/news/2020/12/16/planning-together/.

[31] Donovan R. Rypkema, Caroline Cheong, and Randall Mason. "Measuring Economic Impacts of Historic Preservation: A Report to the Advisory Council on Historic Preservation," *PlaceEconomics*, November 2011, 7. See also Randall Mason, "Economics and Historic Preservation: A Guide and Review of the Literature" (Washington, DC: Brookings Institute, 2005), 17. (Author's emphasis.)

[32] Rypkema et al., "Measuring Economic Impacts of Historic Preservation," 12.

[33] Mason, "Economics and Historic Preservation," 8.

[34] "EcoDistricts Protocol: The Standard for Community Development," September 2017, EcoDistricts: Portland.

[35] Elizabeth Greenspan, and Randall Mason, "Civic Infrastructure: A Model for Civic Asset Reinvestment," PennPraxis for the William Penn Foundation, Philadelphia, March 2017.

[36] The Multiple Benefits of Deep Retrofits, C40 Cities, BuroHappold Engineering. April 2020, 12. An Integrative Business Model for Net Zero Energy Districts, Rocky Mountain Institute: Insight Brief, Ialn Campbell, Victor Olgyay, August 2016. Centers for Disease Control and Prevention, Measuring Healthy Days. Atlanta, GA: CDC, November 2000. Federal Reserve Bank of San Francisco, 2019, "Transforming Community Development through Arts and Culture," Federal Reserve Bank of San Francisco Community Development Innovation Review 2019-2, 187. Interview with Jimeno A. Fonseca, Net-Zero Neighborhoods Workshop, Center for Architecture, New York, New York, December 9, 2019.

[37] Main Street America was founded by the National Trust for Historic Preservation in 1980. See https://www.mainstreet.org/home.

[38] Jennings et al., "Advancing Sustainability through Urban Green Space," 194. Anthony Biglan, *The Nurture Effect: How the Science of Human Behavior Can Improve our Lives and Our World* (Oakland, CA: New Harbinger Publications, 1995), 132.

[39] Interview with David Driskell, Net-Zero Neighborhoods Workshop, Center for Architecture, New York, New York, December 9, 2019.

[40] Scenario planning is a practice that evolved out of the RAND Corporation post-WWII and thereafter as a practice of corporate strategy, e.g., Royal Dutch Shell, vis-à-vis the oil crisis of 1973. Robert Goodspeed, *Scenario Planning for Cities and Regions: Managing and Envisioning Uncertain Futures* (Cambridge, MA: Lincoln Institute of Land Policy, 2020), 20, 22–25.

[41] E. Larson, C. Greig, J. Jenkins, E. Mayfield, A. Pascale, C. Zhang, J. Drossman, R. Williams, S. Pacala, R. Socolow, E. J. Baik, R. Birdsey, R. Duke, R. Jones, B. Haley, E. Leslie, K. Paustian, and A. Swan, *Net-Zero America: Potential Pathways, Infrastructure, and Impacts,* Interim Report, Princeton University, December 15, 2020, 337, https://netzeroamerica.princeton.edu/img/Princeton_NZA_Interim_Report_15_Dec_2020_FINAL.pdf.

[42] Checker, "Green Is the New Brown," 159. See also the work of Isabelle Anguelovski et al. at the Barcelona Lab for Urban Environmental Justice and Sustainability.

[43] Vaclav Smil, *Energy in Nature and Society: General Energetics of Complex Systems* (Cambridge, MA: MIT Press, 2008), 335.

[44] Rypkema et al., "Measuring Economic Impacts of Historic Preservation," 27.

[45] Rypkema et al., "Measuring Economic Impacts of Historic Preservation," 15.

[46] Mason, "Economics and Historic Preservation," 19–20.

[47] Diana Ürge-Vorsatz, Sergio Tirado Herrero, Navroz K. Dubash, Franck Lecocq, "Measuring the Co-Benefits of Climate Change Mitigation," 39, no. 1 (2014): 554, 562–63, 574. Categories of co-benefits from energy-based mitigation policies include: positive health impacts related to indoor and outdoor air quality; reduction of mortality and morbidity due to cold housing conditions; reduction of and increased protection from exposure to noise; reduction of traffic related injuries and improved health from active transport; reduction of mortality due to urban heat island; improved thermal comfort for building occupants; improved productivity of individuals, communities and organizations; access to and affordability of energy services; increased energy security; and economic growth and employment.

[48] Ürge-Vorsatz et al., "Measuring the Co-Benefits of Climate Change Mitigation."

[49] Melissa Checker and Maggie Fishman, "Introduction," I*Local Actions: Cultural Activism, Power, and Public Life in America,* ed. Melissa Checker and Maggie Fishman (New York: Columbia University Press, 2004), 5–6.

[50] Checker, Fishman, "Introduction," 5.

[51] What is Historic Preservation?, National Park Service, accessed on May 31, 2021, at nps.gov/subjects/historicpreservation/what-is-historic-preservation.htm.

Figure 1. Frédéric Druot, Anne Lacaton, and Jean-Philippe Vassal, Tour Bois-le-Prêtre, Paris. © Fabio Lepratto.

Francesco Cianfarani and
Michele Morganti

Preservation Themes in Mass Housing's Retrofit
Climate and Energy in Tor Bella Monaca, Rome

Introduction: Urban Decay, Preservation and Retrofit

This article aims to debate the problem of preservation for postwar mass-housing complexes, particularly in light of their urban decay.[1] The phenomenon of urban decay in contemporary cities is related to mass housing in multiple ways. The physical and social decline of this residential model has been internationally debated since the last fifty years by a vast scientific literature and this topic is still central worldwide. Indeed, mass housing represents a consistent part of the modern global housing stock and it is a model still under experimentation in booming and crowded cities of East Asian countries.[2]

Preservation, a discipline grounded in tools and practices that ensure the diversity and significance of cultural heritage in the built environment, plays a strategic role in processes of regeneration of distressed neighborhoods and communities. However, urban decay of postwar mass housing is one of the most problematic topics to interpret through traditional tools of preservation, at least for two reasons. First, because these tools have to deal with original, short-term planning and design strategies, demonstrated over time as outdated.[3] Today most of postwar mass housing's original features have revealed themselves as unsustainable, also considering the urgency of climate change mitigation and adaptation in cities.[4] Second, the negative narrative associated with such mass housing still generates a shared feeling of disengagement with the cause of preservation. Especially in Western countries, decades of media representation of mass-housing neighborhoods as unlivable, top-down, and crime-ridden environments had heavily influenced the debate on their global cultural legacy.[5]

Recent studies in the field are contributing to expanding the theme of modern heritage preservation to postwar housing, with particular attention to mass housing.[6] Within this debate, current research on building retrofit and climate-proof adaptation is increasingly debating innovative ways to extend the life of mass-housing complexes while tackling their urban decay.[7] The strategic importance of mass-housing stock for the experimentation of contemporary retrofit and climate-proof practices is due to multiple factors. First, the residential sector accounts for 27 percent of global primary energy consumption and is responsible for 17 percent of global carbon dioxide emissions,

Future Anterior
Volume XVIII, Number 1
Summer 2021

making housing one of the most critical areas for the reduction of emissions in contemporary cities.[8] Second, within the global residential stock, mass housing plays a crucial role in building renovation and efficiency.[9] Due to their physical characteristics, mass-housing complexes are one of the main contributors to global operational energy consumption and one of the most exposed to urban climate change.[10] Third, mass-housing stock is usually owned and managed by the public, particularly in Europe and the USA. This makes mass housing a sector where national governments and local authorities can play a vital role in promoting energy efficient and climate adaptation actions, leading through best practices.

Climate change and the associated energy crisis is recasting forms and actions in architecture. In fact, according to Amale Andraos, several notions involved in architecture have taken new forms in the engagement with climate change, including the ideas of technology, infrastructure, embodied energy, and narrative.[11] Similarly, these notions are also altering the conceptual coordinates of contemporary preservation culture. In particular, the topic of the embodied energy is suggesting new interpretations for the assessment of the intangible values of the built environment. Demolition of a postwar housing complex still implies dramatic costs of disposal of waste materials and land clearing. Most importantly, in the case of mass housing, usually built with energy intensive construction methods and materials, demolition implies the loss of the intricate web of consumed, exchanged, or produced energy characterizing its life cycle.[12] Therefore, contemporary retrofit practices become strategic to foster a new goal for the heritagization of mass-housing stock, focused on the cultural and ethical need of retaining its embodied energy while reducing the demand of operational energy.[13]

Topics of neighborhood preservation alongside requirements of climate-proofing, energy efficiency, carbon emission reduction, and adaptation to current lifestyles emerge. Therefore, when it comes to defining successful climate-responsive retrofit practices, important questions arise: what are the most sustainable strategies for the refurbishment of mass-housing complexes? How can these actions help retain the social and cultural significance of one of the most controversial and endangered legacies of the last century? How do we outline new design principles for improving urban and architectural quality through retrofit?

To reply to these questions, this article discusses the current debate and the ultimate proposals for the retrofit and preservation of the Tor Bella Monaca neighborhood in Rome, one of the biggest and most disputed Italian mass-housing complexes. First, the article presents a brief introduction to the topic of mass housing in relationship to phenomena of urban decay and heritage questions. It discusses the evolution of mass-housing preservation culture, identifying most significant interpretations. Second, it illustrates the Italian context. Third, it analyzes the case study of Tor Bella Monaca, reconstructing its history and main urban and architectural features. Finally, it discusses the latest design and research contributions for the renovation of Tor Bella Monaca and how climate-responsive retrofit strategies can be implemented to support preservation goals.

1. Evolution of Mass-Housing Preservation Culture

Postwar mass housing testifies unquestionable cultural values. Significant traces of this legacy can be found globally, in Western Europe, USA, and in the former Soviet countries, in Asia (mainly in India, China, Japan, Korea), Central and South America (Argentina, Brazil, Venezuela), and Africa (Algeria).[14] Many of these projects stand for the uniqueness of their urban and architectural spaces, often paired with advanced experimentation in building technologies and materials.

Though characterized by undeniable design features, postwar mass-housing complexes often resulted in evident problems of technical obsolescence. Indeed, being guided by design values of affordability, construction speed, and prefabrication, mass-housing projects implemented experimental master plans, building methods and technical solutions that are currently obsolete. In addition, the urbanistic premises of these projects—usually mono-functional and mono-income settlements, built in peripheral areas far from job opportunities, transit, and recreational facilities—resulted in marginalized and fragile communities.

Therefore, the widely expressed underappreciation of the mass-housing model in contemporary cities, especially in Western countries, is based on the phenomena or urban decay often associated with it. Early discussions focused on the social, economic, and environmental opportunity of retaining these structures date back to the late 1970s. The center of discussion was in Europe, particularly in France, Netherlands, and Great Britain, where urban renewal policies usually resulted in systematic, large-scale demolitions of mass-housing complexes.[15] Especially the European urban and architectural design culture valued the topic of mass-housing preservation as an important field of experimentation. Belgian architect Lucien Kroll was among the first designers to critically approach the transformation of decaying French mass-housing projects, by developing an "eco-social" methodology, based on residents' participation.[16] Though not primarily guided by energy retrofit goals, Kroll's proposals put the basis for the development of a sustainable and inclusive culture for the transformation of mass housing.[17] In the 1980s, the collaborative work of Groupe Aura, Eckart Hahn, and Arken Arkitekter expanded Kroll's approach to energy retrofit interventions by focusing on the addition of exterior architectural features—like loggias, balconies, greenhouses—to significantly improve the physical and environmental performance of dwellings.[18] All these proposals reinforced the culture of retrofit, by grounding it to the retention of existing social bonds and ecosystems. Most importantly, this body of work helped globally recognize the significance of mass housing's heritage and integrate tools and studies on preservation into topics related to energy and sustainability.

Following these pioneering approaches, contemporary design culture is particularly focused on expanding topics of preservation to mass housing. Current research of French architects Anne Lacaton and Jean-Philippe Vassal has established the most recognized design practices for the retrofit of outdated mass-housing stock. This research stands out as a response to the still diffused, often economically absurd and socially unsustainable, demolition policies for European mass housing.[19] The projects of the Bois-le-Prêtre Tower in Paris, or the Cité du Grand Parc in Bordeaux, arguably the best-known contemporary examples of postwar housing renovation,[20] clearly manifest Lacaton and Vassal's "never demolish" approach.[21] The renovation of these large-scale residential buildings is mainly focused on the aesthetic, functional and energetic performance of ground floors and building envelopes. The latter are significantly improved by adding extra self-supporting structures to generate additional residential spaces, such as loggias and winter gardens.

Lacaton and Vassal's seminal contribution is not primarily motivated by the urgency of preserving mass-housing complexes as monuments. On the contrary, it is mainly focused on engaging the hidden potential for transformation of the mass-housing model and its adaptability to change.[22] This approach to preservation via retrofit is evidently based on a deep understanding of mass-housing phenomenon as part of modern design culture, intrinsically linked to principles of open-endedness, modularity, and adaptability. The innate predisposition to modification in modern buildings makes mass housing fit to incorporate shifts in lifestyles and new possibilities for energy upgrading.

2. The Italian Case Study

To further discuss cultural aspects of global mass housing, modern heritage topics, and contemporary opportunities for the retrofit culture, the Italian case study of Tor Bella Monaca in Rome (TBM), is presented here.[23]

The Italian scenario is particularly worth discussing for several reasons. As in other countries in Europe, the heartland of modern housing experimentation, Italian postwar mass-housing complexes represent a consistent part of the modern built heritage.[24] Also, though not yet widely recognized by national legislations and preservation authorities as heritage, the cultural and social value of this legacy is undeniable.[25] The history of Italian postwar mass housing has been linked to national social welfare programs that aimed to support low-income households and counterbalance the often-poor quality of real estate developments in peripheral areas of cities. Especially in Italy, mass housing had represented, in the words of Miles Glendinning, "a field of the most burning political concern," and "a central focus of agitation to the socially-minded intelligentsia, including architects, city planners, sociologists, and public health reformists."[26] Today, these public complexes still serve as home for hundreds of communities.

Because of its size, location, and urban characteristics, TBM epitomizes most of the traits of Italian mass-housing complexes built between the early 1960s and the 1980s through PEEPs, Piani di Edilizia Economica e Popolare (Low-cost housing plans).[27]

TBM is the result of the first PEEP-approved by the municipality of Rome in 1964.[28] Interventions implemented by PEEPs reflect similarities with approaches that were globally pursued at that time. Not so differently from French *grands ensembles,* Soviet *khrushchyovka,* Japanese *danchi* complexes, or American Public Housing projects, PEEPs resulted in producing unified, mono-class, self-sufficient industrialized housing developments, often far from urban centers.[29]

Indeed, TBM was built in the eastern outskirts of Rome, immediately outside the perimeter of the GRA, the main ring road of the City. The site chosen for construction was a slightly hilly area of Campagna Romana (Roman countryside), surrounded by low-quality private developments with no infrastructure and services.[30] From the beginning of its history, TBM was imagined as the latest, biggest, and fastest public-housing project in Rome originating from the 1964 PEEP. The project, started in 1981 and almost completed in 1984, was planned by the technical office of the last left-wing city administration.[31] TBM's design and construction had to achieve a threefold goal. First, it had to rapidly build affordable rental units for 25,000 people.[32] Second, it had to provide basic infrastructure, services, and green spaces both for TBM's residents and existing communities in the surrounding unplanned neighborhoods.

Figure 2. Views of Tor Bella Monaca during construction. © Elio Piroddi.

Third, it represented the response of the public against the uncontrolled private expansion and proposed a way to stop speculative developments from the consumption of the Campagna Romana.

3. TBM: Five Traits of Italian Mass Housing

The design of TBM can be summarized according to five key elements, traceable in most postwar Italian PEEPs. These aspects clearly represent the broadest Italian mass-housing production, as an expression of the planning culture developed in the nation particularly from the 1960s—the years of the Economic Boom—to the early 1980s—the end of the Years of Lead, the season of internal terrorism and economic deceleration.

The first aspect concerns the adhesion of TBM's planners to the model of the modern city.[33] Though completed in the 1980s, TBM's urban design is still grounded in the myths of modern planning culture. The master plan follows a car-oriented, high-rise, low-density model, implemented by

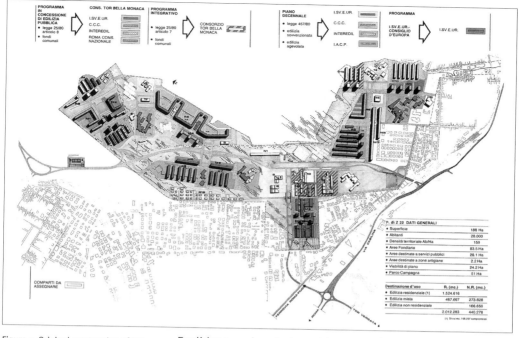

Figure 3. Original master plan of Tor Bella Monaca. © Elio Piroddi.

Euclidean zoning. Its layout is centered on the axis of via di Tor Bella Monaca, an expressway that connects the neighborhood to the GRA ring road. The expressway provides access to five districts—four residential neighborhoods and one service area—characterized by towers, slabs, and *redents,* following a pattern independent of the street layout.

Second, as a product of modern planning culture, TBM can be defined as an "artificial city," an urban and residential model based on a standardized and "normative way of life."[34] Control and normalization of environmental conditions and building performances were among the essential features of modern civilization, mainly spread worldwide through housing. TBM was planned at the beginning of the 1980s, during a historical moment of still perceived climatic stability and energy abundance. Therefore, TBM's designers pushed to the extreme the environmental control of the project towards a sort of "thermal anesthesia."[35] Building form and façade orientations did not consider sufficiently solar energy and local wind patterns, relying completely on artificial systems for thermal comfort. However, since their construction, TBM buildings' envelopes in concrete panels have produced high operational energy costs. In addition, these materials, together with oversized artificial horizontal surfaces—streets, parking areas and impermeable pavements—produce a relevant urban heat island effect.[36] These result in an additional increase in energy demand for cooling, health problems for residents, and reduction of efficiency of drainage infrastructure.

Figure 4. Tor Bella Monaca, view from Viale Duilio Cambellotti after construction. © Wikimedia Commons.

In TBM, the excessive dimensioning of the street sections, green spaces, and parking areas is caused by the standards set by the Roman PEEP and the postwar national legislation for mass housing.[37] As a reflection of the Italian "normative approach" to mass housing, these standards had the goal to provide a minimum but significant amount of streets, green spaces, parking areas, and residential spaces for each inhabitant. Also, the exaggerated extent of TBM was partially justified by the need to connect it with the existing, disordered web of informal private settlements. Therefore, the ground level of the neighborhood is strongly characterized by the presence of several spaces left over after planning—SLOAPs.[38] SLOAPs represent the third trait of TBM as one of the main controversial topics of Italian PEEPs. In TBM, 40 percent of total unbuilt areas is undefined in terms of land use and ownership.[39] Ambiguously identified in the project master plan as *campagna-parco* (countryside-park), the spaces surrounding the built-up areas and street network have no landscape design or function. Over time their out-of-scale size, together with perceived unclear ownership, has generated abandonment and serious maintenance issues.

The fourth key aspect of TBM concerns the questionable design of ground floor spaces of residential buildings. As prescribed by national and regional laws on housing, most of TBM's ground floors were designed to host dwellings — some of them for individuals with disabilities — or private storage units. As a result, local businesses, community services, and recreational spaces in TBM were placed in separate, large-scale monofunctional buildings. This design choice has generated a continuous, blind barrier at the ground floor of the housing blocks and a sense of discomfort and insecurity that contributes to the impoverishment of the neighborhood's social life.

The last key aspect concerns the experimental construction technique of TBM's buildings. To speed up the construction of the neighborhood, residential units were built with an industrialized system of reinforced concrete panels called *coffrage tunnel*.[40] This construction choice is responsible for the already mentioned poor performance of the building envelope and for the lack of diversity of the dwelling units in terms of spatial layout and size.

Over the years, all these planning and design criticalities had contributed to exacerbate social problems of TBM's development and, more generally, Italian PEEPs. Soon after the early allocations, excessive distance from the city center and transit, lack of *mixité sociale* and public amenities, together with discontinuous maintenance policies, led to the physical and social decay of the neighborhood.[41]

4. TBM: Preservation Via Retrofit
The most controversial planning and design aspects of TBM are the result of the unique social, economic, and ideological nature of its program. Interestingly, extending the life of this mass-housing complex may appear a paradox that is prolonging the life cycle of a neighborhood whose original physical structure was determined by a program shaped by specific but obsolete norms and standards.

However, some underestimated and not fully developed design features of TBM's project are rare to find in contemporary Italian peripheral areas, such as large dwellings, expansive views towards the city, and immediate accessibility to green areas. Moreover, the abundance of open spaces and infrastructures make TBM particularly fit as a field of experimentation for climate-responsive retrofit strategies.

First of all, preservation initiatives for TBM should start from changing its reputation, by developing a new storyline, a narrative grounded in the unique and positive aspects of the neighborhood. Today TBM is widely perceived by the Roman public as an icon of social exclusion and as a symbol of the failures of the City's housing policies. Over the last thirty years, disregard for rules of allocations and rent collections, together with illegal squatting and crime episodes have exacerbated the relationship between the TBM's community, the City, and the housing authority. However, though characterized by a current social exclusion, TBM hosts an active and cohesive community of residents, supported by associations and social centers that daily fight for fostering values of legality and solidarity.[42]

In the case of TBM, the urgency of shifting the general negative perception of the neighborhood is clearly manifested by recent discussions about its future. In this regard, in 2010 an ambitious redevelopment project proposed by the City put TBM at the center of the national debate.[43] The project, presented as the largest housing redevelopment in Europe, was based on the idea that preserving TBM through retrofit was an unsustainable strategy in terms of economic, social, and environmental impact.[44] Therefore, the proposal, entirely financed by private developers, planned the complete demolition of the existing residential stock and the construction of a new settlement, with a 25 percent increase in built-up areas. The proposed new master plan, designed by the New Urbanist planner Leon Krier, was inspired by the traditional model of the European compact city. Reactions were polarized, especially because of the social and political implications of the proposal. Parts of the TBM's residents, together with the Roman public and housing authority, perceived the project as a reactionary attack to TBM's history of progressive architecture and social engagement.[45] After four years of public debate, the redevelopment project was found to be mostly socially unsustainable and economically unfeasible and was abandoned by the new City administration.

Nevertheless, Krier's initiative had the merit to trigger off a stimulating debate among citizens, policymakers, planners, and academics.[46] Over the last ten years, significant interdisciplinary research-based projects have been conducted to oppose the negative storytelling about TBM, by demonstrating material and immaterial resources in the neighborhood. Though none of these projects have been implemented yet, they had the merit to recognize environmental, urban, and architectural values in TBM, and to identify cross-disciplinary strategies for its preservation and retrofit.[47] Moreover, the local debate has been supported by several international initiatives, promoted by the UN-Habitat Global Housing Strategy—such as the International Competition on Urban Revitalization of Mass Housing—and the Toledo Declaration.[48] These initiatives have encouraged EU countries—in particular France, UK, Netherlands, and Germany—to undertake transformative actions

ranging from complete preservation to urban regeneration and redevelopment.[49]

Five associated design goals can be recognized within the debate, in consideration of the above-mentioned five traits of Italian mass housing: *urban intensity*; *climate-proof city*; *SLOAP shrinking*; *streetscape activation*; *passive layout.* Through a cross-scale approach, from the urban to the building scale, they can be formulated as follows.

TBM's current low-density, high-rise model does not meet human needs in terms of urban intensity. The achievement of this goal, resulting from a combination of several physical and nonphysical factors—compactness, diversity, density, and connectivity—is of primary importance for building vibrant communities.[50] A successful project should consider the following design actions to foster urban intensity. First, the modern city model needs to increase its urban compactness, to promote walkability and urban vibrancy. Second, it necessitates to enhance its diversity, as well as its functional and social *mixité,* by introducing new dwelling typologies that respond to current housing needs, such as workspaces, dwellings for temporary city users, elderly, and small families. Last, it requires a reduction in the *enclave* effect, by enhancing street networks with the surrounding urban areas as well as the city center.[51]

In the current scenarios of urban climate change, clearly manifested by the increase of extreme weather events, the abundance of open spaces is a valuable resource of climate-proof potential offered by the modern city and, by extension, the mass-housing model. Compared to the limited presence of nature in compact cities, these open spaces can easily accommodate nature-based solutions both at urban and building

Figure 6. Design proposal for the transformation of the streetscape of Tor Bella Monaca © Nicole De Togni, Lavinia Dondi, Elena Fontanella, Agim Kërçuku, Fabio Lepratto, Michele Morganti.

scales. A climate-proof environment is of primary importance to increase health and quality of life of inhabitants as well as create more comfortable spaces, both in terms of microclimate condition and aesthetics.[52] The introduction of trees, rain gardens, water squares and ponds, bioswales, permeable pavements, cool materials, and green roofs and façades can project mass housing into a climate-proof future.[53] In this regard, TBM and similar housing complexes should have a crucial environmental role for a sustainable future of the whole urban system.

Several design proposals for TBM underline the importance of re-scaling and reducing excessive, underused public spaces.[54] SLOAP shrinking is crucial both to avoid the indeterminacy of uses — often cause of informal appropriation and associated crime episodes — and to reduce maintenance budget. In addition, this goal is a fundamental prerequisite for enhancing social control, space protection, and sense of ownership, as described below.

One of the most fragile spaces in TBM is the streetscape. Public/private thresholds need to be activated through an appropriate use of the spaces at the ground level. This would open opportunities for creating both new community spaces and services, such as co-housing and co-working, and new dwelling typologies with semiprivate spaces that act as filters between public and private realms. By successfully managing public/private thresholds, it is possible to increase the sense of ownership, natural social control, space protection, social mixité, and street vibrancy.[55]

Design actions at the streetscape level should be associated with suitable retrofit strategies by relying on the use of passive layouts at the building scale. Considering these issues in a preservation perspective is nowadays necessary in light of the need of meeting the GHG emissions target of the EU for the existing building stock.[56] The transformation of the dwelling layouts, together with a new — or renewed — building envelope, has been identified as an effective design strategy to improve health conditions, indoor thermal comfort as well as the overall functional and aesthetic quality of the building. The expansion of dwellings' living spaces through additional private or semiprivate spaces — winter gardens, loggias, and balconies — allows for a multitude of activities, sometimes defined by the tenants. Added spaces at the envelope extremities act as passive devices — buffer spaces and greenhouses — that increase building thermal performance and reduce energy demand for heating. In addition, the design of a new façade allows the implementation of extra passive devices, such as thermal insulation layers — both opaque and transparent — sun shadings, green or Trombe walls, stack ventilation systems, et cetera. Finally, by working on the exterior layer of the building, construction works can be realized with low-cost prefabrication systems while keeping tenants inside during the entire process.

Conclusions

Today, TBM consists of almost two-square kilometers of human relationships, spaces, matter, and energy to be preserved and regenerated. Its modern layout, open spaces, energy reservoir, and visual and physical relationships with nature make it an archetype of postwar Italian mass housing. As climate change and energy consumptions and emissions are the most crucial and unsolved challenges in cities' future, neighborhoods like TBM have an effective potential to improve their climate-proof and energy efficiency.[57]

The preservation and valorization of mass-housing complexes, such as TBM, requires both the understanding of inhabitants' needs and their direct participation in retrofit practices. Successful retrofit processes must involve communities in several ways: fostering local urban practices through a conscious transformation of urban and building spaces; producing narratives useful for tackling the stigma and creating new shared imaginaries; promoting retrofit living labs and pilot projects through participatory processes. As a matter of fact, housing is one of the most representative aspects of society's transformation. Therefore, preservation actions need to be based on the assessment of the sustainability of the mass-housing model in current social scenarios.

The debate on TBM's preservation suggests significant insights on the contribution of energy efficient and climate-proof design to possible retrofit actions in mass-housing complexes. Nowadays, in light of increasing evidence of the negative effects of extreme weather events in cities, environmental awareness is becoming paramount in many areas, including urban

Figure 7. Current picture of Tor Bella Monaca, Tower R15. © Fabio Moscatelli.

Figure 8. Current picture of Tor Bella
Monaca, from the Roman countryside.
© Fabio Moscatelli.

and architectural design. The physical characteristics of these neighborhoods, featured by a strict relationship among urban, building, and interior scales, identify them as perfect assets to test complex and systemic retrofit actions, based on cross-disciplinary approaches.

Biographies

Francesco Cianfarani holds a PhD in Architectural and Urban Design at Sapienza University of Rome. He is Assistant Professor at the Christopher C. Gibbs College of Architecture, University of Oklahoma, where he conducts studies on housing design and transformation, and adaptive reuse of industrial heritage. Cianfarani is the author of articles and book chapters in the field, including: "The Legacy of the Official Borgate: Design, Reception and Current Life of the Quarticciolo Neighborhood," in *The Routledge Companion to Italian Fascist Architecture*, ed. K. B. Jones and Stephanie Pilat (Routledge, 2020); and "L'architettura del Villaggio Olimpico tra forma della casa e forma dell'evento," in *Quattro Quartieri*, ed. F. De Matteis and L. Reale (Quodlibet, 2017).

Michele Morganti is Assistant Professor of Sustainable Building Design at Sapienza University of Rome. His research and teaching activities focus on the relationships among urban climate change, microclimate, and building energy performance in a cross-scale design perspective, with special interests in housing retrofit. Michele's book *Ambiente costruito mediterraneo: Forma, densità ed energia,* published in 2018, investigates interactions between urban form and energy in the Mediterranean city by means of density. Current studies include spatial metrics for urban energy modeling and climate-responsive design in light of climate change.

Notes

[1] Current literature does not provide universally acknowledged definitions of "mass housing." The article adopts the definition of "international postwar mass housing," referring to public housing projects built between the 1960s and the 1980s. These interventions were usually characterized by large-scale, self-sufficient, mono-class, industrialized developments, mainly built and managed by public authorities. For a concise perspective on international mass housing, see Miles Glendinning, "Multifaceted Monolith: The Hidden Diversity of Mass Housing," in *Images of Power and the Power of Images. Control, Ownership and Public Spaces,* ed. Judith Kapferer (Brooklyn, NY: Berghahn Books, 2012), 47–59.
[2] Raffaele Pernice, "Urban Housing for the Masses in East Asia: Structuring the

Contemporary Cities in Japan, China and South Korea," in *Archtheo '16—Xth International Theory of Architecture Conference 2016,* October 27–28, 2016, Istanbul, Turkey, Proceedings of Archtheo 16, 361–69.

[3] Nicola Belli, "Modern Urban Planning And Dissonant Heritage: The Case Of San Polo," *Art History & Criticism* 16, no. 1 (2020): 82.

[4] The essay mainly focuses on the Italian and, therefore, European context. In this regard, see European Environment Agency, "Urban Adaptation to Climate Change in Europe 2016" (Luxembourg, 2016), https://www.eea.europa.eu/publications /urban-adaptation-2016, accessed June 5, 2020.

[5] Nicholas Dagen Bloom, Fritz Umbach, and Lawrence Vale, *Public Housing Myths, Perception, Reality, and Social Policy* (Ithaca: Cornell University Press, 2015).

[6] See bibliography reported in Lisanne Havinga, Bernard Colenbrander, Henk Schellen, "Heritage Attributes of Post-war Housing in Amsterdam," *Frontiers of Architectural Research* 9, no. 1 (2019): 1–19.

[7] Sustainable retrofit can be defined as the upgrading of the building fabric, systems, or controls to improve the energy performance of a property; see William Swan, Les Ruddock, and Luke Smith, "Low Carbon Retrofit: Attitudes and Readiness within the Social Housing Sector," *Engineering, Construction and Architectural Management* 20, no. 5 (2013): 522–35.

[8] Payam Nejat et al., "A Global Review of Energy Consumption, CO_2 Emissions and Policy in the Residential Sector (with an Overview of the Top Ten CO_2 Emitting Countries)," *Renewable and Sustainable Energy Reviews* 43 (2015): 843–62.

[9] BPIE, *Europe's Buildings under the Microscope* (Brussels: Building Performance Institute Europe, 2011), http://www.bpie.eu/eu_buildings_under_microscope.html.

[10] Tobias Loga, Britta Stein, and Nikolaus Diefenbach, "TABULA Building Typologies in 20 European Countries—Making Energy-Related Features of Residential Building Stocks Comparable," *Energy and Buildings* 132 (2016): 4–12.

[11] Amale Andraos, "What Does Climate Change? (for Architecture)," in *Climates: Architecture and the Planetary Imaginary,* ed. James Graham (Zurich: Lars Müller Publishers, 2016), 297–301.

[12] Sofie Pelsmakers, *The Environmental Design Pocketbook* (London: RIBA Publishing, 2015).

[13] Pere Fuertes, "Embodied Energy Policies to Reuse Existing Buildings," *Energy Procedia,* no. 115 (2017): 431–39.

[14] Florian Urban, *Tower and Slab, Histories of Global Mass Housing* (Abingdon: Routledge, 2012). Miles Glendinning, "The Hundred Years War: a 'Long Century' of Mass-Housing Campaigns Across the World," http://leidiniu.archfondas.lt/en /alf-03/lectures/miles-glendining, accessed June 5, 2020.

[15] As in the infamous case of the American Pruitt-Igoe, the demolition of European estates such as the Immeuble Debussy, at La Courneuve, France, in 1986, symbolized the final proof of modern mass housing's failure in Europe. Raphaële Bertho, "The Grands Ensembles. Fifty Years of French Political Fiction," *Études photographiques,* no. 31 (2014): 1–12.

[16] Simon Guy and Graham Farmer, "Reinterpreting Sustainable Architecture: The Place of Technology," *Journal of Architectural Education* 3, no. 54 (2001): 145–46.

[17] On this topic, Tony Schuman, "Participation, Empowerment, and Urbanism: Design and Politics in the Revitalization of French Social Housing," *Journal of Architectural and Planning Research* 4, no. 4 (1987): 349–59.

[18] The design potential of these strategies has been widely investigated in the last decades. See, for instance, Fausto Novi, ed., *La riqualificazione sostenibile. Applicazioni, sistemi e strategie di controllo climatico naturale* (Florence: Alinea, 1999), 40–42, 158, 160–61.

[19] Craig Buckley, "Never Demolish: Bois-le-Prêt Regrows in Paris," *Log,* no. 24 (2012): 43.

[20] These projects have been developed together with architect Frederic Druot. Ilka Ruby, Andreas Ruby and Deutsches Architekturmuseum, *Druot, Lacaton & Vassal, Tour Bois le Prêtre* (Berlin: Ruby Press, 2012); Karen Kubey, ed., *Housing as Intervention: Architecture Towards Social Equity* (Oxford: Wyley/AD), 42–45.

[21] "Never demolish, never remove or replace, always add, transform, and reuse!" This motto was first laid out in *PLUS,* a design manifesto for the retrofit of mass housing. Fredric Druot, Anne Lacaton, Jean-Philippe Vassal, *Plus: La vivienda colectiva, territorio de excepciòn* (Barcellona, G. Gili, 2007).

[22] Buckley, "Never Demolish," 43.

[23] This study adopts the definition of "Italian postwar mass housing" referring to public housing interventions between 1960s and 1980s, planned with the National Law number 167 of 1962. For a brief recap of public housing policies in postwar Italy, see Nadia Caruso, *Policies and Practices in Italian Welfare Housing,* SpringerBriefs in Geography (Cham: Springer, 2017).

[24] Bloom, Umbach, and Vale, *Public Housing Myths*, 170.

[25] Decreto Legislativo 22 gennaio 2004, n. 42, "Codice dei beni culturali e del paesaggio, ai sensi dell'articolo 10 della legge 6 luglio 2002, n. 137." On the same topic, see also Chiara Dezzi Bardeschi, *Cento voci per il Restauro* (Firenze: AltraLinea Edizioni, 2013), 103.

[26] Miles Glendinning, "Ennobling the Ordinary: Postwar Mass Housing and the Challenge of Change," *Docomomo Journal,* no. 39 (2008): 6.

[27] A PEEP was an urban master plan for social housing introduced in Italy with the National Law 167/1962. Law 167 required municipalities greater that 50,000 inhabitants to build public housing, infrastructure, and services to tackle the dramatic national housing shortage and the unplanned growth of suburban areas. Gaston Ave, *Urban Land and Property Market in Italy* (London: UCL Press, 1966).

[28] This plan envisioned the construction of public housing complexes for roughly 700,000 inhabitants. Today, only in the city of Rome, more than 400,000 people live inside dwellings built through the first PEEP. For an overview of the first Roman PEEP, see Piero Ostilio Rossi, *Guida all'Architettura di Roma Moderna* (Bari-Rome: Laterza, 1991), 158–61.

[29] Glendinning, "Multifaceted Monolith."

[30] For a brief history of the TBM project, see Alessandra Montenero, "Tor Bella Monaca: Il Perché, l'Attuazione e il Divenire di un Grande Piano di Zona," in *Rigenerare Tor Bella Monaca*, ed. Marta Calzolaretti and Domizia Mandolesi (Macerata: Quodlibet, 2014), 52–62; Elio Piroddi, "Operazione Tor Bella Monaca. Un esempio di qualificazione della quantità," *L'industria delle costruzioni* 18, no. 155 (1984): 6–37.

[31] TBM's designers are F. Canali, P. Visentini, and A. M. Leone (general planning), Studio Passarelli (urban design and building coordination). The construction started in 1981. First dwellings were assigned in 1983, after only eighteen months.

[32] Montenero, "Tor Bella Monaca," 57. The complex was planned to host mostly unemployed and evicted families.

[33] The idea of TBM's master plan as a reinterpretation of the modern city model is supported by Elio Piroddi, project coordinator of TBM's building R5. Piroddi, "Operazione Tor Bella Monaca," 6.

[34] On this topic, see Daniel Barber, "The Form and Climate Research Group, or Scales of Architectural Histories," in *Climates*, 303–7.

[35] Carolina González Vives, "Dehydrated Architecture" in *Climates,* 329–37.

[36] Lisa Gartland, *Heat Islands: Understanding and Mitigating Heat in Urban Areas* (London: Earthscan, 2008).

[37] TBM has an overall surface of 188 hectares; 24 hectares are destined to street network (roughly 20 km), 9 for parking areas, and 51 are identified as "countryside park." Alessandra De Cesaris, "Il Progetto del Suolo/Sottosuolo: Ridefinire l'Attacco a Terra di Tor Bella Monaca," in *Rigenerare Tor Bella Monaca*, 145.

[38] "SLOAP—Space Left Over After Planning," *Architectural Review,* no. 920 (1973): 201–66, cited in Piero Ostilio Rossi, "Introduzione," in *Rigenerare Tor Bella Monaca,* 15.

[39] Marta Calzolaretti, "I Temi della Ricerca," in *Rigenerare Tor Bella Monaca,* 75.

[40] TBM's structures were built by using the French industrialized casting technology called *coffrage tunnel* (tunnel formwork), a prefabrication system developed since the early 1960s for the construction of medium to high-rise housing. Implemented for achieving the maximum speed and construction efficiency, the system comprised sets of steel tunnel structures used as formworks for building tubular cells, delimited by two-side loadbearing walls and a floor slab. For more details, see Enrico Mandolesi, "Prefabbricazione," *Enciclopedia Italiana Treccani* (Rome: Treccani, 1961), App. III, II, 474–IV, III, 49; Franco Nuti, *Tecnologie industrializzate e tipi edilizi per la residenza. Metodi di valutazione del rapporto tra fattori funzionali e fattori tecnologici e costruttivi nell'edilizia residenziale industrializzata* (Bologna: Cooperativa Libraria Universitaria, Editrice Bologna, 1984).

[41] On today's social problems of TBM, see Carlo Cellamare, *Fuori Raccordo. Abitare l'altra Roma* (Rome: Donzelli Editore, 2016).

[42] For an understanding of social life of TBM, see Carlo Cellamare, *Periferia. Abitare Tor Bella Monaca* (Rome: Donzelli Editore, 2020).

[43] For more info on the unbuilt proposal by Leon Krier, see "La proposta Krier," in *Rigenerare Tor Bella Monaca,* 50–51.

[44] Comune di Roma, "Programma Di Riqualificazione Urbana 'Tor Bella Monaca,'" 2010, http://www.urbanistica.comune.roma.it/archivio-programma-tor-bella-monaca.html, accessed June 5, 2020.

[45] Rossi, "Presentazione," 14.

[46] As a reaction to the proposal of redevelopment undertaken by the Municipality of Rome, a team of scholars and academics obtained funds by the Italian Ministry of

Education, Universities and Research, to support a study on the urban regeneration of the neighborhood, based on preservation via retrofit. See Calzolaretti and Mandolesi, *Rigenerare Tor Bella Monaca*; Cellamare, *Periferia*.

[47] The attention of the design culture on mass housing preservation and retrofit continues to rise in this period. The Italian Society of Architectural Technology (SITdA) has recently organized a design competition aiming at collecting ideas and projects for a portion of TBM and fostering a cross-scale interdisciplinary approach in regenerative design. In particular, the winning entry, "Tor Bella Assai," identifies some specific fields of actions. The proposal, redefining sequences of spaces and actively involving the ground floor of the buildings, takes the opportunity to act, first, on the hierarchy of semiprivate open spaces between the buildings and the countryside. Second, it focuses on the reactivation of the streetscape along the building complex, including: the transformation of the housing types on the lower floors; the insertion of mixed uses; the reorganization of the accesses; the redefinition of the carriageway and pedestrian areas, through spatial and microclimatic control devices; the implementation of nature-based solutions for buildings and open spaces. See Nicole De Togni, Lavinia Dondi, Elena Fontanella, Agim Kërçuku, Fabio Lepratto, Michele Morganti, "Tor Bella Assai Sei campi di azione strategica per la rigenerazione di TBM," in *Architettura e Tecnologia per l'abitare. Upcycling degli edifici ERP di Tor Bella Monaca a Roma*, ed. Eugenio Arbizzani, Adolfo Baratta, Eliana Cangelli, Laura Daglio, Federica Ottone, and Donatella Radogna (Santarcangelo di Romagna: Maggioli Editore, 2021). Another relevant study in the field focuses on design principles and strategies useful for mass housing stock renovation and retrofit in Rome. Authors tackle the topic of affordable housing through adaptation of building typologies to meet current inhabitants' needs and increasing quality of life in existing neighborhoods. See Federico De Matteis, Maria Rosaria Guarini, and Luca Reale eds., *Roma Cerca Casa* (Santarcangelo di Romagna: Maggioli Editore, 2016). A research-by-design framework on TBM's preservation can be found in the section "TBM. Strategie e progetti per una rigenerazione sostenibile" in *Rigenerare Tor Bella Monaca,* 251–311.

[48] UN-Habitat, *Global Housing Strategy Framework Document,* https://unhabitat.org/; The Toledo Declaration aims to promote the life quality in the renovation of mass housing districts by fostering specific objectives: improve social cohesion, increase urban compactness and vibrancy of urban spaces, develop local economies, promote functional *mixité* and building sustainability, among others; Toledo Informal Ministerial Meeting On Urban Development Declaration, https://ec.europa.eu/regional_policy/archive/newsroom/pdf/201006_toledo_declaration_en.pdf, accessed June 5, 2020.

[49] In addition to retrofit projects and regenerative plans above mentioned, it is worth mentioning Europark in Antwerp, Waterlandplein in Amsterdam, La Courneuve in Paris, Gentiaanstraat in Apeldoorn, Square Vitruve in Paris, El Barrio de la Mina in Barcelona, among others.

[50] ChengHe Guan and Peter G. Rowe, "The Concept of Urban Intensity and China's Townization Policy: Cases from Zhejiang Province," *Cities* 55 (2016): 22–41.

[51] De Togni, Dondi, Fontanella, Kërçuku, Lepratto, Morganti, "Tor Bella Assai."

[52] Milena Vuckovic, Kristina Kiesel, and Ardeshir Mahdavi, "The Extent and Implications of the Microclimatic Conditions in the Urban Environment: A Vienna Case Study," *Sustainability* 9, no. 2 (2017): 177; Hyunjung Lee, Helmut Mayer, and Liang Chen, "Contribution of Trees and Grasslands to the Mitigation of Human Heat Stress in a Residential District of Freiburg, Southwest Germany," *Landscape and Urban Planning* 148 (2016): 37–50.

[53] De Togni, Dondi, Fontanella, Kërçuku, Lepratto, Morganti, "Tor Bella Assai."

[54] "TBM Strategie e progetti per una rigenerazione sostenibile"; De Togni, Dondi, Fontanella, Kërçuku, Lepratto, Morganti, "Tor Bella Assai."

[55] De Togni, Dondi, Fontanella, Kërçuku, Lepratto, Morganti, "Tor Bella Assai."

[56] European Climate Foundation, *Roadmap 2050: A Practical Guide to a Prosperous, Low Carbon Europe* (The Hague: ECF, 2010), http://www.roadmap2050.eu/, accessed June 5, 2020.

[57] Xuemei Bai et al., "Six Research Priorities for Cities and Climate Change," *Nature* 555, no. 7694 (2018): 23–25.

Figure 1. Raymond Graves, Portland Public Services Building, Portland, Oregon, 1979–82, with Portlandia statue by Michael Kaskey, view from southwest along Fifth Avenue, renovated exterior, 2020, by DLR Group. Photograph by James Ewing/JBSA. Courtesy of DLR Group.

Joseph Siry

Graves's Portland Building, 2020
Preservation as Transformation

The city of Portland (Oregon) Public Services Building, generally known as the Portland Building, designed by Michael Graves beginning with a competition in 1979 and dedicated in October 1982, was from its origins acknowledged as a turning point in the history of American and modern architecture. It is cited as the first major work of Postmodern Classicism, which came to define the decade's departure from the conventions and convictions of the Modern Movement that had dominated professional and intellectual discourse in American architecture through the postwar era.[1] The Portland Building also marked a convergence of the Postmodernist rejection of the modernist glass building envelope with the questioning of that form for reasons of energy conservation in the wake of the OPEC oil embargo of 1973, and even slightly earlier, when American architects and mechanical engineers first engaged with rising fuel costs[2] (Figure 1).

Recent reconstruction of the Portland Building, completed in 2020, was premised in part on a deep investigation of the building's energy performance. It was an edifice under critical scrutiny in terms of its shortcomings relative to both the original vision for the structure and to the ways in which its equipment and services as built had been conceptually and technically superseded by sustainable practices that long postdated the building's birth. Based on exhaustive appraisal and analysis of the building's material, spatial, and mechanical condition, the architect for the reconstruction project, the DLR Group, known globally for its advocacy of sustainable design, provided architecture, energy modeling, planning, and interior design services for the Portland Building's renewal.[3] The process is a vivid, compelling case of how the priorities of historic preservation, which focus on fidelity to a building's original material conditions, engage with a situation where those materials had to be rethought to preserve original design intent.

To understand the Portland Building's contemporary retrofit, we need to revisit how energy issues framed the original competition for its design in 1979 and the process of the design's development and construction through 1982. All those architects, engineers, and others who have conceived and managed the retrofit had to work with the disjuncture between the high aspirations for the building and the compromises in its realization that limited their fulfillment. These aspirations

Future Anterior
Volume XVIII, Number 1
Summer 2021

were rooted in both the discourses of Postmodern Classicism in American architecture from the mid 1960s and the priorities of energy conservation from the early 1970s.[4] One prominent point of convergence for these two lines of criticism was the large glass-enclosed office building, by then ubiquitous as one of the most widely known modernist types. By the late 1970s, when the City of Portland came to reconsider the need for a new public services building, national consciousness had embraced energy conservation in architecture as a high priority, and this meant that the large glass building envelope was rethought toward this end.

In Portland the project had become a central concern of the mayor, Neil Goldschmidt (in office 1973–79), who supported the concept of a new building for the city's services as part of a larger effort to revitalize the downtown. Among his priorities for the structure was that it be a "high-tech building" in terms of energy use.[5] This overarching aim of the city as client provided a frame of reference for many design decisions. In June 1979 the city acquired the site, a typical local 200 ft. × 200 ft. sq. block with a city park, called Chapman Square, to the east, along Fourth Avenue, and a transit mall to the west, along Fifth Avenue. The block is between the classically styled Portland City Hall (1895) on the south and the larger, classical Multnomah County Courthouse (1914) on the north (Figure 2). The site is in Portland's historic center on the west side of the Willamette River. It offers views to the Cascade Range on the west and the distant Mount Hood to the east. Around the site were tall steel-and-glass towers, including the Standard Life Insurance Building (1963) by Skidmore, Owings & Merrill directly west of Graves's building and the darker, all-glass Orbanco Bank diagonally opposite to the northwest. This six-sided, twenty-three-story structure, dedicated in April 1980, had almost exactly the same square footage (417,000) as Graves's Portland Building. It featured partially reflective double-pane, energy-conserving glass in 3,870 windows.[6] In contrast to his design for the Portland Building, Graves said: "There are glass towers in this town that can be turned upside down, and they look the same. They are so well balanced that they have neither a top nor a bottom. It seems that that's the way a lot of modern architecture has gone: people producing an ever-slicker, cleaner glass box."[7]

As David Milliken and Meredith Clausen have discussed,[8] given budgetary constraints, Portland decided that the project would be a single contract for design/build, with any proposal developed by a contractor, an architect, engineers, and other collaborators who would be hired as a team based on a bonded bid of a total price for the building's completion by a set time. This was to avoid criticism of public expenditures by

Figure 2. Graves, Portland Building, original site plan. From *Progressive Architecture* 164, no. 2 (February 1983): 108. Zonda Media.

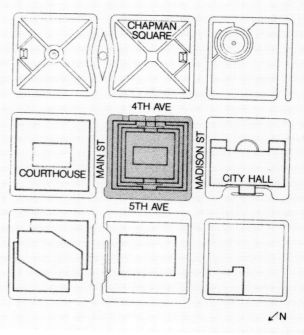

ensuring comprehensive collaboration in order to minimize financial uncertainties that could increase costs. Design/build had entered US architectural practice in the mid-1970s as a response to rapid inflation of building costs in the early 1970s. Only in 1978, after a three-year debate, did the American Institute of Architects allow members to engage as principals in design/build construction. Portland had never done a design/build process and the building was among the country's first larger design/build projects.[9]

The city decided on a national competition, its first for a major civic building. Potential design teams would submit proposals with cost figures based on detailed plans and specifications. These would be assessed relative to the city's 228-page "Program of Facility Requirements," dated July 23, 1979, which specified needs, including energy-efficiency criteria. Designs were to provide 400,000 square feet of space, including 6,000 square feet of commercial space. The budget for the net floor area of 362,000 square feet of useable space was strictly limited to about $22 million or $51 per square foot, which was quite low.[10] The maximum energy utilization rate, or energy use intensity (EUI), was to be 55 kBtu per gross square foot per year, in keeping with the federal Department of Energy's regulations then in effect. Minimum requirements would be indoor temperatures held to 68°–78° F.[11] Echoing the consensus of mechanical engineers for tall glass buildings since the 1950s, the city said to competitors that "The HVAC will be more energy efficient without operable windows."[12] Yet it sought an aesthetically exceptional structure that would be "open, exciting, efficient. A strong bold direct design solution" that would be "expressive of the humanity of the individuals who will use the building."[13] Finalists were selected in part on the basis of their "ability/potential to maximize energy conservation opportunities."[14] Projected costs of heating, ventilating, and air conditioning systems were over 18 percent of the building's total, exceeded only by the superstructure itself (26+ percent).[15]

Graves's ultimately winning proposal was for a fifteen-story building with a grid of 3 ft. × 3 ft.–square windows ten feet on center in its main block. At the council's request, Graves later increased the window size to 4 ft. × 4 ft., and converted the windows to fixed, single-glazed units.[16] He wrote: "the common element of the window has been made somewhat special to the people inhabiting this building as its dimension, sized for the individual, both particularizes the context outside and greatly reduces the consumption of energy within the building."[17] He thus made the individual sealed window into a signature element both of the building's Postmodernist style and its energy strategy. The stepped base, which contained an arcade surrounding rentable spaces for retail stores at street level, increased the building's lateral stability and hence its earthquake resistance.[18] For heating and cooling, the building had a cubic form that the mechanical engineer recommended as most efficient in its high ratio of interior volume to surface area. The structural frame would be columns and beams of reinforced concrete, while the exterior walls were first designed as stucco on cement block. Yet at the council's request, Graves substituted poured-in-place reinforced concrete as a bearing wall around the building's exterior for seismic resistance, working with the reinforced concrete elevator and stair core to insure structural stability. The concrete walls were sealed against the weather with an elastomeric, non-oil-based paint. Their exterior surface was textured to create a pattern of vertical and horizontal joints to suggest the stone coursing found on the adjacent neoclassical civic buildings to its north and south. The concrete's beige color was to suggest stone. Structural bays were 30 ft. × 30 ft.[19] Overall Graves's proposal projected an energy use of 47.07 kBtu per square foot per year.[20] After much discussion and revision, a modified design for the building gained the city council's final approval on April 30, 1980. Construction began in July of that year and finished by October 1982.[21]

The base was clad in blue-green tile. Above, on the east and west fronts, were paired red-painted pilaster-like motifs below a giant tiled evocation of a keystone on the upper floors, originally planned to be rented to private clients. On the building's upper north and south side walls, pilaster-like motifs were crowned by garlands envisioned as light-weight stucco eventually modified and realized in precast concrete. Typical office floors had areas of 23,500 square feet. Sympathetic to its historic context, the building, according to Graves, captured some of the fragments of the city's architectural past, such as its street level arcades, found in the traditional buildings that had been demolished to create the sites for modernist towers. The main west entrance faces a transit mall along Fifth Avenue, with a secondary east door to its lower story on Fourth Avenue, across from Chapman Square in the multiblock park. The competition specified that the roof should be attractive since it would be visible from nearby buildings. Thus Graves imagined pavilions modeled on Roman temples and villas sheltering storage, stair exits, skylights, and mechanical rooms. The final building had a simpler version of this roofscape.[22]

The insulation value of the Portland Building's envelope insured a much lower heat loss and heat gain through wall surfaces relative to a largely glazed building. And even though the windows on office floors were enlarged to 4 ft. × 4 ft. and were unshaded, they provided little more daylight, but they did increase heat gain.[23] A black spandrel glass facing on solid walls was used for the flute-like vertical surfaces of the columnar exterior forms and the surrounding giant square windows (see Figure 1). Yet for the small square windows, which lit interiors, as distinct from the spandrel glass as an exterior wall cladding, Graves wanted to use all clear glass in order to increase natural light, and operable sash to facilitate ventilation. Associates recall the day that he was upset to learn that the city would install darkly tinted glass in the upper floor windows against his wishes.[24] Dark glass would reduce solar gain and summer cooling loads, and thus the size and cost of air-cooling equipment. The city preferred fixed glass as more energy efficient, yet the exterior wall and fixed glass were so tight that summer heat could not easily escape.[25]

Given the heat-retaining exterior envelope and Portland's moderate climate, the building was dominated by internal energy loads and cooling loads to offset heat generated by lighting and office equipment, rather than heat from outside. The volume was divided programmatically into two parts with different internal energy loads: three lower floors containing a large computer center (required in the original program, before the era of ubiquitous personal computers) and upper office floors. The bulk of the mechanical space would be on the second story in enclosed space, not publicly visible, ringing the open small balcony above the information lobby on the first floor. Loads were analyzed and published in 1981, before the building was completed the following year. The three bar charts on the right of Figure 3 show the energy loads noted in kBtu per square foot per year for the entire building (bottom); floors one through three, including the computer floor (center), where loads greatly exceed the target of 60 kBtu per square foot per year; and floors four through fifteen of the office tower (top). The loads in the bar charts are color coded: yellow for electrical, red for heating, and blue for cooling. These were predicted for twelve different design alternatives listed on the lower left. Energy loads for heating and cooling derived from a full range of factors, including internal loads from occupants, lights, and equipment, and loads associated with heat loss or gain through the building envelope. As the middle bar chart on the right shows, on the bottom three floors with rentable commercial spaces around the periphery, the large computer center's machines consumed much energy and generated considerable heat, as was typical of that era. In the restored building, the computer center was removed and its second-floor area serves as office space. Energy loads of the bottom three floors were much larger than the upper office tower's loads because of the computer center's enormous electrical load of 30W per square foot. At first the large quantity of heat recovered from the computer center usable for heating other interiors enabled no use of the electrically powered boiler plant.[26] The new building's energy requirements were quite low (37 kBtu per square foot per year).[27] Its material and mechanical systems met the city's requirements for an energy-conserving building that would be a civic model for best practices in this field (Figure 3).

Now that nearly forty years have passed since its completion, the Portland Building in retrospect remains central to the architectural history of its period, and was, among its other distinctions, listed on the National Register of Historic Places in 2011.[28] Yet the building has had structural problems, and its public interiors were not well received locally in terms of material details and psychological effects.[29] There was tenant dissatisfaction with the small heavily tinted windows in office areas, which were quite dark, giving these interiors, which were home to some 1,300 city workers, an almost cavern-like appearance.[30] Some bemoaned hot and noisy ventilation. By 2010 the building's deficiencies included water intrusion and end-of-life mechanical and electrical systems. It was also built prior to improvements in local seismic codes in the 1990s.[31] After extended debate about its future, when demolition was considered, in 2015 the City of Portland committed to a transformative preservation that represents a contemporary critique of 1980s practices. Significantly, the city did not refer to the project as a "restoration," but rather as a "reconstruction." What began as an effort to halt persistent water penetration developed into a $195-million program for the tower's complete overhaul as an investment in an historic asset, because

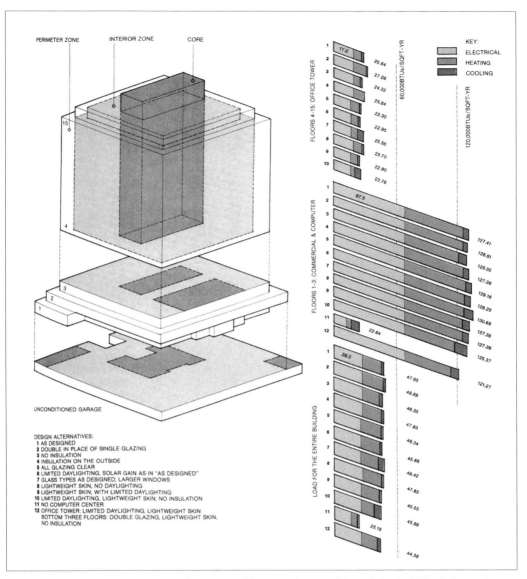

PERIMETER ZONE   INTERIOR ZONE   CORE

15

4

3
2
1

UNCONDITIONED GARAGE

DESIGN ALTERNATIVES:
1 AS DESIGNED
2 DOUBLE IN PLACE OF SINGLE GLAZING
3 NO INSULATION
4 INSULATION ON THE OUTSIDE
5 ALL GLAZING CLEAR
6 LIMITED DAYLIGHTING, SOLAR GAIN AS IN "AS DESIGNED"
7 GLASS TYPES AS DESIGNED, LARGER WINDOWS
8 LIGHTWEIGHT SKIN, NO DAYLIGHTING
9 LIGHTWEIGHT SKIN, WITH LIMITED DAYLIGHTING
10 LIMITED DAYLIGHTING, LIGHTWEIGHT SKIN, NO INSULATION
11 NO COMPUTER CENTER
12 OFFICE TOWER: LIMITED DAYLIGHTING, LIGHTWEIGHT SKIN
   BOTTOM THREE FLOORS: DOUBLE GLAZING, LIGHTWEIGHT SKIN,
   NO INSULATION

KEY:
ELECTRICAL
HEATING
COOLING

FLOORS 4-15: OFFICE TOWER   60,000BTUs/SQFT-YR

1 17.0
2 25.84
3 27.28
4 24.32
5 25.84
6 23.30
7 22.95
8 25.56
9 25.70
10 22.80
   23.78

FLOORS 1-3: COMMERCIAL & COMPUTER   120,000BTUs/SQFT-YR

1 87.5
2
3
4 127.41
5 126.61
6 125.56
7 127.39
8 129.18
9 128.29
10 130.69
11 127.38
12 22.64   127.38
   125.37

LOAD FOR THE ENTIRE BUILDING

1 28.0
2 47.95   121.27
3 48.89
4 46.35
5 47.93
6 46.34
7 45.86
8 48.42
9 47.83
10 45.55
11 45.89
12 25.15
   44.38

Figure 3. Graves, Portland Building, electrical, heating, and cooling loads for the entire building, floors one through three including the computer center, and floors four through fifteen (office tower), according to twelve different design alternatives. Analysis prepared in Center for Planning and Development Research, College of Environmental Design, University of California, Berkeley; Vladimir Bazjanac, Project Director. From *Progressive Architecture* 62, no. 9 (October 1981): 109. Zonda Media.

there was widespread recognition of the building's importance in recent architecture.[32] This most costly single office project in the city's history included the cost of relocating staff.[33]

Meticulous, comprehensive assessments led to the recent, phased project, which began in December 2017 and was completed in mid-2020. The building was totally emptied of its occupants and disassembled down to its structural frame of reinforced concrete. As there was extensive water intrusion and consequent mold issues, the building's walls were radically rethought internally and externally.[34] The renovated interiors were refitted with clear vision glass double-glazed insulated units, and other measures insured that offices would be bright.[35] Before his death in 2015, Graves had included this change among those that he recommended.[36] The glass is clear

Figure 4. Graves, Portland Building, reconstruction, 2019, north interior with clear glass replacing tinted spandrel glass. Photograph by Joseph Siry.

to increase daylighting but it also has a low heat emissivity and a low shading coefficient to reduce the solar gain into the building, and thus the cooling load, which yields a lower electrical load. This solution for the square windows recovers Graves's original design intent for daylighting but with a contemporary glazing unit engineered for optimal thermal performance. Also, where there was black spandrel glass facing solid walls, as in the columnar motifs outside, there is now clear glass to better illuminate office interiors (Figure 4).

For a seismic upgrade, a reinforced concrete shear wall was added up the building's core. To further bolster the resiliency, 110,000 pounds of steel reinforcing bars per floor were added to the structural core and exterior columns. Inside wall insulation thickness increased by eight inches. There was concern that the reconstructed envelope would create a deeper gap between interior spaces and the outer face of the windows, but this tunnel effect was deemed minimal.[37] The reconstruction also included the removal of the interior's dropped planar ceilings so as to permanently reveal the original concrete waffle slab structure characteristic of the period. The original frame plus the added concrete gives the building a larger thermal mass, which increased its capacity to retain internal heat in winter and limit outdoor heat in summer (Figure 5). This effect of interior temperature regulation through the building's material mass is distinct from the effect of the increased insulation

Figure 5. Graves, Portland Building, reconstruction, 2019, reinforcing steel around central core on upper floor, with concrete waffle slab ceiling left exposed. Photograph by John G. Duffy, P.E.

and thus increased R value of its reconstructed outer wall envelope.[38]

The original building had two 300-ton chillers, so a total of 600 tons of refrigeration for its air-conditioning systems. With its increased occupancy and computers, the reconstructed, better insulated building would need 705 tons of cooling. For sustainability, original electrically fired boilers, chillers, cooling towers, and interior ductwork were almost entirely removed. To minimize consumption of fossil fuels in order to meet current Oregon standards for reduction in their use, the restored Portland Building also has no fossil-fueled water boiler or chillers. Instead, both heating and cooling are supplied by six electrically powered combined heat pump and air-conditioning units on the roof. These units are raised on a 4.5-foot-tall platform so as not to disrupt the existing green roof, which was created in 2007. Operating as heat pumps, rooftop units have the capacity to draw heat into the building from outside air even when the ambient temperature is 15° F. This facilitates the structure's use as a warming center for the homeless during the winter in a downtown where the homeless population is substantial and highly visible every day. The system's design was less concerned with cooling than it was with providing adequate heating. Since the capacity of heat pumps in winter tends to be limited, six heat pump/air conditioning units were provided, when only four are thought to be normally sufficient for heating. When operating as heat pumps, these provide warm primary air to two large rooftop air handling units, each has a capacity of 100,000 cfm. There is supplementary heating from fan-powered terminal units near the ceilings inside the offices. Working with the central fan, these units draw air from their plenum whenever their zone requires heat. During the shoulder seasons of fall and spring, and given the fact that temperatures in Portland rarely go above 70°, most of the time the building will be ventilated with unheated and uncooled outside air. At night, when the temperature goes below 60°F., the building's dampers will open to bring in cool air which, given the building's originally large and now enhanced thermal mass, will cool the building down in preparation for daytime occupancy.[39] Air handling units sit in a mechanical penthouse not seen from the street around the building's base, but visible at a distance or from the higher floors of nearby buildings.[40] Its design required multiple meetings with the city's historical committee, among others, and the penthouse is painted a rose beige color to minimize its bulkiness. The adjacent outdoor heat pumps, elevated above the green roof on the east side, have a comparable color. As with other recent changes, the rooftop reconstruction is transformative yet seeks to be respectful from both an environmental and aesthetic perspective (Figure 6).

The Portland Building's reconstruction involved significant changes in its base. After decades of repairs, the base's teal-colored tile cladding, with some tiles damaged, was updated to a larger 2 ft. × 2 ft. grid of glazed terra-cotta rainscreen panels, close in size to what Graves had proposed.[41] The plan also includes enclosing in glass some of the ground floor retail spaces on the north and south sides that formerly faced onto open porticoes, and opening these spaces to the central lobby. This lobby, accessible from the west front, had been almost totally lacking in natural illumination, but it was to be full of sunlight from new peripheral windows. On the east or Fourth Avenue side, facing the city park, the underground parking entrance has been removed and the entrance glassed in to give occupants views of this green space. On the west side, the twenty-five-foot-high hammered copper statue of Portlandia by sculptor Raymond Kaskey was preserved, and protected by scaffolding and plastic wrap during the reconstruction, before being newly unveiled so that it is visible from inside and from an adjacent exterior observation deck[42] (Figure 7).

The most controversial changes in the reconstructed Portland Building occur on the upper exterior. After extensive analysis of possible alternative solutions to the continuing issues of water penetration through the original concrete and tile walls, the project team concluded that affixing terra cotta panels directly to the concrete, which had been the mate-

Figure 6. Graves, Portland Building, reconstruction, 2019, rooftop AERMEC heat pump and air conditioning units on east roof, looking southeast. Photograph by Joseph Siry.

rial solution that Graves originally envisioned, was not now viable to prevent future leakage. Such a solution had also become questionable in the context of current building codes. Simple repair and repainting of the concrete walls were also considered, but the reconstruction took a different approach. On the upper walls, painted concrete and tiled keystone-like surfaces were overlaid with an exterior unitized rainscreen of aluminum panels. Horizontal and vertical joints between the panel units approximate the scoring pattern on the underlying concrete, which had been meant to evoke stone coursing. The original fiber-glass cement garlands on the sides were also re-created in formed aluminum.[43] The colors of the beige and red aluminum panels closely approximate those of the original surfaces, although the aluminum is slightly less bright and reflective than the painted concrete. The added depth of the rainscreen overlaid onto the original concrete wall does change the windows' depth and the walls' surface proportions slightly (Figure 8).

The overall result is a precisely crafted simulacrum of the original exterior surfaces that comprehensively addresses the key issue of water penetration that had resisted earlier repairs and alternative solutions. Michael Graves's firm pledged its support for this change, and outside façade consultants affirmed the soundness of this approach. But the exterior appearance is altered to the point where there was concern that the Portland Building could lose its listing on the National Register.

Figure 7. Graves, Portland Building: (top) pre-renovation view of entrance to parking garage on east base along Fourth Avenue (Photograph: Courtesy of DLR Group); (bottom) renovated Fourth Avenue façade with glazed terra-cotta replacing original tile, and former parking garage entrance converted into window onto parks (Photograph: James Ewing/JBSA). Courtesy of DLR Group.

Oregon's DoCoMoMo chapter, now devoted also to preserving Postmodernist architecture, voiced its opposition. They were concerned that the new metal cladding "will sufficiently alter the building's proportions to diminish its integrity of design and materials."[44] Portland's Historic Landmarks Commission held hearings to review the proposed reconstruction and concluded that replacement of almost all of the visible materials on the building was an "extreme measure," but that it was nonetheless necessary to address the issues that had plagued the structure since its opening. These the commission

Figure 8. Graves, Portland Building, reconstruction, 2019, from northwest, unitized aluminum rainscreen cladding, clear glass windows. Photograph by Joseph Siry.

attributed to the original minimal budget, which had led to unfortunate compromises, especially in terms of the windows and the exterior skin. Portland authorities meant to respect the historical significance of the original building with a solution deemed effective to fully extend its life for another fifty to one hundred years.[45]

Yet, although the Portland Landmarks Commission unanimously approved the exterior reconstruction, the State Office of Historic Preservation may delist it from Oregon's Historic Register because of the material changes. To Peter Meijer, who wrote the Portland Building's 2011 nomination for listing on the National Register of Historic Places, the reconstruction is an "open and sore wound." He thought the original materials could have been kept.[46] Amidst such controversy about this unusual approach to preservation, the city and the architects claim to be transforming Graves's canonical monument to meet today's environmental and material criteria while respecting his design, which was iconic for Postmodernism of the 1980s. In effect, the preservation debate surrounding the Portland Building focused on whether or not to maintain Graves's original material choices, which were themselves compromises that alluded to older conventions of classical masonry architecture represented by the adjacent earlier civic buildings.

The Portland Building's reconstruction resonates with themes characteristic of preserving Postmodernist architecture.

Much has changed since the building opened with fanfare in 1982. At that time, its design embodied the salient critical force of Postmodern Classicism as a rebuttal to the Modern Movement that had defined the preceding decades. In other words, what the Portland Building represented for its city in the 1980s, Rem Koolhaas' Seattle Public Library as a demonstration of Deconstructivist aesthetics did for its city in the 2000s, and the Miller Hull Partnership's Bullitt Center as a net-zero energy building did for Seattle in the 2010s — that is, they all shifted contemporary architecture's paradigm. Yet the cultural moment that gave rise to Postmodern Classicism from the late 1960s to the late 1980s is now valued more as an historical period than as a contemporary direction. Also, the Portland Building predated the digitization of design, fabrication and construction, and the emergence of sustainability and, more recently, resilience as a comprehensive ideal for the built environment. Its pioneering design/build process has also been succeeded by later variants based on shared digital platforms. Indeed the building's restoration represented such a contemporary variant as a close collaboration between a team of architects, engineers, and contractors working under municipal coordination. Finally, the original Portland Building was a municipal project with a limited budget, not directly linked to collateral private investment in Portland's downtown. Today the neoliberal model of public–private partnerships, which has become nearly ubiquitous for urban change worldwide, would more likely lead to a coordinated vision of high-end real estate development over a broader area.[47]

The Portland Building represented an effort to define communal or civic identity that made it locally iconic, and hence worthy of preservation, restoration, or rehabilitation. The solution for preservation needed to respond to the contemporary understanding of how to make a building energy-efficient in ways and to levels not envisioned decades ago. In other words, sustainability has effectively transformed the nature of historic preservation. In this case, commitment to revalue rather than discard the Postmodernist past collided with the building's material difficulties. This set up a tension between authenticity to original materials and an exterior solution that is an approximation, accepted by some but not by all persons involved. Yet as we consider the rainscreen, one other major lesson of the Portland Building's reconstruction relative to the conventions of preservation is that its original design intent was less dependent on its specific materials when built than it was on Graves's distinct formal or stylistic stance. In this key way, the reconstructed building still has the memorable urban presence of its earlier self.

Biography

Joseph Siry is Professor of Art History at Wesleyan University. His recent books are *The Chicago Auditorium Building: Adler and Sullivan's Architecture and the City* (Chicago, 2002), which won the 2003 Society of Architectural Historians' Alice Davis Hitchcock Award for best book by a North American scholar; *Beth Sholom Synagogue: Frank Lloyd Wright and Modern Religious Architecture* (Chicago, 2012), a finalist for a 2013 National Jewish Book Award, Visual Arts category; and *Air-Conditioning and Modern American Architecture, 1890–1970* (Pennsylvania State University Press, 2021). His book in progress is *Energy and American Architecture, 1970–2020; From Conservation to Net-Zero.*

Notes

[1] Early accounts include Eleni Constantine, "The Case for Michael Graves's Design for Portland," *Architectural Record* 168, no. 2 (August 1980): 96–101; Douglas Brenner, "The Portland Building, Portland, Oregon," *Architectural Record* 170, no. 5 (November 1982): 90–99; Lance Knobel, "Graves Deco: Public Services Building, Portland, Oregon, USA," *Architectural Review* 172, no. 1029 (November 1982): 60–67; Karen Wheeler, ed., *Michael Graves, Buildings and Projects 1966–81* (New York: Rizzoli, 1982), 195–205; Susan Doubilet, "Conversation with Graves: The Portland Building, Portland, Oregon," *Progressive Architecture* 64, no. 2 (February 1983): 108–15; David Milliken, "The Portland Building Design/Build Competition: The Consequences of Competitions for American Architectural Design," senior thesis, Reed College, May 1983; John Pastier, "'First Monument of a Loosely Defined Style': Michael Graves's Portland Building," *AIA Journal* 72, no. 5 (March 1983): 232–37; Tod A. Marder, *The Critical Edge: Controversy in Recent American Architecture* (New Brunswick, N.J.: Jane Vorhees Zimmerli Art Museum, Rutgers, The State University of New Jersey; Cambridge, Mass.: MIT Press, 1985), 162–74; and Christina S. Olson, "Living With It: Michael Graves's Portland Building," *Art Criticism* 5, no. 1 (1988): 34–56. Later studies include Laurie Manfra, "Portland Building: The Michael Graves Legacy Remains as Contentious and Confounding as Ever," *Metropolis* 25, no. 8 (April 2006): 166–67; Stan Allen, Michael Graves, and Sarah Whiting, "Michael Graves: The Portland Building, 25 Years Later," Architectural League of New York and the Princeton University School of Architecture, November 2008, podcast; Jayne Kelley, "The Portland Building (Portland Municipal Services Building)," *Journal of Architectural Education* 66, no. 1 (2012): 21–22; Meredith Clausen, "Michael Graves's Portland Building: Power, Politics, and Postmodernism," *Journal of the Society of Architectural Historians* 73, no. 2 (June 2014): 248–69; and Justin Chan, "Change Ahead for Graves's Portland Building," *Architectural Record* 206, no. 4 (April 2018): 30.
[2] See Giovanna Borasi and Mirko Zardini, *Sorry, Out of Gas: Architecture's Response to the 1973 Oil Crisis* (Montreal: Canadian Centre for Architecture and Mantua: Corraini Edizioni, 2007); and Zardini, "A Crisis That Made Architecture Real," *Perspecta 42: The Yale Architectural Journal* (Cambridge, Mass.: MIT Press, 2010): 79–82.
[3] DLR Group, "Postmodern Renaissance: The Portland Building," https://www.dlrgroup.com/work/the-portland-building/, accessed 11 June 2020. PAE (Peterson Associated Engineers) provided MEP engineering design services and KPFF provided structural engineering design services.
[4] The foundational text for Postmodern architectural theory in the United States is generally considered to be Robert Venturi, *Complexity and Contradiction in Architecture,* 2nd ed. (1966; New York: Museum of Modern Art, 1977). Defining accounts of the movement that discuss the Portland Building include Charles Jencks, *The Language of Post-Modern Architecture,* 6th ed. (New York: Rizzoli, 1991); and Heinrich Klotz, *The History of Postmodern Architecture* (1984), trans. Radka Donnell (Cambridge, Mass.: MIT Press, 1988). Among Graves's writings, perhaps the most closely related to the Portland Building was his essay, "A Case for Figurative Architecture" (1982), in Wheeler, ed., *Michael Graves,* 11–13.
[5] On Goldschmidt's administration and downtown planning, see Carl Abbott, *Portland: Planning, Politics, and Growth in a Twentieth-Century City* (Lincoln: University of Nebraska Press, 1983), 167–81, 200–202, 207–28.
[6] Larry Shaw, "Building Dedicated with Modest Ceremony," *Oregonian,* 3 April 1980, C3.
[7] "Graves Aims at Building 'of Human Scale,'" *Oregonian,* 16 March 1980, D1.
[8] See Milliken, "The Portland Building Design/Build Competition," and Clausen, "Michael Graves's Portland Building."
[9] Ivancie, "Design-Build Competition Was a New Step for Portland," *Oregonian,* 28 October 1979. On the national debate among architects, see "Members Vote 3-1 to Extend Ethics to Include Design/Build," *Architectural Record* 164, no. 1 (July 1978):

34–35; "Design/Build Debate Produces a New Code of Ethics," *Architectural Record* 164, no. 1 (July 1978): 55, 57; and Arthur T. Kornblut, "Design/Build Changes All the Ground Rules for Affected Architects," *Architectural Record* 164, no. 2 (August 1978): 57.

10 "Program of Facility Requirements, prepared for City of Portland by Edward C. Wundram of Dielschneider Associates," 23 July 1979. City of Portland, Archives and Records Center [hereafter CPARC]. The author thanks reference archivist Mary Hansen for generous assistance.

11 Request for Bids, Portland Public Service Building, Addendum No. 7, 7 December 1979, p. 2. Milliken, "Portland Building," Appendix F.

12 Request for Bids, Portland Public Service Building, Addendum No. 5, 15 November 1979, p. 7. Milliken, "Portland Building," Appendix F. On sealed windows in postwar tall glass buildings, see Joseph M. Siry, *Air-Conditioning in Modern American Architecture, 1890–1970* (University Park: Pennsylvania State University Press, 2021), 159–92.

13 Dielschneider Associates, Inc., and William C. Neland, Portland Public Service Building, Program of Facility Requirements, 23 July 1979, 7. Milliken, "Portland Building," Appendix E. See Brenner, "Portland Building," 90.

14 "Pre-Bid Information," in Request for Proposals, Portland Service Building, June 1979. Milliken, "Portland Building," Appendix D.

15 Portland Public Service Building, Program of Facility Requirements, 23 July 1979. Milliken, "Portland Building," Appendix E.

16 Steve Jenning, "City Stalls Decision on Project," *Oregonian,* 20 March 1980.

17 "Portland Public Service Building; Building Description by Michael Graves," 7 February 1980, p. 1.2. Milliken, "Portland Building," Appendix I.

18 Milliken, "Portland Building," 71, and Appendix I.

19 Lisa Fleming Lee, "Building *the* Building," *Leading Edge* (Sunar Publication), 1, 1982, 66.

20 Art G. Abela to Allyn Staley, City of Portland Public Service Building by Pavarini/Hofmann, 14 February 1980, p. 2. CPARC.

21 Minutes, City Council Meeting, 30 April 1980, PCA. Steve Jenning, "Council Vote Unanimous: Templelike Building Wins Okay," *Oregonian,* 1 May 1980.

22 Constantine, "Case for Graves's Design for Portland," 100. The city specified: "The building must be designed to be 'looked down on' as it is not likely to be as high or higher than neighboring commercial structures. The roof or roofs are to be considered a major elevation." "Portland Public Service Building, Program of Facility Requirements," 23 July 1979, 8. Milliken, "Portland Building," Appendix E. In Graves's project, large "sconces" marked the roof's junctures with the central main fronts as places from which to view city and landscape, including the distant Mount Hood. These features were not included in the final built design.

23 Pastier, "First Monument of a Loosely Defined Style," 236. On the enlarged windows, see "Energy Analysis; Portland Public Office Building," *Progressive Architecture* 62, no. 9 (October 1981): 108–9.

24 Patrick Burke, quoted in Brian Libby, "A Postmodern Predicament: Will the Renovation of the Portland Building Compromise Its Historic Integrity?," *Architect,* 19 September 2017, https://www.architectmagazine.com/design/a-postmodern-predicament_0, accessed 11 June 2020. See also Antonio Pacheco, "A Graves Situation: DLR Group's Controversial Portland Building Renovations Are in Full Swing," *Architect's Newspaper,* 13 September 2018, archpaper.com/2018/09/portland-building-dlr-group-michael-graves/, accessed 11 June 2020.

25 Graves, in Doubilet, "Conversation with Graves," 111–12.

26 See "Energy Analysis," 108–9.

27 William K. Langdon, "The Interface between Energy and Formal Design Concerns," 248, citing Vladimir Bazjanac, "This Is Where and What," *Progressive Architecture* 63, no. 4 (April 1982): 124; and Graves, in Doubilet, "Conversation with Graves," 110. Graves's structure used less energy in Portland's mild climate than a conventional glass tower, although it consumed more energy than a building of similar size and shape that had a multilayered glass skin designed to maximize natural light.

28 Portland Public Service Building; National Register of Historic Places Registration Form. https://www.nps.gov/nr/feature/weekly_features/2011/PortlandPublicServiceBuilding.pdf.

29 Clausen, "Michael Graves's Portland Building," 263–65.

30 John G. Duffy, P.E., Facilities Mechanical Engineer, Office of Management and Finance, City of Portland, conversation with author, 5 April 2019. The author deeply thanks John Duffy for an extended tour of the reconstructed building's mechanical systems on 12 June 2019.

31 Randy Gragg, "Postmodernism's Seismic Shift: An Icon of 1980s Architecture Is Not as Sturdy as It Looks," *Metropolis* 16, no. 9 (May 1997): 44, 50, 53; and

Christina S. Olson, "Living with It: Michael Graves's Portland Building," *Art Criticism* 5, no. 1 (1988): 34–56.

[32] Ayda Ayoubi, "Demolition Phase Is Underway on Michael Graves's Portland Building," 15 March 2018, City of Portland, Office of Management and Finance, The Portland Building Reconstruction Project, D3 No. 2-2016; "Clarification of $195 Million Project Scope," 5 December 2016. See Howard S. Wright Co., "The Portland Building Reconstruction Project; Final Basis of Design," 14 September 2017, CPARC. Documents on the reconstruction may be accessed at www.portlandoregon.gov. On architects' concerns over the building's fate, see Karri Jacobs, "PoMo Redux," *Architect* 104, no. 1 (January 2015): 83–84, 86, 88.

[33] Andrew Theen, "Portland Building Renovation, at Up to $195 Million, Moves Forward," *Oregonian,* 21 October 2015.

[34] The Portland Building Reconstruction Project, Project No. B00018, 1 August 2016, Development Plan and Operations Manual, Project Charter, CPARC.

[35] Pacheco, "A Graves Situation."

[36] Randall Gragg, "The Portland Building's Ongoing Saga," *Architectural Record* 208, no. 7 (July 2020): 18–19.

[37] Brian Libby, "Portland Building 2.0: City Takes Bold, Non-Historic Approach Restoring Graves-Designed Landmark," *Portland Architecture; A Blog About Design in the Rose City,* posted 20 June 2017. https://chatterbox.typepad.com /portlandarchitecture/2017/06/index.html, accessed 6 February 2021.

[38] Pacheco, "A Graves Situation"; Duffy, conversations with author, 5 April 2019; 12 June 2019; City of Portland, Office of Management and Finance, The Portland Building Reconstruction Project, D3 No. 2016–07 Seismic Solution. 2 December 2016. See also FFA Architecture + Interiors, Inc., The Portland Building; Building Systems and Interior Assessment Index, 11 February 2015, CPARC.

[39] Duffy, conversations with author, 5 April 2019, 12 June 2019. City of Portland, Office of Management and Finance, The Portland Building Reconstruction Project, D3 No. 10-2017 Mechanical System Selection.

[40] Brian Libby, "Visiting the Renovated Portland Building, and Seeing the Light," *Portland Architecture,* blog (portlandarchitecture.com), posted 10 April 2020.

[41] "Rebuild of Portland Building Approved," *nextportland,* blog (https://www .nextportland.com/), posted 11 October 2017.

[42] Ayoubi, "Demolition Phase Is Underway"; Libby, "Visiting the Renovated Portland Building."

[43] Pacheco, "A Graves Situation." City of Portland, Office of Management and Finance, "The Portland Building Exterior Envelope Restoration and Structural Improvements." See also FFA Architecture + Interiors, Inc., "The Portland Building: Exterior Envelope Restoration; Structure Improvements; Assessment Phase I," March 2013, CPARC.

[44] Iain MacKenzie, DoCoMoMo Oregon Vice President, to Hillary Adam, Bureau of Development Services, and members of the Portland Historic Landmarks Commission, 15 June 2017, https://docomomo-us.org/resource/files%2F2qn1vmb6zjeymaxta. pdf, accessed 11 June 2020. See also Libby, "Portland Building 2.0" and "A Postmodern Predicament"; and "Rebuild of Portland Building Approved."

[45] City of Portland, Oregon, Bureau of Development Services, Land Use Services, Notice of Final Findings and Decision by the Historic Landmarks Commission Rendered on 24 July 2017, https://www.portlandoregon.gov/bds/article/648958, accessed 12 June 2020; City of Portland, Office of Management and Finance, The Portland Building Reconstruction Project, D3 No. 08 2017–Floors 4-15 Envelope Solution, 2 December 2016, CPARC; Pacheco, "A Graves Situation."

[46] Meijer, quoted in Gragg, "Portland Building's Ongoing Saga," 19.

[47] See, for example, Jason Hackworth, *The Neoliberal City: Governance, Ideology, and Development in American Urbanism* (Ithaca: Cornell University Press, 2007).

Figure 1. View of Unilever House, 2021. Photo: Author.

Juliana Kei

Retrofitting the Monument of Commerce
Unilever House, London

Introduction

In July 1931, *The Times* newspaper reported on the completion of Unilever House in London and admired it as "The Monument of Commerce."[1] The building's monumentality is manifest through its prominent presence on the Victoria Embankment, its scale (34,000 square feet of floor space), as well as its modern design and fittings. Unilever House's construction was also tied to the historical merger between the British soapmaker Lever Brothers and the Dutch company Margarine Union in 1929.[2] Building upon the notion that Unilever House can be considered both as a monument and a headquarter space for multinational corporations, this article examines its two large-scale retrofitting exercises—first by the multi-disciplinary design practice Pentagram (1980–83) and then by the international architectural office Kohn Pederson Fox (KPF) (2005–2008). The different approaches taken by Pentagram and KPF to inject value into Unilever House are considered: the former sought to accentuate the building's artistic and historical value while the latter focused on reducing, recycling, and reusing. How Lever Brothers' troubled history in colonial exploitations has been reenacted or repressed in these two renovations is also explored. This article further retrieves the polemic writings of Theo Crosby, one of the founders and the then-lead architect of Pentagram, on preservation and retrofitting. Examining his provocative articles such as "Glooming White Elephants" and "Towards a New Ornament," this research situates Pentagram's renovation in the socioeconomic and architectural conditions of postindustrial London.[3] Through this case study, this research seeks to parse out more of the entanglement between architectural values and retrofitting.

Unilever and its predecessor, Lever Brothers, has been an influential patron of arts and architecture. Their architectural and planning projects include the celebrated factory and workers village Port Sunlight (1888) in Birkenhead, which combined Enlightenment visions with industrial paternalism and an idealized image of English vernacular architecture.[4] When William Lever (Lord Leverhulme) purchased the site of 100 Victoria Embankment for the Unilever House, it was expected to be another grand architectural venture. However, a series of business blunders and over-ambitious acquisitions, including the purchase of the colonial mercantile Niger Company, put Lever

Future Anterior
Volume XVIII, Number 1
Summer 2021

Brothers in severe financial strains. Therefore, no building work was even started by the time of William Lever's death in 1925.[5] The plan for Unilever House restarted in 1929 after the merger with Margarine Union, and the need for a larger headquarter space for a corporation manufacturing almost all goods related to fat and oil became pressing.[6] Lever Brother's in-house architect James Lomax-Simpson, who had worked with William Lever on Port Sunlight, directed the project.[7] Although the design of Unilever House was also attributed to the partnership of renowned Scottish architects Thomas Tait and James Burnet, archival materials suggested Lomax-Simpson dictated most aspects of design.[8] The stripped Classicism of Unilever House is also more conservative than Tait and Burnet's other architectural outputs of the time.[9] Unilever House, in short, can be regarded as a structure that embodies the corporation's history and architectural vision.

The plan of Unilever House can be best described as a fan shape with a significant setback from its two frontages facing the Victoria Embankment and New Bridge Street (see Figure 1). Behind the fourteen-bay Portland stone façade was a steel frame structure punctuated by four light wells. Unilever House was well regarded by contemporary critics. For example, Charles Reilly considered it a "good large building" because it looked smaller than it was, due to its setback, proportion, and incurved treatment.[10] In comparison to its prominent façade, the interior space of Unilever House was rudimentary: open-plan office fitted with mass-produced furniture.[11] Only in the entrance spaces and elevators were there more deliberated Art Deco features. Its wartime usage as a military training facility and decades of piecemeal renovations had resulted in poorly planned compartmentations and inefficient circulations.[12] By the 1950s, the company head-office had already outgrown the building, and two adjacent buildings were purchased to provide additional workspaces.[13] In the mid-1970s, Unilever decided to sell the added properties to fund a large-scale renovation of Unilever House.[14]

Glooming White Elephants

Unilever's decision to retain and retrofit Unilever House was an unconventional one in the context of 1970s Britain.[15] At the time, London had suffered from decades of population losses and subsequent urban decay.[16] There was an exodus of established companies and institutions from the City of London.[17] These socioeconomic conditions were also significant to the formation of Pentagram, the designer chosen for Unilever House's first retrofitting job. Today, Pentagram is known as the largest independent interdisciplinary design practice in the world and excels in almost all realms of design, ranging from branding to interior spaces to multimedia campaigns.[18] They are also recognized for their ability, to borrow the words of *The Independent,* to combine "the formal restraint of Swiss modernism with the wit of the Madison Avenue advertising industry."[19] What is lesser known is that in the first two decades of Pentagram's history, under the leadership of Theo Crosby, their architectural outputs were more eclectic and consisted mostly of preservation and retrofitting projects.[20] This profile should be attributed to both Crosby's preservationist stance, and the fact that there was a lack of funds in construction from both the public and private sectors in Britain at the time. Building rehabilitation, retrofitting, and interior renovation became a means of survival for architects in London in the 1960s and 1970s. Pentagram was part of this shift and distinguished itself by providing streamlined design service in graphics, architecture, and corporate identity to attract and retain prestige clients, including the news agency Reuters.[21]

Pentagram's engagement with retrofitting architecture was driven by Crosby's belief that the reuse and revitalization of old buildings provided more opportunities to integrate arts and crafts in architecture.[22] Crosby had been a strong proponent for interdisciplinary collaboration since the postwar era, including organizing the now canonized *This Is Tomorrow* exhibition (1956).[23] Since the 1960s, Crosby had been reusing the ideas he developed to promote postwar Modernism in his preservationist works. He argued that the incorporation of arts and ornaments in the built environment would create a sense of plenty and excitement for a society of leisure. In his 1970 publication *The Necessary Monument,* Crosby elaborated on his theorization of the socioeconomic value of ornaments and monuments.[24] He proposed using the Tower Bridge as a driver for London Southwark's postindustrial urban regeneration.[25] He also positioned preservation as a remedy to the socioeconomic problems engendered by the mass construction and mass planning projects found in the postwar welfare state.[26] In Pentagram's 1975 publication *Living by Design,* Crosby further developed his theory on preservation and retrofitting under the framework of "Glooming White Elephants."[27] He considered one of the biggest challenges found in preservation and rehabilitation of old buildings was when "the site became too valuable (as happens in city centers) or not valuable enough (as happens with country houses)."[28] The task of designers and architects, for Crosby, was to inject value into old structures and retrieve a balance between the building's purpose, its location, and its values.

Although Crosby did not explain what he considered as the values found in old buildings, it is clear that they include artistic value as well as the integrity of manual labor. In his writing, he frequently evoked William Morris's pursuit of "the value and joy of hand work."[29] Crosby also recognized the intertwined nature of the different values found in historical structures. At stake was that Crosby also promoted the exchange of one kind of value with another. In *Living by Design,* he wrote, "To bring a new life to a very large old building requires a creative and complicated structure of uses within which, trade-offs of various values can be made which utilize the potential building fully—and do not distort its qualities."[30]

The exchanges of value, Crosby stressed, offered the necessary commercial answer and to "bring in the increased return necessary to satisfy the owner."[31] In his theory for retrofitting, Crosby considered the integration of arts and architecture could be a means to maintain or even increase the market exchange value of aged structures, and to provide jobs in architecture and its cottage industries. Noteworthy was also that Crosby's ideas would have been received as part of the mainstream of preservation and regeneration practice in Britain at the time—as indicated by the burgeoning "heritage industry."[32] Pentagram's Unilever House renovation was also featured at a Royal Institute of British Architects seminar, in 1985, entitled "Profitable Rehab."[33]

Toward a New Ornament

In Unilever House, Pentagram employed decorative elements as the generator of the retrofitting design. They established an alternative contractual model in which the client, Unilever, directly hired a team of artists, craftspeople, and tradespeople.[34] Pentagram argued that through the individuals' creativity and manual labor, their retrofitting accentuated the Art Deco characteristics, and hence increased the artistic and historical value of Unilever House.[35] Under such a framework, Unilever's in-house architects also maintained more control over the technical aspects of retrofitting, including the schedule and program of works.[36] The architect, meanwhile, served as the coordinator of the different parties who were involved in the project. In practice, the collaboration started by the team choosing a diamond shape pattern found in the building's original marble floor as the motif of the new design.[37] The artists, based on the motif, devised individual designs for the different parts of the building. For example, the glass designer Diane Radford developed a new diamond-shaped pattern for the decorative glass in the main lobby, which was then carried over to the design of the entrance revolving door.[38] The pattern was also modified and applied to fixtures such as railings, ceiling lights, and partition walls (Figure 2).[39] Pentagram's role was to orchestrate the collaborative work and design some elements when opportunities arose.[40] The result was a highly

Figure 2. Main Lobby of Unilever House after Pentagram's renovation. Radford's glass in the background. Photo: Pentagram.

decorative interior that bespoke handcrafted fixtures and orna-ments unified under a similar pattern. Their use of high-quality materials and good craftsmanship also distinguished Unilever House renovation from the "flatness" of PoMo design that was prevalent at the time.[41]

On the one hand, the Unilever retrofitting was a rejection of the rudimentary simplicity found in postwar Modernist design and planning.[42] On the other hand, Crosby, not unlike early twentieth-century Modernists, justified his design by positioning it as a response to economic and industrial conditions. The involvement of independent artists, craftspeople, and tradespeople resonated with the initiatives in promoting small businesses found in Britain at the time.[43] The retrofitting work also corresponded with the establishment of the Crafts Council, in the 1970s, that championed crafts as agents of industrial design. Although it was unlikely that Crosby had read Alois Reigl's *The Modern Cult of Monument* (1903), his approach overlapped with the classification found in the essay: Crosby aimed to increase the artistic and commemorative value of the monumental structure.[44] Crosby also measured the newness value of his additions, seeking to instantiate their purposes in the society that the building stood.

In their effort to upgrade Unilever House as the workspace for a multinational enterprise, Pentagram's performance was not always satisfactory. Although their Art Deco–inspired design offered opportunities to integrate building service elements in theory, their adaptability was limited in reality. For example, inspired by the diamond pattern, Crosby created columns with folded-metal capital that incorporated up-lighting fixtures (see Figure 2).[45] In the office space, Pentagram installed customized drop-ceilings based on the diamond pattern, distinguishing the Unilever office space from the conventional gypsum board suspended ceiling.[46] However, since bespoke elements were used widely in the project, they had to manufacture customized pipes and ducts that were more costly to construct. Other difficulties included predicting the light transmittance of the decorative light and undulating surfaces. Dimmers had to be installed in some areas to calibrate the lighting level, which also increased the cost.[47] However, one may also argue that prioritizing artistic value, over economy and efficiency, was the pursuit that undergirded the Unilever retrofitting.

Elsewhere in the building, Pentagram sought to inject and increase real estate and commercial value through artistic interventions. One of the major changes found in the Pentagram retrofitting was the enlargement of the windows on the top floors. The old bland walls on the top of the building had created an austere crowning for the Classicist façade but also rendered the attic space inhabitable (Figure 3).[48] The tall parapets also obstructed the view of the existing top floor. To add and improve the valuable floor spaces, Pentagram commissioned artist Nicholas Munro to create fourteen twice life-size statues to be placed in front of the new windows to draw attention away from the conversion.[49] They also argued that

Figure 3. Unilever House in 1932. The top of the building was a blank wall and not used as office spaces. Photo: RIBA Photo Library.

the addition reflected Lomax-Simpson's original design intent depicted in a 1929 elevation, which featured fourteen statues on the top parapet.[50] Moving beyond the conventional top-floor addition method that often required a setback, Pentagram demonstrated their ability to exchange artistic value for real-estate value.[51]

It is also worth noting that in addition to Munro's statues, Unilever commissioned a total of 250 artworks during the Pentagram retrofitting. This "art shopping spree," as described by the *Sunday Times,* could be regarded as a continuation of the corporation's long-established patronage in the arts.[52] It also resonated with the Percentage for Art campaign in England put forward by artists, architects, and critics, including Crosby, since 1982.[53] Motivated by similar initiatives such as the Public Art Fund in the United States, the Percentage for Art was hoping to rejuvenate the public realm in postindustrial cities.[54] However, these initiatives in Britain did not lead to a nationwide reform and were instead entrenched with controversies such as Prince Charles interventions in architecture.[55] The limitation of the Percent for Art can also be gleaned from the Unilever House project, where the artworks spoke little about the public realm. Although the works were visible to the public, they were mostly dedicated to visualizing and commemorating the history of the corporation. Moreover, at the time of the Pentagram retrofitting, the Unilever company had been laying off more than 20,000 workers for cost-cutting. [56] The public art commissions,

Figure 4. View of the Staff Canteen of Unilever House after Pentagram's renovation. Photo: Pentagram.

ironically, can also be seen as a mechanism for the corporation to shift their responsibilities to an abstract notion of social responsibilities and away from the welfare of the workers (as seen in the Port Sunlight project).

During Pentagram's retrofitting, the incorporation of arts and craft also inadvertently drew out more tenuous stories about Unilever's relationship with social responsibilities. In his design for the main lobby and staff canteen, Crosby used palm leaves—the raw material for Unilever's soap products—as the design motif (Figure 4). However, it was well known, even during William Lever's lifetime, that the company's expansion to acquire palm and coconut had brought about some of the worst labor exploitations in the South Pacific.[57] There were also artworks that made direct reference to the Lever Brothers' colonial history. A timber relief sent from United Africa International, produced by the Chief Erhabor Emokpae of Benin, portrayed William Lever's African "travels and enterprises" (Figure 5).[58] In the piece, African laborers carried coconuts with their hands, and heads are placed alongside modern machinery and the Sunlight label. Together, they stand underneath an enlarged figure, presumably William Lever, on horseback. The relief signified the company's association with colonial imperialism, but also obscured the much more violent and problematic reality. The United Africa International oversaw the Huileries du Congo Belge, a plantation that William Lever built on the former Congo Free State (land that was formerly directly ruled by Leopold II of Belgium, and where some of the most horrendous colonial atrocities were imposed), between 1911 and 1960. Various forms of conscripted, compulsory, and coerced labor, including child labor, were found in the 750,000 hectares concession the Lever Brothers received from the Belgian government.[59]

Pentagram's renovation also accidentally reenacted the company's colonial past. Crosby asked Unilever's subsidiaries

66

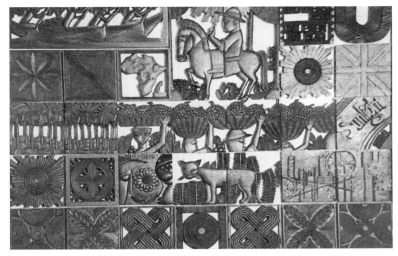

Figure 5. Wooden relief created by Chief Erhabor Emokpae of Benin featured in the Pentagram renovation of Unilever House. Photo: Pentagram.

from all over the world to contribute artworks to celebrate the retrofitting of the London headquarter. This call for participation and collective effort conveniently veneered over the fact that many of these subsidiaries were built upon colonial occupations. These Pentagram additions further highlighted the colonial association of the Unilever House — which was celebrated for its usage of "Empire Materials," the finest materials gathered from different corners of the British Empire, when it was completed in 1932.[60] To solicit gifts from the subsidiaries can also be regarded as an alternative validation of the false belief that the colonies should be grateful for the modernization and industrialization brought by European colonization — a view that William Lever embraced.[61]

Reducing Value

In comparison to Pentagram's use of artistic value to trivialize speculation and exploitations, more questions about values in architecture can also be asked about the subsequent KPF renovation. KPF took a drastically different approach, and their design principle can perhaps best be described as inserting a twenty-first-century hi-tech office architecture behind a 1930s façade. They demolished all the existing structures except the Portland Stone façade and the foundation of the building. The existing lightwells were combined into a large atrium space (Figure 6). This reductive design approach to retrofitting may also be regarded as a reflection of the changing working conditions in Unilever. Due to the developments in telecommunication and automation, the corporation no longer needed the large quantity of office space provided in Unilever House. As part of the retrofitting, Unilever sold the Unilever House to the developer Stanhope and leased back part of the building.[62] Moreover, KPF also removed part of the rear of the building to further reduce the floor area of the building. As a result of this partial demolition, the frontages of Unilever House increased from two to three. A large curtain-wall rear façade was introduced to the expanded rear facade. This opening up of the building is both physical and conceptual: the design seeks to signify a nonhierarchical and globalized network of trade and commerce. Glass walls or semitranslucent partitions replaced Pentagram's highly decorative crafted panels.[63] The boardrooms and meetings, originally located on the top floor of the building, are distributed over different parts of the building, signifying Unilever's new vision of a nonhierarchical, visible, and collaborative workspace.[64] A series of suspended platforms in the atrium spaces that function as meeting spaces and vertical circulation became the main visual element of the retrofitting. An artwork entitled "The Space Trumpet" made by artist Conard Shawcross is attached to these platforms to underscore their sculptural quality.[65] All of the artworks and decorations from Pentagram's retrofitting was removed, and only a few artifacts from the 1930 original structure, including the Pewter panels created by Eric Gill, were preserved.[66] There is no celebration of colonial explorations, yet there is also no reference to the long and troubled history of the building and the corporation.

The theme of reduction is carried over to the process of retrofitting as well: the project paid significant attention to minimize the time required for material delivery, construction waste, day-to-day energy usage, to water run-off from the roof.[67] The project claimed to minimize landfill by achieving 87 percent recycling/reuse rate. They recycled and reused 6000 metric tons of steel, 5500 cubic meters of concrete, and 100 percent of the furniture.[68] Some of the materials were reused in the Unilever House, including most of the steel and the floorings. The furniture and a part of the structure were donated to schools and charity organizations in London.[69] The concrete was sent to a concrete crushing facility to be repurposed and reused in the building industry. In contrast to Pentagram's emphasis on the individuality and meaning of each bespoke piece, KPF treated building materials as a collective whole. To preserve, for KPF, is less about maintaining or modifying the physical entity, but more about conserving the embodied energy found in the existing structure. In considering the relationship between the past and the present in their retrofitting work, KPF prioritized closing the material life cycle, instead of a stylistic dialogue with old architectural expressions. In these two retrofittings, one can find the meaning of "value" shifts from one definition to another. In the Oxford Dictionary, the word *value* can be defined as "the regard that something is held to deserve; importance or worth" or "the numerical amount denoted by an algebraic term; a magnitude, quantity,

Figure 6. Office and Atrium Space after KPF's renovation of Unilever House (2005). Photo: Wikicommon Image.

or number."[70] In Pentagram's retrofitting, the exchange of artistic value and real estate value suggests they adhered to the former definition. In the KPF retrofitting, the dematerialized and decontextualized method reconceptualizes the building and material as numerical amounts. This change in the understanding of value in architecture to the second definition also propelled the reductive approach in an age of environmental awakening.

Conclusion

These two different approaches to retrofitting also tie to the changing notion of the environment in architectural culture. Both designers presented their projects as an attempt to tackle the environmental crisis of their time. The KPF retrofitting aligned the construction process and their design decisions with the aims of reduction, recycling, and reusing, as well as established sustainable building frameworks.[71] Influenced by publications such as E. F. Schumacher's *Small Is Beautiful* (1973), Pentagram and Crosby also presented retrofitting projects, in general, as a means to reduce and reuse.[72] However, from Crosby's writings, one can gauge that the main driver behind the decorative design was a critique of the monotonous and deteriorating built environment of their time.[73] To inject values into decaying old structures, for Pentagram and Crosby, was to ensure the sustainability and viability of the city environment that was under threat.[74]

These two retrofitting projects also offer an alternative means to reflect on the other crisis of our time. The Pentagram retrofitting is an addition to the ongoing debate about architectural heritage and colonial and racial injustice. It also draws attention to how later additions and retrofitting may perpetuate the problematic pasts that architecture embodied. In Britain, where many companies, industries, and institutions are directly or indirectly tied to imperialism, how one should retrofit seemingly conventional old structures such as offices, schools, and houses requires more consideration. At the time of writing, there have been initiatives to remove or at least remark on the colonial connotation of buildings. While these changes are only at an initial stage, there are growing debates and re-envisioning of what street, buildings, and public arts should signify. The Unilever retrofitting by KPF, meanwhile, provokes other difficult questions about the practice of whitewashing—or greenwashing—history. The current methods and criteria stipulated by sustainability and green building regulations lean heavily on the numeric amount of emission and consumption, which may function as a distraction from the historical and cultural connotations of buildings. However, this emphasis on material matters does not necessarily lead to a reduction in meaning: there are more stories to be told in the timbers, steels, and stones extracted from different corners of the empire and by exploited labor. In architectural history, there are emerging scholarships that delve into the colonial material origins and labor implication of building materials in Britain and America.[75] Existing studies in the history of economy and the theorization of new materialism and architecture can also scaffold this shift in architectural research and practice. Somewhat ironically, there are also new projects in former British colonies such as Hong Kong that diligently traces the material, labor, and knowledge network in colonial architecture.[76] While the discussions on these projects do not entirely shift away from colonial nostalgia, they are examples of how architectural retrofitting can critically demonstrate both the collaborations and oppressions found in colonial architecture. These studies and projects highlight that new design approaches can be devised to incorporate the uncomfortable facts about materials and labor in the cycle of reuse, reduce, and recycle.

Biography

Juliana Kei is a lecturer at the Liverpool School of Architecture. She is currently completing a monograph on Theo Crosby with Stephen Parnell and Alan Power to be published by Lund Humphries. Her other research interests include late/postcolonial architecture and exhibitions. As part of the Hong Kong Design History Network, Juliana curated the Hong Kong pavilion of the London Design Biennale, which investigates the future of the history of Hong Kong, held in June 2021.

Notes

[1] Anon., "Unilever House: A Monument of Commerce," *The Times*, July 19, 1932.
[2] Clive Aslet, "Unilever House Blackfriars," *The Thirties Society Journal* 1 (1980): 18–21.
[3] Pentagram, *Living by Design* (London: Pentagram, 1978). Theo Crosby, *Unilever House: Towards a New Ornament* (London: Pentagram, 1984).
[4] Anon., "News in Brief; Unilever House," *Sunday Times*, October 5, 1986. Elizabeth Outka, *Consuming Traditions: Modernity, Modernism, and the Commodified Authentic* (New York: Oxford University Press, 2008), 46–49.
[5] Aslet, "Unilever House Blackfriars."
[6] Aslet, "Unilever House Blackfriars."
[7] Aslet, "Unilever House Blackfriars." Anon., "James Lomax-Simpson," Oxford Reference, 2011, https://www.oxfordreference.com/view/10.1093/oi/authority.20110803100113528.
[8] Aslet, "Unilever House Blackfriars."
[9] For example, in 1933, Tait completed the Royal Masonic Hospital and, in 1934, terrace houses in St John's Wood London, which are both of Art-Deco modern style.
[10] Charles Reilly, "Unilever House: The New Building at Blackfriars," *The Times*, December 12, 1931. Reilly's favorable comment may be attributed to the fact that Lord Leverhulme was a patron of the Liverpool School of Architecture, which he chaired.
[11] Anon., "Steel Furniture at Unilever House by Sankey-Sheldon," *The Times*, July 19, 1932, sec. Advertisement.
[12] "The £37m Face-Lift," *Architect & Surveyor*, May 1982, 5.
[13] "London County Council Metropolitan Management and Building Acts Amendment Act 1868 Section 12 and 13 Licensing of Places of Public Entertainment: Public Control Committee Report by the Architect to the Council," Case No. 2537. Unilever House, Victoria Embankment, E.C. 10th, and 23rd July 1942 in London Metropolitan Archive, folder LMC GLC/AR/BR/19/2537.
[14] Anthony Williams, "Rehab de Lux," *Building*, February 26, 1982, 32.
[15] Royal Institute of British Architects, "Profitable Rehab: A One Day Seminar Held at the Royal Institute of British Architects" (London: Royal Institute of British Architects, 1985).

16 Richard J. Williams, *The Anxious City: English Urbanism in the Late Twentieth Century* (London: Routledge, 2004), 6–8.

17 In the reporting of the Unilever House retrofitting, journalists also remarked that "it was fashionable to talk about relocation" in the late 1960s and early 1970s London. "The £37m Face-Lift," 4.

18 "Pentagram—the World's Largest Independent Design Consultancy," Company Website, 2020, https://www.pentagram.com/.

19 Emily King, "Obituaries: Alan Fletcher," *The Independent*, September 25, 2006.

20 Pentagram, *Living by Design*. Pentagram, *Pentagram: The Work of Five Designers* (London: Lund Humphries, 1972).

21 King, "Obituaries: Alan Fletcher."

22 Theo Crosby, *The Pessimist Utopia* (London: Pentagram, 1974).

23 Crosby, in the current historiography of British architect, is mostly known for his role as the technical editor of *Architectural Design* as well as the organizer of the now canonized 1956 exhibition *This is Tomorrow*. Simon Sadler, "Theo Crosby's Environment Games 1956–1973," in *Exhibiting Architecture: A Paradox?*, ed. Eeva-Liisa Pelkonen (New Haven: Yale School of Architecture, 2014), 99–106. Salomon Frausto, "Sketches of a Utopian Pessimist," *AA Files* 75 (January 2018): 162–68. Stephen Parnell, "Brute Forces," *Architectural Review*, June 2012.

24 Theo Crosby, *The Necessary Monument* (London: Studio Vista, 1970).

25 Crosby, *The Necessary Monument*.

26 Crosby, *The Pessimist Utopia*.

27 Pentagram, *Living by Design*, 174–75

28 Pentagram, *Living by Design*, 174–75.

29 Pentagram, *Living by Design*, 174.

30 Pentagram, *Living by Design*, 174.

31 Pentagram, *Living by Design*, 174.

32 Robert Hewison, *The Heritage Industry: Britain in a Climate of Decline* (London: Methuen, 1987).

33 Royal Institute of British Architects, *Profitable Rehab: A One Day Seminar Held at the Royal Institute of British Architects* (London: RIBA, 1985).

34 Crosby, *Unilever House*.

35 Timothy Olster, "Working with Artists: 3 Case Studies," *The Architects' Journal*, February 1984, 64–66.

36 Olster, "Working with Artists: 3 Case Studies."

37 Crosby, *Unilever House*.

38 Crosby, *Unilever House*.

39 Gavin Stamp, "Inner Light," *The Architects' Journal*, February 1982. Anon., "Service in Style," *Building Services*, July 1982.

40 Olster, "Working with Artists: 3 Case Studies," 64.

41 John Stokdyk, "Maverick with Message," *Building*, May 1988.

42 Crosby, *The Pessimist Utopia*.

43 During the second Harold Wilson government, a Committee of Inquiry on Small Firmsresulted in the Bolton Report. In the following years, to support the growth of small businesses became an issue that was supported by both major parties in Britain. David Kirby, "Government and Policy for SMEs in the UK," *Environment and Planning C: Government and Policy* 22 (2004): 775–77.

44 Alois Riegl, "The Modern Cult of Monuments: Its Character and Its Origins," *Oppositions: A Journal for Ideas and Criticism in Architecture* 25 (Fall 1982): 21–56. Riegl's essay was translated into English in 1982, after the publication of Crosby's writing on "Glooming the White Elephant" and *The Necessary Monument*.

45 Riegl, "The Modern Cult of Monuments."

46 Riegl, "The Modern Cult of Monuments,"24.

47 Riegl, "The Modern Cult of Monuments," 25.

48 Aslet, "Unilever House Blackfriars."

49 Olster, "Working with Artists: 3 Case Studies." "Unilever House London- Unilever PLC," Archival Record at the Unilever Archive, GB1752.UNI/PLC/UH

50 Aslet, "Unilever House Blackfriars."

51 Such a strategy was also found in other Pentagram retrofitting projects such as the Ulster Terrace, originally designed by John Nash, where they created an undulating façade where the largest addition was conveniently found at the top floor where the value was the highest.

52 Anon., "News in Brief; Unilever House," *Sunday Times*, October 5, 1986.

53 Deanna Petherbridge, "Art and Architecture," *Art Monthly*, November 1982. The Art and Architecture campaign was launched after a conference held at the ICA London in 1982, and speakers included artist John Maine and Stephen Lobb, art critic Kate Linker, and architectural critics including Kenneth Frampton, Joseph Rykwert, Charles Jencks, Robert Maxwell, and Crosby.

[54] Kate Linker, "Provision and Persuasions in US Public Art," *Art Monthly,* November 1982.

[55] The Arts & Architecture sought the patronage of Prince Charles. Several of the groups' meetings and newsletters were dominated by the debates on Mansion House redevelopment, which led to discontent from artists and craftspeople due to the dominance of architectural debates. *Arts and Architecture Newsletter* 21 & 27, Arts & Architecture Archive. Royal College of Art Library Special Collection.

[56] Anon., "News in Brief; Unilever House," *Sunday Times,* October 5, 1986.

[57] Jules Marchal, *Lord Leverhulme's Ghosts: Colonial Exploitation in the Congo* (London: Verso, 2017), 234–51.

[58] Crosby, *Unilever House.*

[59] Brian Lewis, *So Clean: Lord Leverhulme, Soap and Civilisation* (Manchester: Manchester University Press, 2009), 183. Marchal, *Lord Leverhulme's Ghosts.*

[60] Anon., "Unilever House: A Monument of Commerce."

[61] Lewis, *So Clean,* 155–56.

[62] The structure was also renamed 100VE after the renovation. Unilever, *100 Victoria Embankment: the Redevelopment of Unilever's London Headquarters* (London: Unilever, 2007).

[63] Unilever, *100 Victoria Embankment,* 34–35.

[64] Unilever, *100 Victoria Embankment,* 25.

[65] Conrad Shawcross, "Space Trumpet [2007]," Conrad Shawcross, 2007, http://conradshawcross.com/blog/project/space-trumpet-2007/.

[66] Christian Brensing, "Unilever House London," *Detail,* 2008, 242.

[67] Lisa Page, "Unilever House: A Bovis Lend Lease Stanhope Alliance Project," Project Report (London: Bovis Lend Lease, 2008).

[68] Page, "Unilever House."

[69] Unilever, *100 Victoria Embankment,* 16–17.

[70] Catherine Soanes and Stevenson Angus, eds., "Value," in *The Concise Oxford English Dictionary* (Oxford: Oxford University Press, 2008), https://search.proquest.com/docview/2137961325?accountid=12117.

[71] The building was awarded "excellence" under BREEAM (Building Research Establishment Environmental Assessment Method).

[72] E. F. Schumacher, *SMALL IS BEAUTIFUL: Economics as If People Mattered* (London: Blond & Briggs, 1973). Crosby, *The Pessimist Utopia.*

[73] Crosby, *Unilever House.*

[74] Crosby has written and exhibited about the decaying urban environment, including his 1973 exhibition at the Hayward Gallery *How to Play the Environment Game.*

[75] Historian Irene Cheng, for example, examines how timber from Burmese teak plantations and British Honduran mahogany forests was used in bungalows in California. Irene Cheng, "Forest, Plantation, Bungalow," in *Marginal Landscapes* (72nd Society of Architectural Historian Annual Conference, Providence, 2019).

[76] For example, the Tai Kwun Centre for Heritage and Art in Hong Kong converts a former colonial prison and courthouse into a public art venue. The bricks of the existing structure, which were produced in northern England in the mid-nineteenth century are reproduced and again shipped from England to Hong Kong for the retrofitting. They also examined the use of Canton (the region of Hong Kong), Amoy (name given by the Europeans to Xiamen, Fujian) and Formosa (Taiwan under Japanese colonial rule) bricks in the existing building. Enid Tsui, "Hong Kong Central Police Station Restoration," *South China Morning Post,* June 15, 2018, https://www.scmp.com/lifestyle/article/2150710/hong-kong-central-police-station-restoration-how-citys-most-ambitious. Purcell Miller Tritton LLP, "The Old Central Police Station and Victoria Prison Hong Kong: Conservation Management Plan" (Hong Kong: Tai Kwun, June 2008).

Figure 1. View of gasoline pumps, product displays, attendant, and entry to Esso gas station store, with interior visible through window wall designed by Mies van der Rohe. Montréal, Quebec, Canada, 1969.

Kai Woolner-Pratt

Mies à jour
The Nuns' Island Gas Station as a Transitional Object

Here, as in our other rituals, modernity's carbon culture is materialized—the body acclimated to the surfeit of coal's heat, conditioned to the touch of congealed oil and natural gas, and joined to a subterranean INFRASTRUCTURE of carbon that delivers these sensations to the skin, ear, and eye.
    —Bob Johnson, "Embodiment"

Every land is unique, whence the need to "recycle", to scrape clean once more (if possible with the greatest care) the ancient text where men have written across the irreplaceable surface of the soil, in order to make it available again so that it meets today's needs before being done away with in its turn.
    —André Corboz, "The Land as Palimpsest"

In 1967, the Esso service station on Nuns' Island *(Île des Sœurs)* filled its first gas tank. Located at the center of a new peri-urban development in the St. Lawrence River, just off the Island of Montreal, the gas station was built by Chicago-based developer Metropolitan Structures to the designs of the Office of Mies van der Rohe (Figure 1). Metropolitan Structures—which emerged out of Herbert Realty Co., the developer of Lake Shore Drive in Chicago—leased the nine-hundred-acre island in 1965. In addition to the gas station, the Office was tasked with the design of three thirteen-story apartment towers—called, respectively, Hi-Rise 1, 2, and 3. (During the same period, the Office was also working with a different, Montreal-based developer on Westmount Square, a mixed commercial and residential project on the edge of Montreal's city center.) Mies's firm had initially also proposed a scheme for the urbanization of Nuns' Island in its entirety.[1] Their proposal was composed of twelve towers along the perimeter of the Island, standing perpendicular to the shoreline, rising through the foliage of the many trees that had not yet been despoliated. The scheme was not accepted—the commission went instead to Stanley Tigerman—but the three Hi-Rise towers were constructed as a sort of fragment of that initial scheme.[2] Similarly, the Esso service station was the first of eight planned stations for the Island, all following the same design.[3] Of these eight planned gas stations, only the building in question has been constructed.

Future Anterior
Volume XVIII, Number 1
Summer 2021

The gas station served the Island continuously from 1967 until 2008, when Imperial Oil erected a larger, standard-issue Esso station just up the road from the Mies service station. By 2008, the Island had seen increased densification, but not to the extent that was anticipated in the initial plans. The gas station was, effectively, no longer able to meet the demand of the Island's residents, and yet proceeding with the construction of the remaining seven gas stations was no longer considered feasible because the master plan for the Island had been abandoned when its ownership changed hands in the late 1970s. The Mies service station thus remains in place as a ruin of very specific conditions in the reification of oil-based mobility in Montreal, which are likewise situated within the broader context of modernization in Quebec, and globally, in the 1960s. The uniqueness of the gas station has been recognized through the induction of the site into Montreal's systems for heritage preservation.[4] It is perhaps not incidental that modernist heritage in Quebec coincides to a significant extent with the history of the Quiet Revolution.[5] The Esso station's retrofit is, therefore, highly instructive for considering the architectural dimensions of Quebec's recent history.

The structure's imbrication with other histories of Montreal's modernist heritage is at once materially maintained and symbolically interrupted by the reconfiguration of the building on other, non-petrocultural terms. After being classified as a heritage building, the structure was the object of a thorough retrofit by Montreal firm Les architectes fabg, completed in 2012. The project reconceives the structure, which had been simply empty for several years, as a community center, providing distinct spaces for seniors and youth in the respective glass enclosures at each end of the building. Services are inserted in the form of monoliths resembling the service core of the Farnsworth House. Containing washrooms, banks of kitchen appliances, and storage space, these elements run parallel to the back wall of each enclosure, leaving most of the interior space free for indeterminate uses.

The air circulating in the interior spaces is thermally conditioned by geothermal wells whose air intake and outtake vents are routed through the cases for the gas pumps, which were originally designed by the Mies Office.[6] The geothermal system also generates most of the energy needed for the building. The symbolism of this retrofit is unequivocal: the ruins of a reckless oil-based modernity, in which Quebec was all too ready to participate as part of its political project of emancipation in the 1960s, must now give way to a more energetically and socially sensitive program. According to Les architects fabg, "The project is not about the faithful restoration of a monument but an interpretation that attempts to communicate the essence of an artistic vision formulated by someone else in response to a world that is no longer the same."[7] But the gas station — rechristened "La Station" upon its reopening in 2012 — was, and remains, a limited gesture within a larger system of energy and transportation infrastructure. Architecture's agency consists here not in the concrete production of a different kind of space, but rather in the rhetorical force of the retrofit's gesture. By reconfiguring the isolated microcosm of La Station, another macrocosm is implied, or even demanded, that would see the revisioning of the Nuns' Island territory as a whole. This project highlights the utility of an architectural retrofit as a prototype for broader projects of sociotechnical repair.

The relationship between the original Esso station's *intrastructure* and its *infrastructure* suggests a disjunction between modernity and modernization. The gas station promises a positive sense of modernity that naturalizes and (re)mediates the violence of Quebec's material and economic "modernization" in the 1950s and '60s. Insofar as Quebec is currently constructing a controversially large hydroelectric plant in the northwest of the province, and continuing to transport (though not refine) oil into and through its territory, Quebec's energy systems are caught between oil and hydroelectricity. Most of Quebec's electrical energy is produced through hydroelectric plants that are situated conveniently out of sight of the metropolitan populations.[8] Despite the centrality of hydroelectricity to Quebec's identity, the province's relationship to oil has indelibly marked its cities: both Montreal and Quebec City have extremely walkable cores juxtaposed with car-dependent peripheries. The entanglement with oil is visible, as well, in major refineries operating at the edges of each city.

How should we situate the rhetorical gesture of the Nuns' Island gas station? By following the retrofit's decoupling from the oil infrastructures implemented in Montreal since the 1960s, this paper revisits narratives that remain latent within the history of the gas station and the Nuns' Island project as a whole. In teasing out the other histories, this article also locates the retrofit of the Nuns' Island gas station within the vibrant discourse on maintenance and repair.[9] While the project improves the functionality of the building, the project's refusal of oil is all the more symbolically weighty because the structure is a decommissioned gas station. Given the rhetorical force of this gesture, the Nuns' Island retrofit might best be considered as an act of sociotechnical repair.[10] Scholars such as Stephen Jackson, Benjamin Sims, and Christopher R. Henke have focused on the way that acts of repair, which may appear to be small and punctual, are always interventions in sociotechnical systems. In the case of the La Station retrofit, the project disavails the visitor of seamless access to oil-based energy with startling elegance, calling attention to Quebec's dependence on oil and offering itself up as a "transitional object."[11] By disavowing its function as a gas station, La Station demonstrates that buildings and even cities could, seemingly easily, be reconfigured on other terms, and highlights the need for the (cosmological) reformation of Montreal's energy and transportation infrastructures.

Territorialized: Measurement and Cultivation

Within the framework of mobility infrastructures, the original gas station is most clearly related to a specific moment within car culture, considered here as a subset of what Bob Johnson calls carbon culture and what Imre Szeman and his colleagues call "petroculture." When Nuns' Island was urbanized in the twentieth century, the surface of the island was treated as a tabula rasa. But like any landscape, it was a palimpsest.[12] The history of human settlement in the area has been recorded in artifacts dating to 4,000 BC. Somewhat more recently, the Island was part of the territory inhabited by the St. Lawrence Iroquois. The conventionally recognized inauguration of Montreal's modern colonial history began with the arrival of Jacques Cartier in 1535, at which time the St. Lawrence Iroquois maintained a fortified town on the Island.[13] In 1652, the French colonial settlement of Fort Ville-Marie was established on what is now called the Island of Montreal. It was amidst this wave of European settlement that, in 1634, Nuns' Island was entered into real estate records as belonging to the French colonist Jean de Lauzon.[14] In 1664, de Lauzon subdivided the Island into three parts, which are recorded as becoming the property of three seigneurs, who established manors on the Island. Shortly thereafter, one of the seigneurs transferred his portion to the sister of one of the other two landowners. When the siblings merged their properties 1668, the Island became divided in a 2:1 split between two seigneuries. In 1706, the Congrégation de Notre-Dame — an order of uncloistered nuns who were active in establishing educational institutions in Ville-Marie — acquired the smaller of the two properties.[15] When the larger seigneurie came up for auction in 1769, the Congrégation successfully purchased it as well, consolidating their ownership of the entire Island (Figure 2).

From then on, the Island was owned and inhabited by the nuns, who exploited the territory for agricultural ends, which included reusing and maintaining houses and outbuildings built by the previous landowners. They undertook agricultural production at a surprisingly large scale: the land hosted not only kitchen gardens, but also orchards and fields of oats and wheat, as well as large numbers of cows, pigs, chickens, ducks, and sheep, whose wool was collected.[16] Education of children

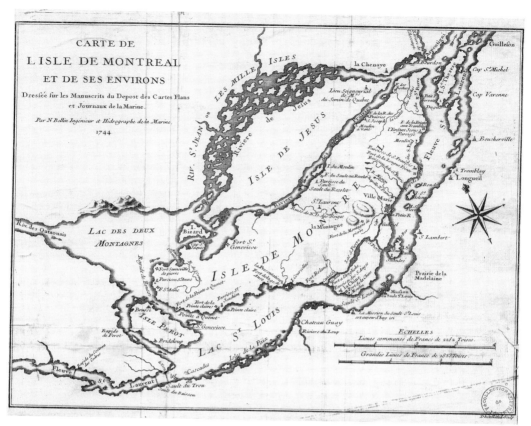

Figure 2. Map of the Island of Montreal, 1744. Nuns' Island is identified as "I. St. Paul" because the island was known as Ile St. Paul until the 1960s. Courtesy of Archives de la Ville de Montréal, BM5-C-26-050A (cropped).

and women being the primary mission of the Congrégation de Notre-Dame, the substantial agricultural yield met the alimentary needs of the convent but was also part of their missionary work. The nun's agriculturalization of the Island persisted through the nineteenth century, only coming to a close in the mid-1950s.

After having sold the Island the previous year, the nuns' barge pushed off from the Island for the last time in 1957.[17] The CMD's decision to cede their land to a real estate developer was taken amidst serious pressures resulting from infrastructural projects at both small and large scales on the St. Lawrence River. Specifically, the possibility of rising waters loomed over the Island in the 1950s. This threat was presented at the large scale by the St. Lawrence Seaway and Power Project and, at the small scale, by the desires of both the federal and the provincial governments to implement hydroelectric dams on the St. Lawrence. In the end, however, neither of these threats materialized. An enlargement of the St. Lawrence Seaway did, in fact, take place in 1957–59, but the concomitant canalization project at Montreal was shunted to the South Shore of the St. Lawrence, sparing any untoward impacts on Nuns' Island while quite literally bifurcating the Kahnawake Mohawk Territory and cutting off the community's access to the river.[18] These prototypical projects—the hydroelectric dams, the St. Lawrence Seaway—constitute vectors of Quebec's infrastructuralization that crystallized when the Nuns' Island territory's changed hands, from a religious organization and a capitalist one. The acute violence within which this transaction took place puts a fine point on the nascent secularization and capitalization that prefigured the Quiet Revolution of the 1960s.

These rhyming narratives of cultural, architectural, and infrastructural modernization condition the established history of the 1960s as a decade in which "Montreal thinks big."[19] The megastructure certainly had its day in a decade that saw the erection of not only the pavilions of Expo 67, most notably the US Pavilion (now the Montreal Biosphere; 1967, Buckminster Fuller) and Habitat 67 (1967, Moshe Safdie).[20] But the 1960s also major urban projects, many of which were explicitly "national," i.e., Québecois, institutions, such as those designed by the local firm David & Boulva, including the Palais de Justice de Montréal (1965–71) and the Théâtre Maisonneuve (1967). Montreal also saw the construction of other large-scale projects designed by international architects—and invested with international capital—such as Place Ville-Marie (1962, Pei Cobb Freed & Partners) and Westmount Square (1964–67, Office of Mies van der Rohe). Many of these buildings are plugged into the extensive network of underground passageways and commercial spaces known as the Underground City (1962). In the same decade, the major infrastructural outlines of the city were established. The Montreal Metro (1966) and the construction of the major highways promoted visions of modern mobility that were at once unified and divergent. The intensification of construction in the downtown was matched by increased construction in the peripheries of the city.

By dealing with the nesting (or at least interlocking) spheres of culture, infrastructure, and structure, the architectural object of the Esso Station on Nuns' Island (1967), and its eventual reincarnation as La Station (2012), can come into acute focus as an expression of social, cultural, and material vectors concerning the modernization of energy systems and, specifically, the establishment of oil as a critical element of 1960s urbanization in Quebec. More concretely, this paper is interested in an anthropological reading of the Nuns' Island gas station as a site that mediates modernity through producing experiences of pleasure, fascination, and devotion that take on an almost explicitly religious or mystical character. Following the intonations of Grimes, a pop star who had her start in Montreal, we might consider the fundamentally magical way in which *we appreciate power.*[21]

The Quebec Housing and Mortgage Corporation, who acquired the Island in 1956, was formed just a year before the sale

Figure 3. Aerial view of Nuns' Island with Champlain Bridge (in foreground), the St. Lawrence River, and downtown Montréal (at left), 1963. Courtesy of Archives de la Ville de Montréal, VM94-EX013-004.

took place.[22] Later on in 1955, the Federal Minister announced the construction of the Nuns' Island Bridge to connect Nuns' Island with the Island of Montreal, which was completed in 1962[23] (Figure 3). The physical implementation of the connection between Nuns' Island and Montreal was matched with a bureaucratic one: in 1956, the corporation was successful in having Nuns' Island merge with the adjacent municipality of Verdun (which has itself since become part of the City of Montreal). Despite all of the necessary conditions coming into place, the developers chose not to construct anything on the Island upon purchasing it in 1956, deeming any construction a bad investment at the time.

Almost a decade later, in 1965, the corporation — now rechristened Proment Corporation — leased Nuns' Island to the Chicago-based developer Metropolitan Structures, which planned 10,000 rental units for the Island (Figure 4). It was at this juncture that the Office of Mies van der Rohe entered the equation. By the end of the 1970s, Metropolitan Structures had only managed to build 3,000 units; finding the economic and political context to be unpropitious, they broke the lease. Proment took control of the Island once again, but changed tack from building rental units to building condominiums, a form of housing that gained traction in Montreal's housing market in the 1980s.[24] The urbanization of the Island has taken place

Figure 4. Aerial view of Nuns' Island after the construction of the first phase of housing and infrastructure (gas station is visible as the flat white roof across the highway from dense housing), Montréal, 1971. Courtesy of Archives de la Ville de Montréal, VM94-B091-001.

in this piecemeal manner up to today, with Proment opening a thirty-six-story tower as part of an "ecological" development project on the northernmost tip of Nuns' Island in 2020.[25]

Constructed: The Architectural Object

While many of the projects produced toward the end of Mies's life quite directly reiterate an existing typology, the Esso Station effects a minor, but distinct, swerve within the design language that the Office—not to mention Metropolitan Structures, and, for that matter, the Museum of Modern Art in New York—so vigorously sought to promote. Given that the car was an important topic within architectural culture and design since the beginning of the twentieth century, it should perhaps not come as a surprise that the Esso Station was not the first "drive-in" to issue from the Office of Mies van der Rohe.[26] Produced shortly after Mies's relocation to the US, the design for the Cantor Drive-In Restaurant for Indianapolis (unbuilt; 1945–46) achieved its open plan using the same sort of trusses as at the canonical Crown Hall (1950–56) and the unbuilt Staatstheater Mannheim (1952–53). But the Esso Station adopted a different approach, not using external trusses but rather a structural system closer to that of the Neue Nationalgalerie in Berlin (1968) and the unbuilt Bacardi Headquarters for Santiago de Cuba (1959). In contrast to each of these buildings, the Esso Station deploys transparent enclosures on each of the far ends of the structure. The plan of the pavilion can be read as an adjustment of the first floor of a residential or commercial tower on the model of Lake Shore Drive, but with the enclosed services pushed to the far ends of the plan to allow for increased circulation in the central section. Especially with its liberal use of brick — which is typically used to enclose mechanical services in the towers — the composition of the Esso Station reads more readily as an acephalous tower than as a fully coherent pavilion, which tended to be executed exclusively using a steel frame with glass. However, the Esso station's authoritative aura can be challenged on purely functional grounds: despite the careful modulation of Miesian design ideas, the gas station's circulation simply did not function well. In the original construction, there were five pumps arranged along three sides of the rectangular central Island. Reasonably, there were two pumps on the west side and two along the east side, but with the addition of a fifth pump on the south side, the circulation of vehicles was rendered confusing and problematic.

Equally difficult is the legibility of the building as an architectural object, because the Nuns' Island Esso Station is unequivocally a concretization of much larger sociotechnical systems, namely the construction of mobility infrastructures that facilitate oil-based societies in Montreal and throughout the world. The petrocultural drive to establish intensive mobility in and through energy and transportation infrastructures manifests in full force at Nuns' Island.[27] The automobile, which structures the entire logic of the Island itself, is placed at the very center of the service station. The central section of the gas station, sheltered by the roof but open on two sides, contained the five gas pumps, as well as a small, enclosed pavilion for the attendant. This foregrounding of the movement of cars at the center of the composition — effectively bringing cars inside the building — produces a strange, almost transgressive, aesthetic effect. A site of rarified stillness intersecting with potentially vigorous movement: a cheetah in a cage — or a car crashing through the glass walls of the Barcelona Pavilion. Reckoning with Mies's legacy by displacing the repressed elements — i.e., the *ordinary* elements — into the center of its visual regime calls to mind a recent project of Andrés Jaque, who suggests that we can "account for," "know," and "access" Mies's "basement."[28] The disinterment of an undisclosed and complex imaginary within Mies's architecture is in large part what motivates this paper. At the Barcelona pavilion, this repressed alterity is the uneasy reality of labor, bodies, and economies that underwrites the visual, spatial, and material precision of the Barcelona Pavilion. Given that the retrofit of the Esso Station necessitated the remediation of the site, the repressed "basement" is, in this case, quite literally, oil. That the project treats oil with almost religious reverence reflects the way that oil is not only a material substance or a sociotechnical system but, especially in the contemplative precincts of the Nuns' Island Esso Station, even experienced as a cosmology.

Retrofitted: Animation and Iconoclasm

The relationship between the gas station's structure and its infrastructures (highways, bridges, pipelines, canals) is circuitous in its semantic entanglement, but what remains clear is that the service station-cum-shrine served to aesthetically codify, and socially naturalize, the movement of bodies within a society predicated upon oil-driven mobility.[29] The gas station at Nuns' Island at once naturalizes and *supernaturalizes* the automobile. By this bad-faith logic, oil would never have been extracted, transported, or processed; the gas station is designed to make gasoline seem to burst forth freely and abundantly, like a darkly sacred spring. It probably remains underestimated within environmental thought the extent to which our enthrallment to oil is continuous with the histories of magic. What is oil, anyway?[30] Infinite energy has been interpreted as the alchemical idea at the heart of the modern financial system: getting something for nothing.[31] Equally, perhaps, it is the animating force that pervades the aesthetic delights of the gas station — where the driver breezily interfaces with an intensively global infrastructure.

Rather than representing modernity in its triumph over the urban and peri-urban territory of Montreal, what if the Nuns' Island gas station were, instead, a shrine that served to invoke a remote (or even absent) modernity? The magical valences of the gas station are nowhere more evident than in this shrine-like environment. But, crucially, *gods change*. This is a fact to which the history of architecture provides an excess of testimony. A religious, or mythopoetic, interpretation of this building allows a parallel to be drawn between the work of transitioning towards renewable energies and the histories of, for instance, the Reformation. In the Germanic lands and the Low Countries, reformers' iconoclastic injunctions saw the removal of iconography from church sanctuaries;[32] in some cases, this even went as far as whitewashing existing frescos on the interior walls.[33] There are many similar histories of shrine conver-

Figure 5. "Maison des générations—Île-Des-Soeurs," retrofit by Les architectes fabg, Nuns' Island, Montreal, 2011. Courtesy of Steve Montpetit.

sion throughout the world, such as the Celtic "holy well" and the Greek and Italic *nymphaeum,* instances of pagan nature cults being inducted into Christian frameworks. If the gas station was designed as a shrine to an oil-driven modernity, then its retrofit makes present a world defined by degrowth through reforming the building's energetic *intra*structure.[34]

I would propose reading the original structure—imbricated as it is in a natural landscape predicated upon mobility—as something approaching a shrine (Figure 5). In the case of the building's original use as a gas station, the individual approaches the sacred site and draws up liquid from the earth, which erupts as abundant potency. The circulation of liquid and gaseous fluids through underground pneumatic systems calls to mind those fountains and grottoes of the Renaissance garden. Early modern architects, drawing on classical texts, manipulated air and water through mechanical means to produce a variety of effects, from simply transporting water and generating underground winds to creating musical effects and moving automata. Both in underground grottoes and above-ground gardens, these systems produced movement and sounds—signs of life—where there were none. The *pneuma* that circulated within Renaissance automata is ambiguously animistic, and its viewers were inclined to feel that where there is breath, there is life.[35]

The concept of animation is a key topic in art history's anthropological turn.[36] This body of scholarship has focused above all on images, and the concept has only partially made its way into architectural history.[37] Working between the bidimensional image and the architectural object, Caroline van Eck expands the framework of animation to account for fetishistic and otherwise inexplicable behavior toward sculpture.[38] The author invokes British psychoanalyst Donald Winnicott's concept of the transitional object to problematize "the tendency of individual human beings to attribute life to inanimate artefacts."[39] For van Eck, the transitional object "takes the place of the mother's breast as the primary focus of affection" and "inhabits an intermediate space between the living body itself and the image that was made after it."[40] This transfer of intimate affections to an object whose appearance lets it hover at the edge of life is, I argue, a useful framework for considering the Nuns' Island gas station.

The Nuns' Island gas station does not appear to be animated by consciousness, as a figurative sculpture might, but rather by the movement of *life itself*. The play of movement across mechanical and pneumatic systems participates in a slightly different history of animated objects. As an elemental fluid, oil serves to animate the automobile and the gas station, as well as the energy and transportation infrastructure in which both are imbricated, and even society itself. More concretely, the flow of gasoline physically animates the hydraulic machinery of the pump, and its combustion enables the pneumatic systems of the automobile. The technological history of the gas station is rooted in the pneumatic and hydraulic infrastructures of antiquity, and the automobile finds its origins in the equally canonical history of the automaton. In this sense, the automobile is a prototypical "curiosity."

The "transitional object" referred to in the title of this article picks up on van Eck's repurposing of Winnicott's theories, but also signals the discourses and narratives of transition away from dependence on oil.[41] These two gestures of transition are less disparate than they may appear. The gas station, as it was originally constructed and used, gave access to a source of vital energy, oil, that seemed to be limitless, but has since turned out to be not only finite but also critically liable to misuse. The Promethean petroculture of the 1960s, exemplified by the luxury of the Nuns' Island gas station with its custom-built pumps, must *mature,* must grow out of its raw dependency on boundless liquid nourishment. In this sense, the 2012 retrofit of La Station qualifies as a "transitional object" in both senses: it conserves a generally fetishistic posture toward the architectural object while severing the connection to oil, its liquid energy source.

The imagistic meaning of the term is often forgotten, but when Heidegger asserts that nature is framed as a "standing reserve" — i.e., nothing more than a resource — he was imagining an oil storage tank.[42] Whatever one's degree of sympathy for Heidegger's writing, the image is apt here. In the case of the Esso gas station, nature — as standing reserve — is drawn up from the earth itself by pumping oil's liquid essence from an underground tank. By contrast, in the retrofit project, the same underground cavern previously occupied by an oil storage tank has been emptied, and its airs have been mobilized by a geothermal pump for heating and cooling the interior environment of the community center. Like the gas pump, the geothermal well draws from underground depths, but instead of bringing up liquid, it comes up with air. Like the Renaissance grotto, the geothermal system activates a chthonic cavern as a tempering device within technical systems for moving air.[43]

By comparing this retrofit to the more capacious architectural histories of shrine conversion and the Protestant Reformation, we can clearly see that when the service station was transfigured, its altered form demanded that the overall economy of Nuns' Island — if not the planet in its entirety — be likewise reordered along similar lines. (As above, so below.) Both for the sake of illusion and for the continuation of human inhabitation of the planet, a transition away from petroculture will entail technological magics whose energetic source is of an unlimited duration. Thinking of the conversion of the gas pumps, the duration of the geothermal well is unlimited whereas that of the oil well is, by nature, limited. The planet that freely powers the geothermal well is not the same as the planet that struggles to expel the last dregs of oil. A renewed world, with a different economy of signs, should be transfigured — not only through a retrofit of this sacred shrine, but also by means of a reformation of its infrastructures.

Transfigured: Architecture and Agriculture

One possibility for the transfiguration of Nuns' Island's oil-fueled urbanism consists in a recuperation of a dropped thread at the very center of the modernist canon. In his essay "Notes Toward a History of Agrarian Urbanism," Charles Waldheim proposes a significant revision to the scholarship on twentieth-century urbanism. Through reference to Ludwig Hilberseimer, Frank Lloyd Wright, and (more curiously) Andrea Branzi, Waldheim renews the link to agriculture that, he argues, has always been at stake in twentieth-century dealings with the urban-rural interface. More precisely, he emphasizes what he calls "a conflation of suburb and region — a suburbanized regionalism."[44]

Hilberseimer passed away in 1967, immediately before the construction of the buildings on Nuns' Island, and by all accounts, he was not involved in the production of the gas station, the high-rise towers, or the scheme.[45] Yet his legacy remains implicit within it. The initial urbanistic scheme is maintained in fragmentary form by the Mies towers, which are situated in tight conjunction with mobility infrastructures — the design of the towers makes a show of integrating underground parking — and with the "green" components of Nuns' Island latent suburbanized regionalism. For Waldheim, the memory of Hilberseimer as a stringent rationalist obscures the Hilberseimer who thought deeply about the generative potential of an interlinking of urban form and agricultural territory.[46] There is also a historiographic distortion of the urban/rural binary within mid-century planning discourse: according to Waldheim, "Many 20th-century urban planning projects aspired to construct an agrarian urbanism — in some cases to reconcile the seemingly contradictory impulses of the industrial metropolis with the social and cultural conditions of agrarian settlement." The twentieth-century "tower in the green" is cast, here, in a different, striking, and ultimately much-needed light. Through returning to this moment at which modernist discourses had not completely decoupled the urban from the rural, or the suburb from the region, we are given the chance to conceptualize transition not as yet another radical break, but rather a historically-situated recuperation of a recent bifurcation in the history of urbanism.

The tower in the green — which is implemented at Nuns' Island in palpably fragmentary form through the three Hi-Rise towers — is readily seeded with another imaginary: the tower in the farm. These two imaginaries not only overlap and coalesce in Waldheim's reading, but, as well, the existing "green" provides a new sort of highly constructed tabula rasa: a blank slate whose soil needs only to be tilled in order to support the agricultural imaginary which remains tantalizingly latent, just under the surface of the apparently still existing carbon-based urbanism of Nuns' Island. The transition of Nuns' Island's landscape away from its petrocultural schema should, in other words, be nearly instantaneous: the "green" is, here, a readymade agricultural field. Such a recuperation would, then, be twofold. Not only would the agriculturalization of Nuns' Island accord with the degrowth schema invoked by this highly evocative retrofit of the Nuns' Island service station, but would recuperate an existing, though neglected, feature of the "tower in the green," which is typically remembered as being among the most hegemonic forms of modernist urbanism. By re-remembering the urbanistic schema imposed upon Nuns' Island as not only petrocultural but also agricultural, the transition toward a Nuns' Island predicated on degrowth suddenly snaps into focus as not a remote possibility, but rather something more immediately proximate, in the (nearly-)here and (nearly-)now.

Received: Pending a New Narrative

Despite the architectural object's *intra*structural energetic transition, does La Station truly depart from the petrocultural infrastructure of Nuns' Island when the site remains difficult to access except by car? As a community center, La Station remains somewhat underutilized, but as an object of Montreal's heritage, but the building itself continues to attract visitors, thereby fulfilling its rhetorical function as a transitional object.[47] While the retrofit project is extremely compelling on its own merits, this project nevertheless highlights the usefulness of architecture as a mechanism for making broad sociotechnical systems more legible and tangible. The disjunction of a degrowth-oriented microcosm and a stubbornly petrocultural macrocosm at Nuns' Island highlights the way that this tension between cosmological paradigms can become acutely manifest through an architectural retrofit. As a closed system, the La Station retrofit cannot fulfill its premises, yet by staking its claim to a decarbonized world, the project makes present a broader cosmological shift. La Station is effective as an act of repair that intervenes within the larger sociotechnical systems of petroculture.

The art historical discourse on animation allows us to get a better handle on our relationship to the gas station as a medium by which the visitor can literally touch larger sociotechnical systems that otherwise remain invisible and undisclosed. In the original building, the liquid petroleum that is transported so rapidly across the earth's surface is suddenly ready to hand in the form of the gas pump; in the retrofit, the visitor senses in the air the real possibility of a built environment predicated on decarbonization and degrowth. In each instance, transscalar imaginaries are brought down to size in a tangible way. Both before and after the retrofit, the structure is a transitional object through which we relate to invisible worlds. This perspective casts into relief the difficult enchantments by which oil's viscous mineral power has saturated the fundaments of our everyday habits and experience.[48] Although La Station might still be mired in an engulfing petroculture, it is possible to tease out other histories that complicate the sense of fossil fuel dependence as a primarily rational problem to be solved. Extending van Eck's attention to the cultic relation to statues, architecture comes to the fore as a key site for the affective appropriation of sociotechnical systems. Although retrofitting a building's *intra*structure is not commensurable to a complete reformation of planetary energy *infra*structure, architecture's capacity to communicate culture at a somatic level can nevertheless be leveraged to mobilize retrofit as a tool for reconditioning and recalibrating cultural norms and expectations.

Figure 6. Photograph of a site-specific project by artist Joe Namy, entitled "Automobile," for the 2016 Biennale de Montréal (BNLMTL 2016) at La Station—Centre intergénérationnel, on Nuns' Island, Montreal on September 21, 2016. Courtesy of Kim Förster.

It is in this specifically cultural sense that La Station functions as an act of sociotechnical repair: in acculturating and acclimatizing the visitor's body to air that is conditioned by the geothermal well—rather than by mechanical air conditioning—the retrofit conveys a bodily, affective knowledge of a decarbonized built environment. It is important to remember that technologies such as geothermal air ventilation and automata were well-developed in Roman antiquity and tackled again with renewed vigor in the Renaissance. While architecture's transition away from carbon may seem to be predicated on innovation, this process might (also) be a matter of recuperating existing touchstones that are central, if obscured, within canonical architectural history. La Station carries forward other histories that are more aligned with the prerogatives of transition and decarbonization, which can be remembered not as remote possibilities but as tangible realities. These narratives reinforce the significance of the Nuns' Island gas station as a transitional object that begins to make present a fully post-carbon—albeit subjunctive—future that is rooted in a different past (Figure 6).

Biography
Kai Woolner-Pratt is a PhD student in the Department of Art & Art History at Stanford University. He previously studied philosophy and literature at the University of King's College and the Albert-Ludwigs-Universität Freiburg. In 2017–19, he worked as a program assistant at the Canadian Centre for Architecture. His current research interests include the role of urban images in early modern cosmographies, the

conjunction of iconography and climate science in Renaissance botany, and the material reception of California counterculture in rural British Columbia.

Notes

I would like to offer my thanks to the editors, peer reviewers, and other contributors for making this a very special experience. I am also grateful to Maria Zinfert, Kim Förster, and Barry Bergdoll for generously providing feedback on earlier versions of this article. All errors and confusions in the text are mine alone.

[1] A model of this scheme is shown and discussed in Anne Cormier, "L'Île des Sœurs. Le plus merveilleux domaine résidentiel de l'Amérique du Nord," *ARQ: La revue des membres de l'Ordre des architectes du Québec* 71 (February 1993): 18–19.

[2] This scheme owes a great deal to the urbanistic ideas of Ludwig Hilberseimer. See Jean-Louis Cohen, "Mies urbaniste, de Détroit à Toronto. Un retour monumental à Berlin," *Collège de France*, filmed June 10, 2020, https://www.college-de-france.fr /site/jean-louis-cohen/course-2020-06-10-18h00.htm.

[3] The developers had come to a financial arrangement granting exclusive rights to Imperial Oil for the provision of fuel on Nuns' Island—the material extravagance of the gas stations functioned effectively as a sort of *noblesse oblige* between corporate entities.

[4] The service station was classified as an "Immeuble patrimonial cité" in 2009. See "Fiche du bâtiment: Station-service de Mies van der Rohe," Le Grand répertoire du patrimoine bâti de Montréal, Direction de la culture et du patrimoine de la Ville de Montréal, http://patrimoine.ville.montreal.qc.ca/inventaire/fiche_bat.php?id _bat=9999-21-0007-01. For documentary evidence of the logistical mechanisms for heritage classification in Montreal, see also "Station-service de Mies van der Rohe," Conseil du patrimoine de Montréal, http://ville.montreal.qc.ca/pls/portal /url/page/cons_pat_mtl_fr/rep_citations_cons/rep_consultations/cons_st _services_mvdr. The conservation of modernist heritage is particularly robust within the ecology of Montreal's architectural culture: there is a Canada Research Chair for urban heritage at UQAM, which also offers a well-regarded graduate program in modern architecture and heritage. Particularly, France Vanlaethem con- tinues to champion Quebec's modernist heritage—including the Nuns' Island Gas Station—as professor emerita at UQAM and as a founder of Quebec's very active Docomomo chapter.

[5] The Quiet Revolution *(la Révolution tranquille)* is an expression that encompasses the wide-ranging reformation of Quebec society in the postwar period. Until the 1950s, many of Quebec's institutions remained under the authority of religious or- ganizations such as the Congrégation de Notre-Dame, the order of nuns who owned "Nuns' Island." Changes were swift and many, as Quebec rapidly secularized and, in the process, established new and unique institutions that are fundamentally dis- tinct from their equivalents in English-speaking Canada. The shirking of ecclesiasti- cal authority was matched by a refusal of Ottawa's hegemony in Quebec's affairs. This nationalist and frequently separatist discourse remains integral to Quebec's identity and public sphere today.

[6] See FABG website, http://arch-fabg.com/project/esso: "De nouveaux puits de géothermie fournissent la majeure partie de l'énergie requise pour chauffer et cli- matiser le bâtiment. Les gaines de ventilation circulant sous dalle sont également raccordées aux pompes à essence qui sont en fait des prises d'air frais. En tirant parti du principe du puits canadien, l'air est préchauffé (ou pré-refroidi) en circulant sous terre avant d'être admis dans le bâtiment." ["New geothermal wells provide most of the energy required for heating and cooling the building. The ventilation ducts under the slab are likewise connected to the gas pumps, which are, in fact, intake vents for fresh air. Drawing on the 'Canadian well' technique, the air is preheated (or pre-cooled) by having it circulate underground before being brought into into the building."]

[7] See *Canadian Architect*, May 1, 2014, https://www.canadianarchitect.com/mies -van-der-rohe-gas-station-conversion/.

[8] By far the largest plant is the James Bay Project, a set of five dams constructed, starting in 1971, on waterways near Hudson's Bay. Hydro-Québec, Quebec's state electrical utility, is a major exporter of energy to New England, New York, Ontario, and New Brunswick.

[9] Especially in the past decade, there has been a vibrant and robust discourse on maintenance and repair. See: Penny Harvey and Hannah Knox, "The Enchantments of Infrastructure," *Mobilities* 7, vol. 4 (2012): 521–36; Christopher R. Henke, "Situ- ation Normal? Repairing a Risky Ecology," *Social Studies of Science* 37, vol. 1 (Feb. 2007): 135–42; Cymene Howe, Jessica Lockrem, Hannah Appel, Edward Hackett, Dominic Boyer, Randal Hall, Matthew Schneider-Mayerson et al., "Paradoxical Infrastructures: Ruins, Retrofit, and Risk," *Science, Technology, & Human Values* 41,

no. 3 (May 2016): 547–65; Brian Larkin, "The Politics and Poetics of Infrastructure," *Annual Review of Anthropology* 42 (2013): 327–43; Benjamin Sims, "Things Fall Apart: Disaster, Infrastructure, and Risk," *Social Studies of Science* 37, no. 1 (February 2007): 93–95; Sebastián Ureta, "Normalizing Transantiago: On the Challenges (and Limits) of Repairing Infrastructures," *Social Studies of Science* 44, no. 3 (June 2014): 368–92.

[10] Christopher R. Henke and Benjamin Sims, *Repairing Infrastructures: The Maintenance of Materiality and Power* (Cambridge, Mass.: MIT Press, 2020); Stephen Jackson, "Rethinking Repair," in *Media Technologies: Essays on Communication, Materiality, and Society*, ed. Tarleton Gillespie, Pablo J. Boczkowski, and Kirsten A. Foot (Cambridge, Mass.: MIT Press, 2014): 221–39.

[11] I am using the term "transitional object" to refer to the psychoanalytic concept developed by Donald Winnicott, but particularly as it has been deployed by the art historian Caroline van Eck. At the same time, I mean to signal that La Station retrofit's is inscribed within the contemporary project of energy transition, and that retrofits of modernist architecture can, in general, be considered "transitional objects" that ideally function as hinges between carbon and post-carbon energy regimes.

[12] André Corboz, "The Land as Palimpsest," *Diogenes* 31, no. 121 (1983): 12–34.

[13] The Viking presence in the Americas circa 1000 AD has been firmly established at L'Anse aux Meadows National Historic Site in Newfoundland, Canada. Historians continue to investigate evidence of Viking travel along the Atlantic coast of North America to Chitzen Itza. Montreal's position on the St. Lawrence leaves open the remote but important possibility of Viking maritime travel as far inland as Montreal in the same period. See Valerie Hansen, *The Year 1000: When Explorers Connected the World—and Globalization Began* (New York: Scribner, 2020).

[14] If I emphasize the significance of records here, it is to stress both the tenuousness of these claims to ownership and the fragility of their dependence upon paper media and infrastructures of organization. See Zeynep Celik Alexander, "The Larkin's Technologies of Trust," *Journal of the Society of Architectural Historians* 77, no. 3 (March 2018): 300–318.

[15] The CMD was founded by Marguerite Bourgeoys, a female colonist who continues to hold a significant place in the historical imaginary of modern Quebec. The canonization of Bourgeoys under Pope John Paul II in 1982 qualified her as the first female Roman Catholic saint to issue from Quebec and Canada.

[16] "En 1916, elle produit 4412 livres de porc, 5340 livres de bœuf, 1402 livres de veau, 17 152 gallons de lait, 3758 livres de beurre, 298 volailles et 132 douzaines d'œufs !" ["In 1916, this resulted in the production of 4,412 pounds of pork, 5,340 pounds of beef, 1,402 pounds of veal, 17,152 gallons of milk, 3,758 pounds of butter, 298 fowl, and 132 dozen eggs!"]. See Centre d'histoire de Montréal, "Les soeurs quittent leur île," Le journal de Montréal (Montreal, QC), March 31, 2018.

[17] The nuns, as well as their various agricultural workers that they hired, accessed the Island by barge; no bridge was built until 1962.

[18] Daniel Macfarlane, *Negotiating a River: Canada, the US, and the Creation of the St. Lawrence Seaway* (Vancouver: UBC Press, 2014).

[19] André Lortie, ed. *The 60s: Montreal Thinks Big* (Montreal: Canadian Centre for Architecture, 2004). See also Dustin Valen and Michael Windover description of SAH 2021 Annual International Conference Panel, "The 60s: Canada Thinks Small," accessed June 20, 2020, https://www.sah.org/2021/call-for-papers#sixties.

[20] Canada was awarded the 1967 International and Universal Exposition only in 1962. In 1962–63, Nuns' Island was the proposed site for Expo 67 before Saint Helen's Island *(Île Sainte-Hélène)* was selected. See Archives de Montréal, "Chronique Montréalité no 6 : de l'Île Saint-Paul à l'Île des Sœurs," YouTube video, 6:07, https://youtu.be/wTTHgQBWm8I?t=310. For a thorough discussion of Expo '67, see Inderbir Riar, "Expo 67, or Megastructure Redux," in *Meet Me at the Fair: A World's Fair Reader,* ed. Laura Hollengreen, Celia Pearce, Rebecca Rouse, and Bobby Schweizer (Pittsburgh: Carnegie Mellon University Press, 2014): 255–70.

[21] Grimes, "Grimes—We Appreciate Power (Lyric Video)," YouTube video, 5:42, https://youtu.be/gYG_4vJ4qNA.

[22] Despite the similarity in name to the Canadian Mortgage and Housing Corporation (CMHC) state agency, the QHMC was a fully private corporation.

[23] Eventually, it was renamed the Champlain Bridge, and was replaced by a new Champlain Bridge in 2019.

[24] Jacques Lacoursière, *L'Île-des-sœurs : d'hier à aujourd'hui* (Montréal: Éditions de l'Homme, 2005).

[25] See Proment website: http://proment.com/en/evolo-x/.

[26] Especially interesting here is the extent to which car culture has been an object of fascination at higher registers within architectural discourse, such as in Aldo Rossi's Polaroids. See Aldo Rossi's photo, "View of a street from a car windshield, United States," https://www.cca.qc.ca/en/search/details/collection/object

/488165. Collection Centre Canadien d'Architecture / Canadian Centre for Architecture, Montréal. © Eredi Aldo Rossi / Fondazione Aldo Rossi.

[27] Carola Hein has termed such spaces "petroleumscapes." See Carola Hein, "Oil Spaces: The Global Petroleumscape in the Rotterdam/The Hague Area," *Journal of Urban History* 44, no. 5 (September 2018): 887–929.

[28] The installation *Phantom: Mies as Rendered Society* (2012–13) was realized by Andrés Jaque and the Office for Political Innovation for the Fundació Mies van der Rohe. It is now held in the collection of the Art Institute of Chicago, in the city where Mies based his US career. The project is given careful articulation in Andrés Jaque, "Mies in the Basement: The Ordinary Confronts the Exceptional in the Barcelona Pavilion," *Thresholds* 43 (2015): 120–278.

[29] This tension inherent to social histories of architecture is described in a compelling way by Alina Payne: "After all, Michel Foucault's seminal first essays took architecture as their departure point. . . . In these narratives architecture becomes the ultimate document: not only does it represent, but it contains, codifies, and shapes behavior and therefore cultural and social practices. These new perspectives have been very fruitful for architectural history in giving a new orientation and impetus to building-type studies. Yet they have done little to reconnect it to an art history more concerned with the representation of society and culture than with the active agents of societal change." Alina Payne, "Architectural History and the History of Art: A Suspended Dialogue," *Journal of the Society of Architectural Historians* 58, no. 3 (September 1999): 296.

[30] Environmental discourses tend to speak of the history of petroleum as coextensive with industrialization, even if we know well that it is not. For an interesting philological discussion along a longer historical axis, see Grantley Macdonald, "Georgius Agricola and the Invention of Petroleum," *Bibliothèque Humanisme et Renaissance* 23, no. 2 (2011): 351–63.

[31] Carl Wennerlind, *Casualties of Credit: The English Financial Revolution, 1620–1720* (Cambridge, Mass.: Harvard University Press, 2011).

[32] Joseph L. Koerner, *The Reformation of the Image* (Chicago: University of Chicago Press, 2004).

[33] Angela Vanhaelen, *The Wake of Iconoclasm: Painting the Church in the Dutch Republic* (University Park: Pennsylvania State University Press, 2012).

[34] I would like to suggest a modernism that "makes present" modernity, along the lines of an "icon" as described in Hans Belting, *Likeness and Presence* (Chicago: University of Chicago Press, 1994).

[35] See, for example, Alessandra Nova, *The Book of the Wind: The Representation of the Invisible* (Montreal: McGill-Queen's University Press, 2011).

[36] This body of scholarship places an aporia around the ontological status of the image in order to enable a more fundamental rethinking of the image's agency. By addressing modern aesthetics as continuous with non-modern — e.g., cultic, animistic, fetishistic — cultural forms, the epistemic authority of modernity is, in anthropological art history, put up for debate. This has taken place not only through theoretical reframing (an anthropological orientation to the image) but also on thoroughly historical grounds, through empirical research on epistemic slippages. See, for instance: David Freedberg, The Power of Images: Studies in the History and Theory of Response (Chicago: University of Chicago Press, 1989); Hans Belting, Likeness and Presence: A History of the Image before the Era of Art (Chicago: University of Chicago Press, 1994); Alfred Gell, Art and Agency: An Anthropological Theory (Oxford: Clarendon Press, 1998); and W. J. T. Mitchell, What Do Pictures Want? The Lives and Loves of Images (Chicago: University of Chicago Press, 2005).

[37] Animation is a major topic in the writing of architectural historian Spyros Papapetros, whose considerations of animation are broadly situated within the Warburgian mode.

[38] Caroline van Eck, *Art, Agency and Living Presence: From the Animated Image to the Excessive Object* (Chicago: University of Chicago Press, 2015).

[39] van Eck, *Art, Agency and Living Presence,* 351.

[40] van Eck, *Art, Agency and Living Presence,* 347, 346.

[41] For example, the Transition Town movement, organized by the Transition Network, was founded in 2007. See https://transitionnetwork.org.

[42] "Nature becomes a giant gasoline station, an energy source for modern technology and industry." Martin Heidegger, trans. John M. Anderson and E. Hans Freund (New York: Harper & Row, 1966), 50.

[43] See Barbara Kenda, "On the Renaissance Art of Well Being: Pneuma in Villa Eolia," *RES: Anthropology and Aesthetics* 34 (Autumn 1998): 101–17. And thinking of underground elemental spaces defined by windy heat, we might count: the Renaissance grotto, the oil well, the gas station storage tank, the geothermal well — and hell.

44 Charles Waldheim, "Notes Toward an Agrarian Urbanism," *Places Journal*, November 2010, accessed June 30, 2020, https://placesjournal.org/article/history-of -agrarian-urbanism/.

45 Tim Russell, *Fill 'er Up! The Great American Gas Station* (New York: Crestline Books, 2012), 124.

46 Ludwig Hilberseimer, *The New Regional Pattern: Industries and Gardens, Workshops and Farms* (Chicago: P. Theobald, 1949).

47 Given that the most vibrant uses of the building since its reopening in 2012 have been for cultural events, it would be worth considering repurposing the building as a cultural institution.

48 Bob Johnson, "Embodiment," *Fueling Culture*, ed. Imre Szeman, Jennifer Wenzel and Patricia Yaeger (New York: Fordham University Press, 2017), 124–27.

Figure 1. Stall of the Volkart Brothers Refrigeration and Air Conditioning Department at the Indian Motion Picture Exhibition, Bombay, 1939. Source: *Volkart Brothers Engineering News*, vol. 4 (June 1939), 2. Dep. 42/155, Volkart Brothers Company Archive, Winterthur City Archives, Winterthur.

Priya Jain

Selling Comfort
Volkart Brothers and Origins of Air Conditioning in India (1923–1954)

"Of the climate you are the tool,
You are, in fact, a perfect fool.
We show you how to keep quite cool,
Get air-conditioned now—it pays!"[1]

The above excerpt is from a longer poem that appeared in the February 1936 issue of the *Volkart Brothers Engineering News* — a then-fledgling newsletter of the Indian establishment of the Swiss merchant house Volkart Brothers (VB).[2] The richly illustrated monthly publication included articles on engineering products and services the firm offered in India (which included present-day Pakistan and Bangladesh) and Sri Lanka. Owing to the technical nature of the products, VB felt it was necessary to facilitate knowledge-sharing in the form of a newsletter among its clients, five branch offices in Bombay (renamed Mumbai in 1995), Calcutta (renamed Kolkata in 2001), Madras (renamed Chennai in 1996), Lahore and Karachi, and smaller agencies in over forty other cities. VB was founded simultaneously in Winterthur, Switzerland, and Bombay, India, in 1851, by Swiss brothers Salomon and Johann Georg Volkart. By the end of the nineteenth century, it had become one of the largest trading firms in colonial India.[3] It exported raw materials (cotton, coffee, coir yarn, etc.) from India to the European continent, Great Britain, and East Asia, and also imported Western manufactured goods (textiles, consumer products like soap, paper, watches, etc.) to the Indian subcontinent.

Starting in the 1880s, VB diversified its commercial activities in a move to spread financial risks.[4] Alongside the traditional pillars of its business, namely, cotton and produce (coconut, coffee, pepper etc.), it started trading in other areas like engineering goods. However, their first attempt at the establishment of an engineering division in India from 1888–92 failed due to financial losses, and the second attempt (with greater emphasis on agricultural machinery) from 1908–20 also proved to be ultimately unsuccessful owing to market competition.[5] It was in 1923, at a time when the colonial Indian government finally gave due attention to industrialization, that a third and successful VB engineering division was set up with its head office in Bombay. It included departments for mechanical, electrical, milling, textile and agricultural equipment, as well as one for refrigeration. Along with the sale of

Future Anterior
Volume XVIII, Number 1
Summer 2021

products like household refrigerators, soda fountains, and commercial freezers, the refrigeration department designed and installed industrial humidification (and de-humidification) plants and soon forayed into the incipient market for "comfort" air-conditioning.[6]

The 1920s and '30s saw a rapid gain in the popularity of air conditioning in Europe and America—from specialized industrial applications initially, to a growing number of buildings like movie theaters, offices, and even homes.[7] VB's refrigeration department played a formative role in bringing this new technology to India. In the words of a VB executive stationed in India, it "helped the ubiquitous ice box [get] replaced by the household refrigerator and the *punkhas* [fans] and *khus khus tatties* [water coolers] give way to air conditioning"[8] (see Figure 1). VB installed some of the earliest air conditioning plants in India in 1934 at the Regal Cinema and the Taj Mahal Hotel in Bombay, using imported Frigidaire and Kelvinator equipment.[9] Up until 1954, when it formed a partnership with the Indian business house Tata Sons to create "Voltas" ("Vol" from Volkart and "tas" from Tata Sons), VB relentlessly marketed air conditioning and installed it in a number of buildings across the country.[10]

This article takes a deeper dive into VB's company archives to analyze the perspective of those tasked with selling "comfort." It reveals that the promotion of air conditioning in India by VB engineers and merchants extended discriminatory colonial views about race, climate and civilization. In fact, the development of air conditioning in India in the early years, strengthened the association of thermal comfort with exclusivity based on social status and economic class. The seemingly mundane practices of "retro-fitting" existing buildings, and "future-fitting" new buildings to accept air conditioning, were impacted by the technology's biased sociocultural framing that extended from the colonial to the postcolonial eras. An analysis of VB's internal communications sheds light on their more cautious privately-held attitudes toward air conditioning, which at times, contrasted with their enthusiastic public promotion of the technology. The critical analysis of air conditioning's origins in India, as presented in this paper, adds to a wider non-Eurocentric appreciation of the entwined history of architecture and climate in a global context.

The Ideal Country for Air Conditioning
Recent scholarship on colonial and postcolonial architecture has spanned numerous disciplinary terrains, including, among others, medicine, technology, race studies, climate science, and physiology. This multifaceted analysis had enabled an understanding of how the production of architectural forms is in-

herently political and historical. Scholars like Jiat-Hwee Chang have shown how the supposedly neutral category of "tropical architecture," based on regional and climactic specificity, and associated most with mid-twentieth-century discourse, was in fact, a product of long-held and racially biased colonial beliefs.[11] Historian Mark Harrison has countered that, up until the late eighteenth century, British traders in India had more confidence in their ability to endure the Indian climate and made few racial and environmental distinctions.[12] However, as the English East India Company moved from trade to imperialism, the punishing military campaigns of the nineteenth century put more focus on the survival and health of British soldiers. This, along with the rise of environmental determinism in the nineteenth century in disciplines of medicine and geography, led to a coupling of race and environment. The colonial apparatus thus evolved to first fear, and eventually ameliorate, the Indian climate. The design of military barracks and hospitals with high ceilings, ventilated basements and strategically positioned windows and verandahs, reinforced the link between environmental performance, health and governance.[13] Miasma theories in the early nineteenth century and the identification of disease-causing microbes later on assisted the rise of a physiological explanation of race. More importantly, they sanctioned state intervention in the form of colonial "city improvement trusts" and extended racially charged notions of the environment to the urban realm.[14]

Ideas coupling race and environment extended well into the early part of the twentieth century when air conditioning made its debut on the world stage. American geographers like Ellsworth Huntington, in his book *Civilization and Climate,* published in 1915, reiterated prevailing negative views on tropical areas when he stated that "denizens of the torrid zone are slow and backward, and we almost universally agree that this is connected with the damp, steady heat."[15] Optimal climatic conditions were seen as necessary not only for progress, but for preventing the supposed racial degeneration of the "white man" in the tropics—they were important for the sustenance of the entire colonial framework.

Air conditioning made it technically possible to modulate not just indoor temperature but also humidity—this differentiated it from prior environmental solutions that mostly focused on temperature. The promise of a wholly man-made indoor climate that reproduced the best aspects of weather anywhere on earth, thus held great appeal for the colonial mission. VB proclaimed in its marketing literature that India was "the most ideal country for air conditioning"—both its long oppressive summers and humid monsoons were readily ameliorated by this new technology.[16] However, some of the first installations of air conditioning equipment in India, much like the case in Europe and America, were not in homes or public buildings, but in factories where precise environmental conditions were critical for manufacturing. The first Carrier brand air conditioning plant in India was installed in 1923 at a British ammunition factory in Kirkee, near Bombay.[17] Several other textile mills with air conditioning reported a 4–8 percent increase in worker productivity.[18] Field experiments indicated that even the apparent racial disadvantage of the natives could be overcome in an air-conditioned factory where "the Indian labor [was found to be] as efficient as any other."[19]

Yet as VB tried to create a market for comfort air conditioning, which it believed had larger business prospects in colonial India, data on increased worker efficiency was both inapplicable and insufficient. Also insufficient were claims of a superior indoor environment based solely on the parameters of temperature and humidity, since the native population did not regard their climate and its damp heat with as much negativity as the colonizers. Nonetheless, the refrigeration department at VB tried—they cited "the limited acclimatization capacity" of the human body as a scientific fact and claimed that "the Indian will suffer from the heat nearly as badly as any foreigner."[20]

A closer look at VB's archival records indicates that in addition to temperature and humidity control, they emphasized equally, if not more emphatically, the two ancillary benefits of air conditioning—air filtration and noise control. In a lengthy 1936 article, *VB Engineering News* proclaimed that even when the weather was not "too unpleasant," those with air conditioning would be "glad not to hear shouting hawkers or other noises from the street and to avoid dust and air drafts which [would] otherwise disturb."[21] In another article, air conditioning was credited for improving worker efficiency due to its ability to prevent illness by shutting out undesirable noise and dirt in the outside air. More importantly, as the article added, this resulted in a "quiet and clean office adding greatly to the prestige of the owner."[22]

As VB pitched comfort air conditioning along these lines of noise and air quality, it focused on the modern Indian elite—often addressing the "lawyers, doctors and other professional men" in their newsletters.[23] As opposed to America, where the inability to open windows had incited lively "fresh air" debates between ventilation and air conditioning engineers in the 1920s, in India, the unwholesomeness of the tropical colony air was never in question.[24] In the Indian context, VB stressed the "absorption of germs," treatment of "asthma, hay-fever and certain skin diseases" and filtration of the "dusty outside air" as supremely desirable benefits.[25]

The ability to literally shut oneself off from objectionable smells, sounds, and people implied not merely a move toward greater physical comfort, but a larger psychological, social and cultural change to the Indian way of life. VB did not merely have to sell air conditioning, they also had to do the cultural work of, as the company newsletter put it, "getting Indians 'air-conditioning-minded.'"[26] This latter, more ambitious, goal meant that air conditioning was framed as aspirational — in colonial India, this ostensibly benign environmental technology was clearly marketed and installed on racial and class-based lines.

In its newsletter, there were some counter-references — that air conditioning was not a "privilege of rich men," that it was "not a luxury but a necessity."[27] VB often cited these in reference to the numerous theater installations, where "the comfort of air conditioning could be enjoyed by patrons of four-*anna* [pence], eight-*anna,* and more expensive seats."[28] However, it can be argued that air conditioning of cinema halls, both in India and in the West, had been successful precisely because of fear of intermingling with lower classes in close quarters, and the apparently noxious, sweaty odors thus produced.[29] When technical constraints did not demand such an intermingling, and in fact facilitated separation, as in class-segregated railway carriages, air-conditioning was blatantly provided only for the upper class.

In 1940, when VB installed an "ice activated" system in seven new first-class carriages of the North Western Railway finished in stainless steel and *shisham* wood, with fixed hermetically sealed windows, they ensured that headroom was not lost to pumps and ductwork which were conveniently located in the adjoining non-airconditioned second-class and servants' carriages[30] (Figure 2). The conditioned compartments with their "tight-fitting" doors and floors of felt and rubber were thus ensured to be "cool, dust-free and noise-reduced" while the servants' carriages with their low ceilings and persistently noisy pumps, accommodated both the controls and the attendants who made the system run smoothly.[31]

Even in office applications, while VB valiantly advertised their new portable Carrier units in 1937 as "within the scope of all pockets," it was only on very rare occasions that spaces other than those for upper management (executive offices, boardrooms etc.) were conditioned.[32] In fact, a common advertising target was the *Burra Saheb* (Chief Officer), depicted as "not worried about the money he spends on personal comfort" to get a "cool, clean room with a minimum of disturbing noises — a place where he can work with quiet efficiency"[33] (Figure 3). A newspaper account even remarked that burra sahebs "were foregoing their tiffin time siesta because they prefer to

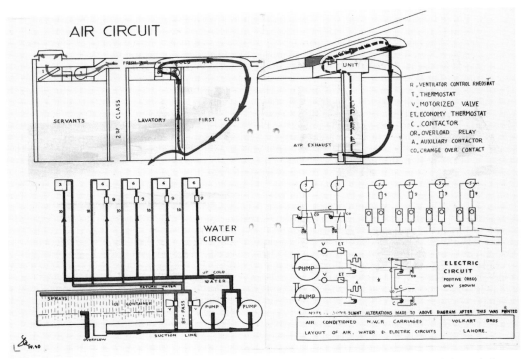

AIR CIRCUIT

Figure 2. A schematic drawing of the air conditioning of first-class carriages of the North Western Railway, Lahore, 1940. Source: *Volkart Brothers Engineering News,* vol. 5 (April/May 1940), 9. Dep. 42/155, Volkart Brothers Company Archive, Winterthur City Archives, Winterthur.

stay and work in a cool room!" and equated conditioned air to pure water, a basic necessity that "all civilized countries" were embracing.[34]

It is ironic that these conditioned spaces with their pure filtered air, sealed from the unhygienic outdoors, often had to be fitted with smoke extraction systems to counter heavy indoor smoking. One such system was installed at the Reserve Bank Building in Bombay in 1939—in other instances, liberal quantities of fresh air were introduced to dilute the smoke in cinemas, conference rooms and railway cabins.[35]

VB engineers recognized the architectural and socio-cultural barriers to a fuller embrace of air conditioning. They acknowledged that Indian rooms "were specially built for airi-ness" and that many in India simply had not taken to air con-ditioning "because it meant they would then be compelled to keep their windows shut."[36] Yet, by casting the sealed interior as superior, as not only cool but also clean, quiet, and sepa-rate, they were hoping to overturn long-held behavioral norms. Moreover, as shown above, despite universalizing claims of India being the "ideal country for air conditioning," marketing and growth of the novel technology was predicated on exclu-sivity and class, a sociocultural (and not purely physiological) connection that has been hard to shake off since.

Retro-Fit: Impediment and Opportunity
The early phase of VB's air conditioning trade in India can be understood as the decades of 1920–30s. During this

time, the majority of installations were retrofits—installed in existing buildings, often in a piecemeal manner with the goal of minimizing alterations and cost. While integration of air conditioning equipment with new buildings was desirable, it was prohibitively expensive and rare. This section analyses the architectural implications of retrofits—what were some of the changes to the layouts and finishes of interior space brought on by air conditioning? It also questions the sociocultural implications—if only a few spaces could be conditioned, how were they determined?

Air conditioning in existing buildings necessitated accommodation of large plant rooms, intensive plumbing, and ductwork. This spatial demand was often blamed by the VB engineers for the "slow progress of air conditioning in India."[37] Hence, they constantly strived to market smaller equipment that could be seamlessly integrated in existing buildings. One of the earliest units of this kind—a new "Floor Type Air Conditioner" was installed in the VB Manager's office in 1935 (Figure 4). Designed to look like ordinary furniture in shape, size and color and to "harmonize with the decoration of the room," these were a lot like present-day fan coil units, incorporating tubes, fans and filters all packaged in a cabinet sized box.[38] For larger rooms many such units were placed directly in or hung from the ceiling of the room to be conditioned.

By 1937, VB had acquired exclusive trading rights for Carrier products in India and began to aggressively market and install their more portable units which could be "installed

Figure 4. Floor-type air conditioner in Volkart Brothers' Manager's Office, 1936. Source: *Volkart Brothers Engineering News*, vol. 1 (February 1936), 4. Dep. 42/155, Volkart Brothers Company Archive, Winterthur City Archives, Winterthur.

in practically any room at short notice" and could be readily moved "as easily as an ordinary refrigerator."[39] At the Bombay Mutual Building, "deep walnut, satin-gloss, cold-rolled steel cabinets" that housed the air conditioning equipment were placed directly in a large office area for middle management.[40] Such open office layouts for senior staff were a result of air conditioning constraints — lack of intervening walls or partitions allowed the conditioned zone to stay connected. Open railings, as in this building, were used instead to demarcate interior space (Figure 5).

Despite claims about the ease of relocation, the supposedly portable air conditioning units were fairly fixed — they needed extensive plumbing connections that were often underemphasized in the marketing literature.

A close working relationship between the air conditioning engineer and the architect was essential to coordinate the "decorative scheme," particularly in large installations where a central ducted system was still the optimum choice. At the New Metro Cinema in Bombay, ductwork was "hidden above the elaborately decorated false ceilings" and at the Reserve Bank of India, it was placed in the corridors to minimize impact on the conditioned conference and board rooms, with supply and return air grilles arranged neatly to "match the structural design and interior decoration"[41] (Figure 6). At other locations, ingenious solutions were found to make retrofits more feasible, like at the existing New Empire Theater in Calcutta where the

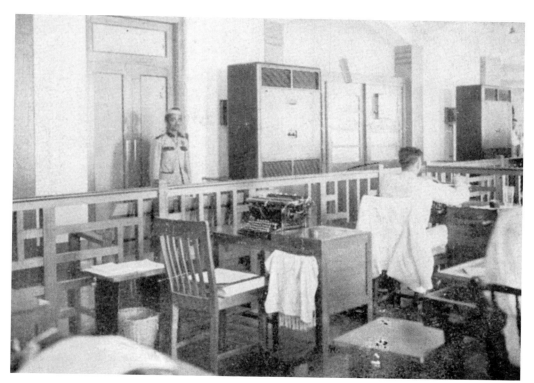

Figure 5. Multiple cabinet-sized floor-type air conditioners in the offices of the Bombay Mutual Building, 1940. Note the open office layout and railings used to partition the space. Source: *Volkart Brothers Engineering News*, vol. 5 (February 1940), 3. Dep. 42/155, Volkart Brothers Company Archive, Winterthur City Archives, Winterthur.

plant room of the adjacent new Lighthouse Theater was used to condition both the new and existing theaters.[42]

Only a few non-theatre buildings in the prewar period had air conditioning from scratch—at the new five-story Scindia House Building in Bombay, a large plant in the basement catered to each floor separately, necessary due to varying occupants on the different floors[43] (Figure 7). Architecturally though, these early air-conditioned new office towers, much like the case in other postcolonial Asian countries like Singapore, were undistinguished from the prevalent tropical art-deco style, featuring a high proportion of solid surfaces and smaller punched windows that protected the building from excessive solar heat.[44]

Other installations by VB in this period, highlighted the undisputed advantage air conditioning brought to spaces driven by technical needs, that could not be ventilated otherwise—like the windowless safety vault at the Bank of India, soundproof studios at the All India Radio and an electrical and testing laboratory at the Engineering College in Guindy.[45]

As VB engineers worked on devising solutions, it was more than just the buildings that were constantly retrofit—even existing technologies from the ventilation and humidification world, were at times "retrofitted" and re-appropriated to meet the budgetary and sociocultural needs of the Indian client. An example of this was the "Fan Humidifier" initially devised and

Figure 6. Board Room in the building of the Reserve Bank of India, Bombay, 1939. Note the careful placement of grilles above the doors. Source: *Volkart Brothers Engineering News*, vol. 4 (June 1939), 3. Dep. 42/155, Volkart Brothers Company Archive, Winterthur City Archives, Winterthur.

patented by VB for use in industrial applications and later marketed as a "Fan Cooler"—pitched as an inexpensive comfort cooling alternative to refrigeration-based systems and one that could be deployed in the drier, northern parts of the country.[46] This is ironic since VB had gone to great lengths in early years to distinguish comfort air conditioning from mere humidification, that was based on more traditional concepts like the *khus khus tatties* of India, and lamented the poor performance of such systems for comfort cooling even in northern cities like Delhi.[47] As they grappled with ground realities though, the need was realized for smaller, more economical solutions like the "fan cooler," better culturally attuned to the local market— that did not make exacting demands, like sealing windows, on the Indian consumer.

Future-Fit: Aspiration and (Un)necessity
The impact of the Second World War on a trading company like VB that relied entirely on transfer of goods between continents was severe—shortages of many engineered western products spurred them to invest in more indigenous manufacture in India.[48] This was bolstered by the turbulent political climate at the end of the war as India finally gained independence from British rule in 1947. As independent India embarked on a technoscientific mission of nation-building, there was an increased demand for engineering goods and services. Therefore, despite

Figure 7. Exterior view of the Scindia House Building Bombay, 1939. Source: *Volkart Brothers Engineering News*, vol. 4 (January 1939), 3. Dep. 42/155, Volkart Brothers Company Archive, Winterthur City Archives, Winterthur.

some initial hesitation about future prospects, VB invested in new factories and offices in many Indian cities.

A telling saga about air conditioning that unfolded at one of VB's proposed new offices in the city of Kanpur sheds light on the technology's evolving impact on architecture and reveals privately-held attitudes toward air conditioning by engineers and agents that relentlessly marketed it[49] (Figure 8). In late 1946, as the VB Engineering Department in Bombay worked up schemes for conditioning the Kanpur office building, the head office at Winterthur directed them to choose a "low cost plant from the point of view of publicity" to demonstrate the affordability of air-conditioning in the Indian market.[50] The engineers complied, and proposed to leave some spaces non-conditioned—these included, in addition to the lavatories, reception, *tiffin* room and cashier's office, rooms for the "sepoys and other menials" and the "junior typists."[51]

Records indicate that some reservations were expressed about leaving the "subordinate staff" out of the conditioned zone, yet it was summarily justified based on functional constraints—the "sepoys and menials" usually shared the reception with constant reopening of the entrance doors making it hard to create a sealed zone.[52] The same applied to the cashier and "junior typists" who were either constantly

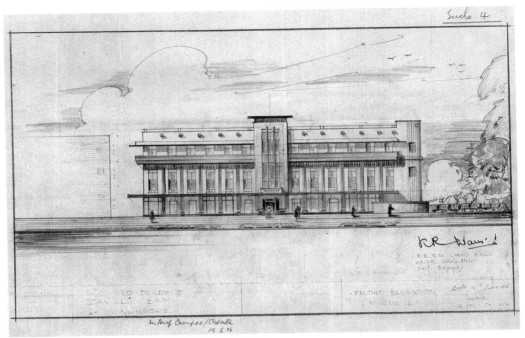

Figure 8. Architectural rendering of the front elevation of the Volkart Brothers New Office Building, Kanpur, 1946. Source: Dep. 42/807, VB Company Archive, Winterthur City Archives, Winterthur.

receiving visitors or shuttling between different parts of the office. Ultimately, equipment shipping delays and concerns over the high overhead costs of this in-house expenditure subverted the entire scheme. VB decided to install small individual air conditioning units instead, in just the Agent (Chief Officer) and the Assistant Agent's offices.[53] In the selective application of air-conditioning, necessitated here by economic constraints, VB was unable to avoid the inequitable sociocultural patterns around the technology that it had itself helped construct and promote.

The deliberations between VB engineers and the building's architect, K. R. Irani, also reveal how the façade became the battleground for conflicts between style and efficiency. The engineers bemoaned the wide verandah provided by Irani around a large part of the floor—they blamed it for cutting down natural light in the interior. This justified their push for an open office layout with minimal closed partitions that, of course, also made it easier and more economical to condition the space. Moreover, as noted by the engineers, it also allowed "clerical staff to not be out of sight."[54] The engineers also criticized the high, ill-positioned canopy that let in too much sun on the south and west, recommending a *chajja* (sunshade) instead, directly above the windows, or canvas awnings, both of which were shot down by Irani as "detrimental from an architectural point of view."[55]

The above account, while unique in that it was the office premises of an air conditioning firm itself, is typical of the unresolved architectural issues around air-conditioned Indian buildings in the early years of the technology. This was affirmed by another account a few years later, when, in 1951, the Bombay government implemented massive electricity cuts extending over two years, allowing air conditioning only for medical uses.[56] This caused a major upheaval in the VB Head Office Building in Bombay, which had been retrofitted in previous years such that it was now "built for air conditioning."[57] Many of the management offices had been planned without access to an exterior wall, and being windowless, were now left with no ventilation. Ultimately a standby generator was sanctioned to provide temporary relief to these offices.

In another memo relating to a different VB building, Peter Reinhart, who was overseeing the India operations, recommended the Winterthur head office to sanction funds for the "apparently unproductive air conditioning." He noted that the better working conditions might "reduce complaints about India's conditions from the European staff." Conditioning the firm offices, in his opinion, would also resolve "the rather abnormal situation that we sell air conditioning and do not use it ourselves." That these expense requests were classed in the "desirable" as opposed to the "absolutely necessary" category by the head office indicates that VB itself had a tepid attitude toward air conditioning in India, a contrast from the wholehearted endorsement they projected publicly.[58]

There had always been skeptics of air conditioning in India — during this time a growing number of architects, civil engineers and administrators, both local and foreign, advocated for a passive approach — a "tropical" modernism as it came to be known later.[59] Air conditioning was not fully rejected though — in fact the idea of "future-fit" emerged — buildings designed such that they could be mechanically conditioned a few years down the line, but would still be fully functional without it in the meantime. The high-profile New Secretariat Building in Calcutta, designed by architect Habib Rahman, and believed to be the tallest building in Asia when constructed in 1954, was designed for "future air-conditioning"[60] (Figure 9). With a relatively narrow floorplate and three-foot deep *brise soleil,* the building provided natural shade, light and ventilation, while a huge basement anticipated future air conditioning equipment.

In other structures like the National Physical Laboratory (NPL) in New Delhi, only parts of the building were conditioned. As a result of this contingent conditioning, many traditional design features such as single-loaded corridors, verandahs and solid facades never really disappeared, at the same time that newer products like wall insulation never gained wide acceptance in India[61] (Figure 10). One can argue that this hybrid

Figure 9. Habib Rahman, New Secretariat Building, Kolkata, 1954. Source: Habib Rahman Archives.

Figure 10. Master, Sathe, and Bhuta, Rendering of the National Physical Laboratory, New Delhi, 1947. Source: *Journal of Scientific and Industrial Research,* vol. 6, no. 1 (January 1947): Cover page.

approach was more socioculturally attuned to the Indian context, though it also intensified the equation of comfort with economic class and social status. Selective conditioning in buildings, like at NPL, continued to be reserved for senior officers while regularly omitted for the junior employees.[62] In many ways, the colonial framing of air conditioning as exclusive and discriminatory led directly to, in fact, laid the foundation for the postcolonial years.

The post-independence Indian approach to air conditioning was thus markedly different from some other Asian countries like Singapore that embraced it universally, even making it a strategic part of their nation-building.[63] In fact in a 1947 memo to the Carrier Corporation, VB officials acknowledged that the Indian government considered air conditioning "not of absolute essentiality to the progress of the country."[64] As a result, air conditioning never took off in India to the same extent that it did in Singapore, though it continued to make small inroads, particularly in the industrial, institutional and commercial sectors. VB still wanted to maintain business holdings in India, though in the post-independence era with stricter rules for foreign firms, they had to form a partnership in 1954 with the Indian business house Tata Sons to create "Voltas." Voltas, to date, remains one of the largest air conditioning manufacturers in India, and in the mid-1950s they launched a popular line of window air conditioners aimed at the Indian residential market.[65]

Acclimatizing to Comfort

The historical analysis of air conditioning in India, as presented in this paper, furthers our understanding of the key ways in which a technology thought to be "universalizing" is actually rooted in the peculiarities of place.[66] Air conditioning was adopted in India according to previously existing patterns of exclusion, often intensifying them. In colonial India, the marketing of air conditioning based on class and status continued long-held views about race and civilization. In the postcolonial era, a mix of political and economic conditions ensured only a partial embrace of the technology. This extended the hierarchical model established before and resulted in hybrid buildings that were architecturally and mechanically cooled at the same time. This selective conditioning furthered the association of air conditioning with privilege.

Another result of this history is that, unlike many parts of the world which have recently witnessed a resurgence of passive cooling features in buildings, in an era of anthropogenic awareness, it can be argued that in India that link was never fully lost. In the second half of the twentieth century, the growth of air conditioning in India remained slow—in fact, many estimates place the current use of residential air-conditioning in India at only 5 percent as opposed to 90 percent in, for example, the US and Japan.[67] However, the past decade has seen rapid growth—a technology once perceived unnecessary in India, by none other than those who marketed it, is gaining wider adoption, and the reasons are not only physiological but largely sociocultural.[68] A century of strategic marketing and limited access has turned air conditioning into an unshakeable aspirational goal of the burgeoning Indian middle class. Much like in the 1930s, air conditioning is desired more for the social and economic status it represents than merely for its ability to cool.

This critical analysis of air conditioning's origins in India is useful, not only for enabling a deeper historical understanding but also for informing the country's more rapid embrace of the technology in the twenty-first century. Recent research and policies on environmental comfort in India have acknowledged that blind adoption of foreign models may not be useful. Acknowledging that Indians are more acclimatized to the country's warm weather, the national government recently issued an advisory to manufacturers to keep the default setting of air conditioners at a warmer 24-degree Celsius (as opposed to 20- or 21-degree Celsius in Europe and America).[69] Other attempts have seen a revival of more traditional techniques for cooling and a parallel stress on natural ventilation. Innovations in fans and evaporative systems, like the use of terracotta tubes to cover entire building facades, are on the rise.[70] Also gaining popularity are "mixed-mode" buildings, much like the hybrid buildings of the mid-twentieth century, which rely on both active and passive means, so that air conditioning is used only periodically.[71] For this selective use of air conditioning to be based on climatic extremes and not class divides will require un-learning decades of social conditioning. It will require that we confront what constituted the "making," "selling" and "meeting" of ideas of human thermal comfort in India and its entanglements with race, class and privilege.

Biography
Priya Jain, AIA, is an assistant professor in the Department of Architecture and is associate director of the Center for Heritage Conservation at Texas A&M University. An architect licensed both in India and the US, Jain has worked professionally for fifteen years on the restoration and adaptive use of a diverse range of historic buildings. Her current research and teaching lie at the boundaries of preservation design, theory, and practice in a transnational context. She is particularly interested in institutional sites and buildings of the recent past. Her work has been supported by the Historic Preservation Education Foundation (HPEF) and published, among other venues, in the *Journal of Architectural Education* (JAE) and *Arris: Journal of the Southeast Chapter of the Society of Architectural Historians.*

Acknowledgments
I would like to thank Michael Rezzoli at the Stadtarchiv, Stadt Winterthur (Winterthur City Archives, Winterthur), Switzerland, for facilitating access to and obtaining copyright permissions for materials from the estate of Volkart Brothers. I would also like to acknowledge Mr. Ram Rahman for allowing me to use material from the archive of his father, Habib Rahman. I am thankful to the *Future Anterior* editors and reviewers of this article for their valuable feedback. My deepest gratitude is also due to the Glasscock Center for Humanities Research, Texas A&M University for a grant that covered the travel expenses for this research.

Notes
[1] "Get Airconditioned Now—It Pays!," *Volkart Brothers Engineering News,* vol. 1 (February 1936), 7, Dep. 42/155, Volkart Brothers Company Archive, Winterthur City Archives, Winterthur. Volkart Brothers hereby shortened to VB.
[2] The first issue of the *VB Engineering News* was published in December 1935. It was intended as a monthly newsletter sent to all "Branches, Agencies, Dealers and Friends" of the VB Engineering Department to "cement the various parts of the extensive Organization more closely together and permeate it with a spirit of co-operation and mutual understanding," *VB Engineering News* (December 1935), 2.
[3] For a comprehensive account of the VB firm history. see Walter H. Rambousek, Armin Vogt, and Hans R. Volkart, *Volkart: The History of a World Trading Company* (Frankfurt am Main: Insel Verlag, 1991) and J. Anderegg, "Volkart Brothers 1851–1976: A Chronicle" (unpublished manuscript, 1976), typescript, Winterthur City Archives, Winterthur. For a more analytical discussion of VB's India operations from the business history perspective, see Christof Dejung, "Bridges to the East: European Merchants and Business Practices in India and China," in *Commerce and Culture: Nineteenth Century Business Elites,* ed. Robert Lee (New York: Routledge, 2011), 93–116, and Christof Dejung, "Worldwide Ties: The Role of Family Business in Global Trade in the Nineteenth and Twentieth Centuries," *Business History* 55, no. 6 (2013): 1001–1018. On trading in colonial India, see Tirthankar Roy, "Trading Firms in Colonial India," *Business History Review* 88 (Spring 2014): 9–42.
[4] Rambousek, Vogt, and Volkart, *Volkart,* 78.
[5] Rambousek, Vogt, and Volkart, *Volkart,* 214, and Anderegg, "Volkart Brothers 1851–1976," 238.
[6] "Introduction," *VB Engineering News* (December 1935), 2.
[7] For histories of air-conditioning, written largely from the perspective of its growth in America, see Gail Cooper, *Air-conditioning America: Engineers and the Controlled Environment, 1900–1960* (Baltimore: Johns Hopkins University Press, 1998), and Salvatore Basil, *Cool: How Air Conditioning Changed Everything* (New York: Fordham University Press, 2014).
[8] R. H. Schuepp, Memorandum, 1977, quoted in Anderegg, "Volkart Brothers 1851–1976," 339.

9 Anderegg, "Volkart Brothers 1851–1976," 409.

10 Rambousek, Vogt, and Volkart, *Volkart,* 160; Anderegg, "Volkart Brothers 1851–1976," 593.

11 See Jiat-Hwee Chang, *A Genealogy of Tropical Architecture: Colonial Networks, Nature and Technoscience* (New York: Routledge, 2016); Jiat-Hwee Chang and Tim Winter, "Thermal Modernity and Architecture," *The Journal of Architecture* 20, no. 1 (2015): 92–121; and Jiat-Hwee Chang, "Thermal Comfort and Climatic Design in the Tropics: An Historical Critique," *The Journal of Architecture* 21, no. 8 (2016): 1171–1202.

12 Mark Harrison, *Climates and Constitutions: Health, Race, Environment and British Imperialism in India 1600–1850* (New Delhi: Oxford University Press, 1999).

13 Peter Scriver, "Imperial Progress: On the Impracticality of Problem-Solving in Colonial Indian Building," *Fabrications* 11, no. 2 (2001): 20–45. See also Jiat-Hwee Chang and Anthony D. King, "Towards a Genealogy of Tropical Architecture: Historical Fragments of Power-knowledge, Built Environment and Climate in the British Colonial Territories," *Singapore Journal of Tropical Geography* 32 (2011): 283–300.

14 For a discussion of colonial-era "improvement trusts" in Indian cities, for Bombay, see Farhan Karim, "Domesticating Modernism in India, 1920–1950" (PhD diss., University of Sydney, 2012), 2.3–2.35; for Calcutta, see Swati Chattopadhyay, *Representing Calcutta: Modernity, Nationalism and the Colonial Uncanny* (New York: Routledge, 2006); and for Delhi, see Jyoti Hosagrahar, *Indigenous Modernities: Negotiating Architecture and Urbanism* (New York: Routledge, 2005).

15 Ellsworth Huntington, *Civilization and Climate* (New Haven: Yale University Press, 1915), 2.

16 The phrase about India as the "ideal country for air-conditioning" was used in "Air Conditioning in Railway Carriages," *VB Engineering News,* vol. 1 (September 1936), 4.

17 "Air Conditioning Explained," *VB Engineering News,* vol. 2 (October 1937), 6. Reprinted from *The Times of India,* September 30, 1937.

18 The estimates of a 4–8% increase in Indian factory workers' efficiency as a result of air conditioning appear in references like "Industrial Development in India," *The Indian Journal of Social Work* 1, no. 2 (September 1940): 268; and Radhakamal Mukherjee, *The Indian Working Class* (Bombay: Hind Kitab Ltd. Publishers, 1945), 233.

19 Gilbert J. Fowler, review of *Developing Village India: Studies in Village Problems,* Special Number of *Indian Farming,* 1946, *Current Science* 16, no. 4 (April 1947): 131.

20 "Modern Tendencies in Air Conditioning," *VB Engineering News,* vol. 1 (February 1936), 3.

21 "Modern Tendencies in Air Conditioning," 3.

22 "Our Carrier Air Conditioning Exhibit At the Office Efficiency Exhibit, Bombay, in November 1938," *VB Engineering News,* vol. 3 (December 1938), 3. This article states: "Tests by business offices and insurance companies show that proper indoor temperatures increase office efficiency by approximately 28% and reduce loss of time due to illness by approximately 45%."

23 "Modern Tendencies in Air Conditioning," 5.

24 For a discussion of historical debates between "fresh" and recirculated air, see Cooper, *Air Conditioning America,* 51–79.

25 "Modern Tendencies in Air Conditioning," 5.

26 Modern Tendencies in Air Conditioning," 3.

27 "Scindia House, Bombay: Office Air-Conditioning in India Reaches 'New High,' Largest Office Installation by Volkart Brothers for Indian Shipping Company's New Building," *VB Engineering News,* vol. 4 (January 1939), 3.

28 "The Lighthouse Theater, Calcutta. Air Conditioning Installation by Volkart Brothers Carrier Department," *VB Engineering News,* vol. 4 (October 1939), 3.

29 For a discussion of how crowding and intermingling in motion-picture theaters in America played out, see Cooper, *Air Conditioning America,* 80–109.

30 "Air Conditioned Carriages of the North Western Railway," *VB Engineering News,* vol. 5 (April/ May 1940), 7.

31 "Air Conditioned Carriages," 7–10.

32 "Amalgamation of Interests in India of Carrier Corporation (the Pioneers of Air-Conditioning) and Volkart Brothers)," *VB Engineering News,* vol. 2 (March 1937), 5. An early but rare example of an office building that was fully air conditioned was the Bombay Electric Supply & Tramways Company, which housed more than 450 employees. This installation was not done by VB but was referenced in "Air Conditioning Explained," 7.

33 "Mr. Burrah Saheb and Air Conditioning," *The Eastern Economist* 30, no. 2 (May 30, 1958): 1025.

34 "Atmosphere to Order," *VB Engineering News,* vol. 2 (August 1937), 6. Reprinted from *The Times of India,* July 8, 1937.

35 E. A. Bertsch, "Another Air-Conditioning Installation by Volkart Brothers—This Time It Is for the New Reserve Bank of India, Bombay," *VB Engineering News,* vol. 4 (June 1939), 3. More liberal amounts of fresh air circulation to counter cigar and cigarette smoke were planned in various projects, like an office installation in 1937, where a Carrier "Weathermaker" unit was suspended from the ceiling, "An Interesting Air Conditioning Installation," *VB Engineering News,* vol. 2 (June 1937), 7.

36 "Air Raid Precautions in Bombay: The Part That Can be Played by Ventilation and Air Conditioning," *VB Engineering News,* vol. 4 (November/ December 1939), 4.

37 "Modern Tendencies in Air Conditioning," 4.

38 "Modern Tendencies in Air Conditioning," 4.

39 "Carrier Portable Summer Air Conditioners Type 50D," *VB Engineering News,* vol. 2 (June 1937), 7.

40 "Carrier Self-Contained Air Conditioning Units Eliminate Structural Alterations," *VB Engineering News,* vol. 5 (February 1940), 3.

41 See "The New Metro Cinema, Bombay: Air Conditioning Installation by Volkart Brothers Carrier Department," *VB Engineering News,* vol. 3 (June 1938), 2; and E. A. Bertsch, "Another Air-Conditioning Installation by Volkart Brothers," 3.

42 "The Lighthouse Theater, Calcutta," 2.

43 "Scindia House, Bombay," 3.

44 Chang and Winter, "Thermal Modernity and Architecture," 100.

45 See for example, "Air Conditioning Installation for the Safe Deposit Vault of the Bank of India's New 'Round' Building, Bombay," *VB Engineering News,* vol. 1 (May 1936), 8; for soundproof studios, "Scindia House, Bombay," 3, and Ram K. Vepa, "Acoustical Design of Broadcast Studios," *Journal of the Institution of Telecommunication Engineers* 2, no. 1 (December 1955): 40–44; and for laboratory conditioning, see "Air Conditioning Plant for the New Electrical Laboratory and Standard Test Room at the Engineering College, Guindy (Government of Madras)," *VB Engineering News,* vol. 2 (January 1937), 7 and G. P. Contractor, "Some Observations on Laboratory Planning," *Journal of Scientific and Industrial Research* 5, no. 4 (October 1946): 155–66.

46 The "fan humidifier" was marketed as a patented VB product for use in mills, go-downs, and storage rooms in *VB Engineering News,* vol. 1 (February 1936), 8. The same product was later marketed as a "fan cooler" for potential comfort cooling in "Air Conditioning in Railway Carriages," 6.

47 "Modern Tendencies in Air Conditioning," 4. A notable early project of so-called humidification-based comfort cooling was installed in the Delhi Legislative Assembly in 1935. This was cited as a failure with "hot, stuffy atmosphere after the installation," and a "typical example of sound principle getting discredited by wrong application." The air conditioning for this Assembly was also discussed in "The Indian Legislative Chambers," *Current Science* 6, no. 10 (April 1938): 487–89.

48 Rambousek, Vogt, and Volkart, *Volkart,* 155.

49 The city of Kanpur was referred to as "Cawnpore" in colonial times. VB archival data uses the former spelling Cawnpore.

50 VB Winterthur to VB Calcutta, 19 November 1946, Dep. 42/807, VB Company Archive, Winterthur City Archives, Winterthur.

51 VB Calcutta to VB Winterthur, 20 November 1946, Dep. 42/807, VB Company Archive.

52 VB Calcutta to VB Winterthur, 21 November 1946, Dep. 42/807, VB Company Archive.

53 VB Calcutta to VB Bombay, 1 February 1947, Dep. 42/807, VB Company Archive.

54 VB Bombay to VB Calcutta, 23 November 1946, Dep. 42/807, VB Company Archive.

55 VB Bombay to VB Cawnpore, 29 November 1946, Dep. 42/807, VB Company Archive.

56 VB Bombay to VB Winterthur, 22 November 1951, Dep. 42/808, VB Company Archive.

57 VB Bombay to VB Winterthur, 22 November 1951, Dep. 42/808, VB Company Archive.

58 Peter Reinhart to VB Winterthur, 26 February 1948, Dep. 42/809, VB Company Archive, 4.

59 For a discussion of how developments in air conditioning and climatic building design in the mid-twentieth century followed a simultaneous path, see Daniel Barber, "Tomorrow's House: Solar Housing in 1940s America," *Technology and Culture* (2014): 1–39, and Chang, "Thermal Comfort and Climatic Design in the Tropics," 1171–1202. For a contemporary critical account of air-conditioning in the Indian context, see W. C. Thoburn, "House Construction and Thermal Comfort in the Subtropics," *Journal of Scientific and Industrial Research* 13A, no. 11 (November 1954): 521–31, 575–82; and S. L. Kumar, "Comfort Studies in Residential Buildings and Offices in India," *The Journal of the Institution of Engineers (India)* xxxvii, no. 4, pt. 1 (December 1956): 267–99.

[60] "Tallest Building in Asia," *Indian Concrete Journal* xxviii (June 1954): 197.

[61] "The National Physical Laboratory, India: Opening Ceremony, January 21, 1950," *Journal of Scientific and Industrial Research* 9A, no. 4 (April 1950): 110–14; "National Physical Laboratory," *Science and Culture* xxiv, no. 3 (1959): 14; "Harnessing the Elements for Prosperity: Volkart," *Marg* 7, no. 1 (December 1953): unpaginated advertisement.

[62] The period from early to mid-twentieth century of the origins and ascendancy of air conditioning was marked by an ambivalent and shifting attitude toward "thermal diversity" — exposure to range of indoor climactic conditions versus a steady state of "comfort" conditions. Air conditioning engineers in the early days strove to create constant conditions in conditioned spaces, minimizing drafts, etc., but at the same time had to counter public fears that constantly moving from outdoors (or other non-conditioned spaces) to conditioned interiors was detrimental to one's health. So they usually dismissed the latter as non-consequential, but also often used the same argument to make a case for central conditioning as opposed to a piecemeal approach. The concept of "thermal diversity" is explored in various texts, including Lisa Heschong, *Thermal Delight in Architecture* (Cambridge, MA: The MIT Press, 1979); and Elizabeth Shove, "Social, Architectural and Environmental Convergence," in *Environmental Diversity in Architecture,* ed. Koen Steemers and Mary Ann Steane (New York: Spon Press, 2004), 19–30.

[63] Chang and Winter, "Thermal Modernity and Architecture," 101.

[64] R. H. Schuepp, "Long, Long Ago," *We: The Voltas House Magazine,* vol. 2 (1955), reprinted in *We,* vol. 16 (1979), Dep. 42/98, VB Company Archive.

[65] "Top Ten Air Conditioner Brands in India," Business Maps of India, accessed May 15, 2020, https://business.mapsofindia.com/top-brands-india/top-ac-brands-in-india.html. The window air conditioner launched by Voltas in 1955 was called "Crystal." It soon became the bestselling room air conditioner in the Indian market.

[66] The post-modernist, anti-regionalist critique of air conditioning is summed up most popularly by Kenneth Frampton who referred to the "ubiquitous air conditioner" as the "main antagonist of rooted culture." Kenneth Frampton, "Towards a Critical Regionalism: Six Points for an Architecture of Resistance," in *The Anti-Aesthetic: Essays on Postmodern Culture,* ed. H. Foster (New York: New Press, 1998), 27. For a discussion of sociocultural impacts on air conditioning, see Gail S. Brager and Richard J. de Dear, "Historical and Cultural Influences on Comfort Expectations," in *Buildings, Culture and Environment: Informing Local and Global Practices,* eds. Raymond J. Cole and Richard Lorch (Oxford: Blackwell Publishing, 2003).

[67] "Making the World Hotter: India's Expected Air Conditioning Explosion," *The Straits Times*, accessed June 15, 2020, https://www.straitstimes.com/asia/south-asia/making-the-world-hotter-indias-expected-ac-explosion.

[68] Sanyogita Manu, Yash Shukla, Rajan Rawal, Leena E. Thomas and Richard de Dear, "Field Studies of Thermal Comfort Across Multiple Climate Zones for the Subcontinent: India Model for Adaptive Comfort (IMAC)," *Building and Environment* 98 (2016): 55–70.

[69] "India Sets 24 degree Celsius as Air Conditioning Default," accessed March 17, 2020, https://www.coolingpost.com/world-news/india-sets-240c-as-air-conditioning-default/. For national competition see "Global Cooling Prize," accessed May 20, 2020, https://globalcoolingprize.org/.

[70] Amani Al-Aidroos and Tom Page, "India has a Looming Air Con Headache: Does Antiquity Hold the Solution?" CNN, accessed June 20, 2020, https://www.cnn.com/style/article/india-air-conditioning-ant-studio/index.html.

[71] Manu et al., "Field Studies of Thermal Comfort," 55–70.

Roundtable Discussion
Retrofitting Research: A Global Conversation on Challenges and Opportunities

The following conversation was recorded over Zoom on February 18, 2021, bringing together most of the contributors to this issue of *Future Anterior*.

FALLON SAMUELS AIDOO: I'm so glad that all of you were able to spend this time with us today. One of the challenging things about having a conversation across geographies is finding a time zone and slot that can somewhat work for everybody. So I appreciate everyone taking time to join us.

And I want to also acknowledge the fact that there are some contributors to this journal who were not able to join us, and so I don't want to present this conversation as comprehensive of all the voices that are even just a part of this journal, let alone all the many voices that are part of this conversation well beyond this particular call for papers from this volume of *Future Anterior*.

That said, I figure it's about time that Daniel and I introduce ourselves and give you a little bit more background than perhaps you found Googling and such. I don't believe that I know any of you in any kind of personal way, so that's both exciting and daunting, to be honest.

I, Fallon Samuels Aidoo, am an assistant professor of Planning and Preservation at the University of New Orleans, and that has put me in a position of trying to bridge the gap between the conversations on the built environment from a kind of planning perspective with that of the kind of architectural field from which I originally hail.

And so a lot of my perspectives on the issue of retrofit are derivative of being that bridge, particularly as it relates to discourse and scholarship on how to address risks and hazards of various kinds. And the fact that I'm situated at a university that has a Hazards Research Center, which is very actively involved in climate, refugee resettlements, and managed retreats and has conducted for the city of New Orleans a study of building elevation and how that relates to flood risk.

So I'm kind of steeped in all things, what to do about our built environment, but I'm also not in community with, here at my institution, people who come from architecture and heritage fields. So I'm really excited to engage in these conversations with all of you. And I look forward to understanding how our different worlds intersect and what nexuses we can forge forward.

Future Anterior
Volume XVIII, Number 1
Summer 2021

DANIEL BARBER: Great. I'll follow on that. Thanks, Fallon, for starting us off and thank you all for joining us. I'm really looking forward to this conversation, which I really think is a way to both give everyone a chance to reflect on their research and methods and strategies and perspectives relative to the challenges of this kind of interdisciplinary, dare I say emergent, research arena around questions of energy and preservation and retrofit.

I'm an associate professor of Architecture at the University of Pennsylvania, where I also chair the PhD program, a program that is officially in architecture, but also absorbs projects in landscape architecture and historic preservation, and we could even explore some of those institutional challenges by which we subsume too many things under architecture and all too frequently, right? And we are certainly kind of guilty of that in the formation of the program at Penn at the same time that we have a great preservation program, as I'm sure many of you know, and serve that PhD of course quite effectively.

I've just written a book on modern architecture and climate, looking at a set of developments across the '30s, '40s, and '50s that understands the kind of design methods and strategies that aims to condition the thermal interior and am increasingly compelled by and drawn to projects that are rethinking the life of buildings beyond their moment of construction into their use, into their sort of broader life span.

Having no formal training whatsoever in preservation discourse, but picking it up as I can from various journals and other venues. So, really interested to follow on this discussion and continue to develop the issue accordingly.

Maybe we'll have a practice here of passing it on as we go. Does that make sense? So I'm just going to elect the person next to me on my grid to introduce—And the idea here is we'll start with this kind of brief introductions, and then we'll get into the broader discussion. But, Joseph, you are next to me, so if you can take it and then when you're done, just pass it on to whoever's next to you and we'll go like that.

JOSEPH SIRY: Thank you. This is the first time I've ever seen fellow contributors to a journal issue. I've never had this experience before. It's really kind of nice.

I'm Joe Siry. I teach History of Modern Architecture at Wesleyan University in Middletown, Connecticut. And most of my scholarly work has been on Louis Sullivan, Andrew Sullivan, Frank Lloyd Wright. And some of that scholarly work has helped to support preservation efforts of their buildings.

But most recently I've been working on a book on air-conditioning and modern American architecture from the

1890s to the 1970s. And that's just finished, that's just out. And beyond that I'm interested in what happens to American architecture in relation to energy issues from the 1970s on. That has led me to work on retrofitting of 1970s and 1980s buildings for energy reasons and other reasons.

And I guess next to me is Michele Morganti.

MICHELE MORGANTI: Thank you. Thank you very much. I'm very glad to be here with you with Zooming. I am Michele Morganti. I am a seasoned professor in Building Design for Sustainable Architecture at Sapienza University of Rome and I hold a PhD in Energy and Environment from the Barcelona School of Architecture at UPC BarcelonaTech and from Sapienza University.

My particular focus of interest in research is the relation among urban climate change, microclimates, and energy in building design as a whole with a special interest in the public housing field, in particular I'm developing currently some studies within the Territorial Fragilities Project from Polytechnic of Milan and these studies include regenerative design with a cross-field approach aiming at defining new methods and new tools reliable and effective in order to support public housing renovation and . . .

I wrote a book a few years ago about the relation between form, density, and energy in the built environment in general with a special focus in sustainability of the urban form and of the special metrics that describe relations between these two categories.

SUSAN ROSS: Thank you for the invitation. Since I only wrote a book review for this issue, I feel privileged to be invited as a contributor to this panel, but this is a conversation that I want to be part of. I'm a licensed architect in Quebec. I worked for twelve years in the private sector, eight in Montreal, four in Berlin, before joining the Canadian federal government for eleven years as a conservation architect, after completing my graduate studies specializing in the conservation of the built environment.

It was in the federal context that I really started to engage with asking how to connect heritage and sustainability. At the time, in the early 2000s, I think a lot of our policy work was fairly cutting edge. We were looking at social and cultural sustainability, as well as environmental sustainability. This was part of trying to influence the emerging focus on rating systems.

I have since, in my own research, shifted more to the intersections of modern heritage and sustainability, so it interests me to hear about some of Joseph and Daniel's areas of focus.

Currently I am more focused on questions around waste and heritage, so not as much on the energy and carbon discussions directly, but indirectly quite a bit. I have organized a related symposium, a special issue of a journal, and a webinar and if people are interested in that part of the discussion, I can share a few resources.

I almost forgot to tell you that I am an associate professor in the School of Indigenous and Canadian Studies at Carleton University in Ottawa. That is my full-time position now, which means that I get to teach and do research on all these things. I'm also cross-appointed with Carleton's School of Architecture and Urbanism.

Going back a little bit to what Fallon suggested about being in a different place, I was hired to do heritage work as an architect in the School of Canadian Studies, since 2016 we're Indigenous and Canadian Studies. This has been an interesting place to become part of bridging a lot of things. Thank you.

And since everybody next to me on the screen has spoken, I'm going to go for Jessica.

JESSICA MORRIS: Thank you very much, Susan. It's a pleasure to be here with you all. I am an architect and practitioner in New York City. I am a product of the MARCH [Master of Architecture] Program at the University of Pennsylvania and took advantage of all of that cross-disciplinarity that I think the school provides opportunity to access.

I have recently taken on the role of co-chair for the Planning and Urban Design Committee with AIA New York. A lot of the work that I do is in the city here. I do have a day job doing some work for the city with pandemic recovery public health outreach.

But coming to this discussion, what brought me here was a case study looking at 2050 net-zero scenarios, so thinking kind of in the framework of future perfect, future anterior and recognizing that preservation is very much the present-day discussion between the future and the past.

I've always kind of taken up the position that preservation is a radical activity in the everyday, and I think most preservationists do not necessarily consider themselves radicals. So the recognition that how we work on preserving our assets is very much aligned with the types of practices that will drive smart growth in the thirty-year project to a new energy future.

I think recognizing that cultivating anchors of the past, things that people know and love from a community-based perspective of the social science aspect of what drives preservation activities really also aligns with these smart growth strategies from a bottom-up perspective, while at the same time recognizing that the gaps in economic analysis and understanding co-benefits (from a health perspective of both preservation activities and smart growth practices) are not well understood.

And ultimately those types of bottom lines are what drive policy to support these parallel sets of practices.

So I'm a little bit of an outlier in a big way and not an expert on anything, but interested in asking a lot of questions of folks who have deep histories in these practices towards a, you know, future perfect, right? Retrofit is a part of that.

I'm going diagonally across. This is like *Brady Bunch,* for the record. Francesco?

FRANCESCO CIANFARANI: Hello, everyone. Thanks so much, Fallon and Daniel for this great opportunity. Nice to meet you all. My name is Francesco Cianfarani. I'm Assistant Professor of Architecture at the Christopher C. Gibbs College of Architecture at the University of Oklahoma, OU, Norman, and a PhD in the field of Architecture and Urban Design gained at Sapienza University of Rome.

I joined OU in 2018 and since 2018 my teaching and research agenda has focused on affordable housing opportunities in the Oklahoma region. Right now, I'm particularly focused on studying and evaluating the HUD programs for the renovation of distressed public housing communities and neighborhoods, and I'm particularly focused on studying Choice Neighborhood Initiatives, especially in Tulsa, Oklahoma.

Over the last ten years, I was particularly involved in exploring multiple occasions for understanding and researching the topic of urban decay, of European mass housing, and particularly Italian postwar mass housing. The idea of postwar mass housing has always been central in my studies and in my interests since I was a student because I think it's a unique idea in the history, modern history of architecture and urban design, but also because it deals with the functional, aesthetic, and technical aspects that deal not just with the dwelling and building scales, but also with the infrastructural scales. I've always been fascinated by this idea of mass housing as an urban infrastructure for model living.

So when I was a PhD student and an adjunct in Italy, I participated in a series of national research groups and publications focused on the assessments of guidelines for the urban and social regeneration of decaying postwar mass housing complexes. My particular focus within these groups was related to mapping different strategies on how to preserve the cultural and the social values of these modern neighborhoods.

Our research goal was defining design guidelines to retain some of the values of these neighborhoods while transforming them in terms of energy performance upgrades. So I decided to apply to the school, to the *Future Anterior* call, with my colleague Michele Morganti, because I think that the topic of the decay of postwar mass housing is really important and central also for bridging the gap between preservation culture and retrofit culture, and also for establishing a new perspective on these topics.

So, I think that that's it. I can pass the words to Yat. Thank you.

JULIANA YAT SHUN KEI: Hello. Hi. Good afternoon. I'm in London. Thank you again for the opportunity. I'm really looking forward to our discussions and yeah, I think it's a privilege to be able to discuss with other contributors to the journal.

I'm a lecturer in architecture at the University of Liverpool. I was also trained as an architect, but my PhD was in History of Design, so I think my consideration was something of a slightly smaller scale, and in my studies I also take either an object or a word as a way of unfolding the power dynamics or beyond that.

I really love that Jessica's talking about preservation as radical. I was drawn to, like, 1960s and '70s radical architecture. And as I developed my research interests, it began to bring me into community efforts and radical preservation projects, and I ended up studying buildings like the Shakespeare's Globe in London, which is radical in its own right of reconstructing a sixteenth-century theater in central London in the 1990s.

My work is mostly thinking about this intersection between preservation, historical construction material in the context of postmodern architecture. So I see myself as a traditional architecture or urban historian with a focus on late twentieth-century architecture culture.

I think there's a few of us left. Priya is here I think.

PRIYA JAIN: Thank you, Yat. I'm sorry I was late, but I'm really happy to be able to join from Texas, especially since we've been having power outages for the last three days. So it's really ironic and interesting to join a forum on climate in the middle of all that.

But I'm here in Texas. I'm at Texas A&M University. I'm an assistant professor in the Department of Architecture and the associate director of our Center for Heritage Conservation here.

I'm an architect. I have worked in Boston and before that in India for a few years. In my work, which involves retrofitting and reuse of many nineteenth- and twentieth-century buildings, the idea of climate has always been integral. We had to insulate — kind of figure out how to insulate these mass masonry buildings back in the Northeast, so that was when I really kind of started noticing the importance of how people — you know, how to get people comfortable in buildings and the challenge of retrofitting them. But . . . This was an issue that always interested me.

But in academia, I've been focusing on twentieth-century buildings in India, where I originally am from. And that was because, you know, some of the projects I worked on were modern-era buildings and kind of the issue of modern heritage is still very threatened in India, so that's something that I wanted to focus on.

As I started getting more into understanding twentieth-century architecture in India, especially in the post-independence era, which is after 1947 in India, it became clear that, you know, I had to engage with issues of air-conditioning and climate because the histories of those are so intertwined. And it was actually when I was researching the first Indian MIT, which . . . was modeled after MIT, that I kind of got into this—gone down the rabbit hole of chasing this architect who was invited to India and then, you know, he collaborated with an engineer in Switzerland who worked for a firm that was—supplied a lot of the initial air-conditioning equipment to India. So that was kind of how I chanced upon their archives, and the stuff I was reading was just so interesting that I felt like I had to tell a story around it and I responded to the call from *Future Anterior*.

So I'm really happy to be here. And some of the things, you know, that are included in my paper is just how the very technical issues of air-conditioning were so intrinsically tied to ideas about race, class, and how those have really continued from the colonial era to the post–colonial era and still have so much relevance. And the way some of these things are viewed in India, climate, comfort, so that's what my paper talks about. And I'm really happy to be here and hear from all of you.

Are we picking the next person? I don't know who has spoken?

AIDOO: Yes.

JAIN: I don't know who has spoken.

AIDOO: We've got *[crosstalk]*

KAI WOOLNER-PRATT: I think I'm the only person left, maybe, right? Kai. Hi, everybody. Yeah, it's really exciting to be here. I really am very happy to be in this group. I think a bit like Jessica said, I also feel like a bit of an outlier in a certain way *[laughs],* in a few ways I guess.

I'm really coming more from art history. My undergraduate studies were kind of in cultural studies and architecture in Halifax at University of King's College. And then I lived abroad for a few years and I came to work in Montreal at the Canadian Center for Architecture. At the same time that this research project called Architecture and/or the Environment—is that right? *[laughs]* Yeah—was going on, where Daniel Barber was one of the members, along with seven other scholars.

That really made an impression on me. So the short story is that through working at the museum, I ended up deciding to kind of go back and study more intensively and do a PhD. So now I'm on my way to Stanford to the Art History Department, so not to the Architectural History Department. They don't have any architectural historians there, so what I would be doing there is to work on architecture, but really from art history.

I'm really interested in bridging discourses on architecture, especially around really pressing issues like the topics that we're dealing with in this conversation, but bringing in art historical scholarship and methodologies and concepts as well as kind of early modern perspective. So that's what I propose to do at Stanford, to work between the History of Science Department and the Art History Department on architecture, but from those angles. So that's really what I brought to this paper in the issue. And I think that's what I can bring to the conversation today as well.

So I don't have any, you know, very on-the-ground experience with preservation. That's not precisely my background. But I can bring the things that I'm familiar with, which is more this art historical perspective and the issues around infrastructure, infrastructural turn and so on. So, yeah, that's where I'm coming from. But I'm in Montreal. I'm in Montreal right now, and very eager to cross the border into California. It's so cold here. *[laughs]*

ROSS: Well, hi from Ottawa, where it might be even colder. [laughter]

WOOLNER-PRATT: Yeah.

AIDOO: You all have pushed your Canadian weather system to the Gulf Coast, and so we're all feeling like we're a little bit in the experience of the Canadian climate at this point in time.

I live here, but I'm not originally from New Orleans or the South and so I'm a little bit more accustomed to it, or at least I have the clothes and the shoes to be able to move around.

I think that we've got such an amazingly diverse group of people as part of this conversation. I was remiss when I started by not adding much about the kind of work that I do.

And so I'll just add that I have very broad interests, but generally my research is focused on places that are rather marginalized in both the historical record as well as historic preservation. And so that's put places that are of significance to Black, Indigenous, and other people of color kind of at the center of my work, but not the exclusive subject of my work.

I started with my dissertation research in Philadelphia and looking at degradation of the real infrastructure and architecture of that city. And I've actually come rather circuitously to the diversity of preservation in Philadelphia just by learning how—learning the different sponsors of retrofit and preservation activity.

From the public sector I think it was really interesting, Francesco, about HUD. You know, its predecessor was actually really key in making it possible for grassroots organizations founded by gender minorities and racial minorities in Philadelphia to participate in these kind of high society preservation activities in Philadelphia, at the same time foundations were starting to play a bigger role in preservation practice.

And so it was quite an interesting experience to be a kind of young Afro-Latina circulating in the, quote/unquote, archives of elite Philadelphia philanthropists and finding the records of, you know, Jewish and Black and gay community organizations. And you're like, "How did that even—" You know, definitely not something one expects to find in somebody's file cabinets.

So I think that it drives home for me the importance of us having conversations like this to better understand which are the methods by which we all document preservation practice and policy and practitioners, and where do we draw, whether it is art history or have national heritage conversations in other parts of the world, where do we draw our discursive frameworks, as well as our methodological tools.

Daniel and I figured that we would start big and give you all—not necessarily everybody to jump in on every single question because we would certainly be here much longer than two hours if we did that. But if you felt compelled to contribute on one front versus another, we give you an opportunity to kind of take a step back from your specific papers and think—be able to contribute something related to where you were coming from in that research.

I know some of you kind of incorporated that into your introductions, but if you wanted to add anything that would inform where we go from here. Is it something that you learned from that particular process of coming at this case study or this larger study that you drew your paper from that tells us what the challenges are for us as a field, if we were to give ourselves that kind of framing. And then maybe drill down from there into the specifics around particular methods and tools and such.

So Daniel, did you want to lead us off, or did you want to let folks just start jumping in?

BARBER: I'm happy to have people jump in. I'm struck as we were going through the intros by the fact that of course Fallon and I are the only ones here to know what all of you have written. So I think we're just going to be stuck with that, right, rather than spend more time clearing that up. But I say that in the sense — in the spirit of feel free to bring in some of the details, you know, from your project as again has already begun to happen.

But as you respond to some of these questions. And I think we can't stay certainly at this larger scale on thinking about the specific kind of methodological and research strategies that have been important for you as scholars and potentially as architects or preservation professionals to think about these intertwined aspects of energy and climate in the context of preservation practice. Jessica, go ahead.

MORRIS: Fallon, to jump off of what you said in a way and sort of play on words that I think is very apt in regards to this intersection and understanding if retrofit is proper in preservation framework. It is not conservation. It serves a function.

I think the fact of preservation activities as being performative, that they are very much about engaging community stakeholders, various groups that find identity in — cultural identity in artifacts, buildings, pieces of infrastructure. So I think performance of a practice of preservation, but at the same time the retrofit market is very much driven by building energy performance. And that reality creates, I think, a parity across things that don't typically get looked at together. Kai, your perspective on the infrastructure, infrastructural turn, I think is that functional aspect of practice and buildings, containers for living or for lifestyles. The social function of architecture starts to become something that is measurable in a performance aspect kind of way.

So, from the sort of identity politics of performing preservation, considering, Fallon, your dive into the archive and who was there, who was represented and how that finds its way to a present-day point of action is — that for me is the starting point and the nexus of what really ties the type of climate-based activities centered on retrofit and preservation to the sort of social science side of who this is for and how it happens ultimately.

How that relates to the work that I've put forward in the volume of *Future Anterior* is — I did not mention this in my introduction — is by looking at the Gowanus Canal as a case study in New York City, which in 2010 was designated a superfund site that was taken as the place of imagining a 2050 net-zero neighborhood. So going from a superfund with a long history of environmental degradation from the very types of companies that were really investing in improving mass transportation and access to other sorts of forms of energy — there is sort of residue of industry and the modernization of industry around the canal—that fast-forward to what is our kind of new green industry and how much of an authentic past you really need to maintain or preserve, not only from a life cycle perspective in measuring the sort of valued assets of today, but also in a kind of authentic cultural atmosphere of a historic district. But performance is the practice that I think ties the two together.

AIDOO: Jessica's remarks make me think a little bit about, Francesco, your discussion of the kind of social mass housing projects that you've been involved in. If you wouldn't mind talking a little bit about how differently or not working in a research collaborative in Europe on that subject has been to working on it here in the United States as it pertains to HUD-funded housing renovation.

CIANFARANI: Yeah. That's a very important question, Fallon. Thanks for sharing it.

Basically I'm at the beginning of my experience here at OU in exploring new possibilities for setting a preservation agenda during huge transformation projects that involve the distressed communities like the ones for the Choice Neighborhood Initiatives.

Right now I'm in the process of working together with people in search of a team. . . .

Basically it is not a case that the topic of mass housing and the decay of the topic of mass housing is explored in our paper . . . basically I'm working on this paper with Michele Morganti who is an architectural engineer with a background in sustainability and a background in environmental assessments. And I'm an architect with a background in adaptive reuse projects and studies on architectural heritage, modern and contemporary history.

I think that especially the topic of the decay of postwar mass housing and the problem of heritage of postwar mass housing needs to be explored by a team, by multiple teams of people that can offer different perspectives. This is something that we see as a problem when we discuss current preservation cultures that particularly endanger modern heritage like public housing. We think that retrofit can really be an opportunity for that type of heritage to be studied, to be shared, to be saved, to be better, and to be better considered by the public, by the institutions, by the community in general.

MORRIS: Francesco, can I ask you to clarify when you say mass housing do you mean public housing, social housing? I think it has different kinds of names globally, and if you can clarify what you mean by mass housing just so that we're understanding the bracket of what it is you're talking about.

CIANFARANI: Yes, Jessica. Thanks for the question. Basically that's not a shared definition of postwar mass housing, but in our paper we framed this as public housing projects that were mainly managed and sponsored by public authorities, characterized by high-rise residential developments in . . . in the face of great modern transition and experimentation of new technologies and new typologies from the 1960s to the 1980s.

In Italy we basically related these studies to a particular national law, which is the law 167 that was really focused on producing possible mass housing complexes for Italian cities. In the American context that can be compared to the American public housing of the 1960s and 1970s or, for example, in England to the City Council Projects or in France to the Grands Ensembles.

We think that actually this topic has a great—really offers great opportunities for also setting up a preservation agenda because first of all, it's still managed by the public, especially in Western countries, and the public can really play a role in fostering good practices for retrofitting, in sharing group practices for retrofitting also with the private sector. It is also a great opportunity for exploring these types of topics in terms of retrofit because public housing is really characterized by scale and by a series of infrastructures that really make it . . . connected to also other private settlements and other private residential stocks in cities.

MORRIS: . . . .

BARBER: Sorry, Jessica. I think there's a few people that have been trying to get in. I wonder if we might want to initiate, as a point of organization, I don't know if people are familiar with the sort of stack process, like rather than keeping your hand up you could just type "stack" into the Chat, and we'll know who's next on the list just in the interest of giving everybody a chance to chime in.

I saw that Kai and Yat Shun were both—well, at least unmuted yourselves, which I always take to be a sign of interest. And Susan as well. So I don't know if we want to go in that order briefly or Jessica, if you had an immediate quick response, but I want to make sure we get everyone.

JESSICA: Sure. And then I'll sit back for a while. Francesco, I think one of the things that came up in the case study that I brought to the table was in energy systems analysis needing a boundary and that that boundary in some ways needed to in a New York setting include a NYCHA campus. NYCHA is the public housing entity here that is sorely in need of deep energy retrofits. It needs to function better from a building performance perspective.

But it also has a very real social function within the eco-system of not only climate mitigation strategies, but adaptation strategies and building resilience. So you know, I think the inclusion of the type of infrastructure that you're talking about, housing infrastructure, state-sponsored housing infrastructure, not as a singular entity that gets worked on separately, but inclusive of these larger strategies for preservation-based tactics. So the social function of the type of infrastructure that you're talking about as a sort of necessary point of inclusion in a larger preservation story is what I'm hearing.

MORGANTI: Can you hear me? Okay. I just want to add a reaction from the first intervention from Jessica that talks about the retrofit in relation to preservation and then . . . markets and related to performance for buildings, performance for energy and environment in general.

I think that our contribution to the call that talks about the mass housing is particularly interesting because as Francesco said . . . can be a hinge [?] between very different fields working together to understand the problem of urban decay in relation to preservation and in relation with the problems of climate adaptation and energy efficiency in our cities.

And we read this problem in mass housing as an opportunity and not as a problem because we believe that there are a lot of resources in this kind of neighborhood typically based on mass housing.

But in addition I want to say that if we want to understand the significance of retrofit in the case of mass housing today, probably we need to go beyond the traditional meaning and significance of retrofit as it is in the technology field. I believe that we can also intend the retrofit as an upgrading to current needs, but these needs are not the typical technology needs. We need also to look at adapting this district to current housing demands, to enhancing the sense of community, to increase — of course — the energy efficiency and the indoor and outdoor comfort, but also fostering the resilience to climate change.

So I think that we need to consider retrofit in a broader sense, and this is crucial for the preservation of heritage like mass housing. Because retrofit leads the way to some preservation themes that today are crucial in light of climate change. First of all they have an innate predisposition to modification as they are modern in the sense of the original design that they were made and also because of the presence of resources and in terms of space, in terms of *[sound drop-out]* . . .

CIANFARANI: We lost Michele. Yes, Daniel.

BARBER: Hopefully he'll make it back, but—

AIDOO: Yeah. Kai, did you want to continue with this train of thought or did you want to pivot to another topic?

WOOLNER-PRATT: I think in a way I would like to continue with this train of thought because I think something that I've been thinking about a lot, maybe naively, is what is retrofit. And I think that's going to be a relevant question right now. And I think I could be the one to put—to pose that, I guess. Naively. *[laughs]*

But I think what I've been thinking about especially as I mentioned this kind of discourse on infrastructure. So my project was about a retrofit of a gas station in Montreal from being used, you know, as a gas station to a community center, which entailed the kind of complete disconnection of the building from the larger infrastructures of oil conveyance and the transportation infrastructures of the highway and so on that were kind of integral to that object and instead they established the geothermal wells that would heat and cool the building and also supply power to the building. So it was a—it really went from—it's a very kind of schematic retrofit in the way that it's so extreme, and I think that that opened up certain things for me that are maybe a bit more again like diagrammatic.

So I've been thinking about that relationship between the building and its infrastructure, and kind of the point of my essay is that if you're going to retrofit a building, especially this building, a gas station, it kind of demands something much broader at least in this case, of retrofitting the territory and the infrastructure systems that it's embedded in.

I think that's something that I've been thinking about a lot is that architecture is almost an interface in a way and the retrofit, again, I'm thinking in my specific case, seems to serve as like an interface and as a kind of more discursive or like rhetorical position that suggests this broader shift and that enacts it at the scale of the gas station, but given its kind of intense imbrication in all those systems, it really doesn't quite make sense in isolation, right? Which is how it's been produced.

So I guess thinking of infrastructure there's a kind of a question I want to pose, which is, like, how do we think about the relationship between retrofit, repair and maintenance? I guess that's more coming from that infrastructural turn, so I don't know if it's something that's familiar to people. It's not something that I'm an expert on by any means, but there is a kind of—there is a way in which I think architecture can be theorized more in terms of the tools that have been developed in terms of infrastructure. And this issue of repair, I think it brings out something interesting because people tend to emphasize the way that repair is continuous but also very adaptive.

And so I think this limit between a kind of punctual intervention of a retrofit and a more ongoing process of repair, I think there's a fluidity in the boundary. And so I'm kind of interested in that. For me that's a little bit unclear where the line is. And I think it also brings up, like, what is the goal. There is a kind of evolutionary dimension to retrofit where things are kind of in flux and constantly changing.

There's a really interesting paper by a lot of authors, one of whom is Cymene Howe, and she—they kind of conclude with this call for imagining an infrastructure that's more inherently flexible or that's more open to transformation or readaptation, that somehow is produced in a way that anticipates its own demise or kind of ruination but also transformation.

And so I think there's something for that in architecture as well. I guess this, yeah, this line between an object and its systems I think that's—that's what I've been thinking about. So I guess in terms of what retrofit is, that's how I've been thinking about it.

I guess the question is like what is that relationship between retrofit, repair, maintenance. Where do we draw those boundaries and—

BARBER: I appreciate how you're also bringing that into our discursive foundations if you will, sort of disciplinary backgrounds that we—I guess speaking for myself, I think it's easy to relate to a discourse on infrastructure that has been a part of our field for some decades if not centuries, right, but this question of repair and retrofit we feel, again speaking for myself, somewhat less prepared to encounter just based on our kind of literature that's been informed. I feel like I'm speaking too generally amongst a very diverse audience, but this presents some challenges to crossing all those boundaries. It's a very insightful framework.

AIDOO: Susan and Yat, did you want to piggyback off of one of—

KEI: I can develop on what Kai says of what is retrofitting. The project—the paper I wrote is kind of writing about one building that goes through retrofitting two times in the past fifty years. And I think it's kind of a context wherein both cases we might say the architect does the right job of his time.

The first time is in the 1980s or late 1970s when the UK was promoting this kind of small business, craftsmen, and they have used the retrofitting exercise to create—to reinsure this traditional craft—arts and crafts into the renovation of this building which is the Unilever House in London, which has its own history about object and network that I will come back to.

And the second time was in the 2000s by Kohn Pederson Fox and they really took on the banner of reusing energy consumption. So this building is everything of a high grade of energy performance and every single material is being recycled, everything is about reducing the emissions.

In both contexts, we might argue that the architect really took the concept of retrofitting in his time very well, but in both cases, it — and my paper kind of uses it as a question of how difficult it is to properly retrofit a building.

In the case of the first renovation by Pentagram, when they are celebrating these arts and crafts ideas, they recreated palm trees, which are the resources for . . . the Unilever Organization in the building as the motif. And there are also a lot of other exercises of reenacting the colonial tendency of that building, which we can talk about in our context today of being very critical of all these artistic expressions.

But maybe also equally problematic is when KPF did the building they were thinking about only the material life cycle and they demolished everything inside of the building except the facade and inserted this kind of high performance steel concrete sustainable architecture into the building. And for them, the material history is about . . . energy.

And right now it's just like — I love the question that Fallon and Daniel said because I think it's like I don't know how to answer many of these things. As an architectural historian we are not very well-equipped in talking about things that — like in terms of the embedded meaning of material energy. Like somehow the Pentagram one was easy for me to talk about pointing to the countries of this very offensive motif. But then like every piece of the material, including the original structure, was from the Empire, right, and then the second time (the Pentagram renovation) also from the Empire. The third time it was being crushed out and reinvented as seeing the Empire does not exist.

And I think I'm just going back to what I think, Kai, you used a word of infrastructure and I think I was talking about a network just because mine are crushed concrete. But I think we are thinking about quite similar things in terms of how we can expand this discussion to a territorial cultural network of things. Yeah, so that is kind of what I wanted to add to it.

AIDOO: Susan, I know you've been waiting.

ROSS: Yes, although with everyone who has spoken since, I have a different response now. I do want to first go back to one initial response to the archive question, and just say I want us to remember to think about the physical building itself as an archive. And in some ways that works well as a way of responding to Yat Shun's remarks just now. It also connects to things I am trying to do by looking at waste and heritage, including by studying demolition in order to understand what we are losing when we lose materials that we don't reuse.

Another thing to Kai's question about making the connection between retrofit, repair, and maintenance, is about use and reuse, and how we conceptualize those two. This is something that I have been discovering through discussions around waste as part of discard studies. Giving more value to materiality and to material energies, which don't necessarily ever get lost, can inform the way that we conceptualize use and reuse. Maybe we are missing the fact that reuse is just continued use. The materials retain their value. Stone remains stone. And even if as an architect or a preservation planner we are thinking differently about how a material is being used by us, it is good for us to remember what it essentially is. So recognizing more essential material values.

But I also have one more thing I wanted to add into that—well, probably three more things. But just one more, and then I'll let someone else speak. In talking about mass housing, one of the questions that comes up is who really effectively leads in the retrofit of social, public, or other ways of talking about mass housing.

It is clear in many ways that people in preservation have not been leading, and yet we are confronted now, that this is our next heritage. I know that here in Ottawa we are starting to lose projects that were experimental housing projects from the energy-crisis era. We have to be conscious that in that era, the people leading were housing experts, or energy experts working in housing. We have the equivalent of HUD, the CMHC [Canada Mortgage and Housing Corporation], and their heritage is important for us to understand and to recognize. Heritage professionals weren't very engaged in that.

And now that housing heritage may be lost. In Canada, there is a profession now emerging, which does not quite have the right name yet, but it is called heritage planning. It has a broader purview than architectural or heritage conservation or historic preservation. But people who do heritage planning likely don't quite have the planning breadth of training and knowledge.

We need to engage more with this idea of heritage planning. Many jobs now call for a heritage planner, and yet if you look at the qualifications, I don't think they realize they need traditional urban planners.

And so, I am following you, Fallon, because you're bridging into that world, right? Organizations like the Canadian Urban

Institute are doing interesting things that intersect between preservation and climate change, and neighborhood planning and housing, and yet they don't see themselves as a heritage organization. Those are all my responses to several points. And, for Kai, I know that gas station in Montreal, too.

AIDOO: Before we jump into the next round of stacked entries in the Chat, I just want to, you know, use this as a point of pivot to one of the questions that really animated Daniel and I as we started thinking about what we wanted this very first foray — as far as a journal issue to be, which is kind of: what is the audience for this kind of work?

You know, you're raising this, Susan, this matter of the new practitioner as, you know, whether their title is heritage planner or not, this being someone out there whose responsibilities may necessitate a body of knowledge that does not yet exist as a body of knowledge so much as a network of information and resources and who is responsible as you kind of put it, who's responsible not just for the actual practice of preservation, but who's responsible for assembling and curating that body of knowledge for that practice.

And certainly I wouldn't say that this journal or any one journal is actually the kind of executor of that action in the sense of being the curator of this really global body of knowledge that has many different kinds of cultural and regional inflections. But there does seem to be a need for institutions and individuals to serve in that role.

One of the challenges of course then is the question of "What kind of tools and techniques and exchanges of information are central to that action?" And so if it is let's say the CCA or these public entities that are the owners of these assets, what are they in need of in terms of techniques? What are they — what should they or are they employing?

When I think about some of the projects that each of you have studied in your articles, I think about the degree to which there is an opportunity for other conceptions of the archive to be a much greater part of our work. And so with mass housing that could be the actual community of tenants of these buildings, right, and their knowledge. And in, whether at least the kind of experimental projects from different eras these grassroots networks of these practitioners whether they're housing experts or social workers or whatever. You know, these are also resources that could be deployed as part of our practice of writing this history and retheorizing preservation as repair, as retrofit, as maintenance or so forth.

But I do — I just wanted to put this question of audience in the forefront of our minds as we continue talking because maybe the word is not "audience" but, you know, "user" or something much more pragmatic than audience. But certainly what is the kind of use value we could say of this body of knowledge?

So, that aside, we've got Jessica, Priya, and Joseph.

MORRIS: Fallon, I appreciate where you kind of took that, and I think, you know, occupants might be in one way the audience or the user, but the practitioner in another way is also very much the audience for the discourse.

Considering Susan's position of kind of use and continual use as a way into your provocation about use value and in an economic term non-use value or public good — you know, I would suggest that the audience of practitioners that may have interest in engaging are not only climate scientists, architects, preservationists, but also cultural anthropologists who need to — geographers, the soft side of science, along with engineers who are calculating these performance metrics that steward or that often drive bottom lines in what a true performance improvement or engineered retrofit on a building is.

At the same time, from a preservation practice perspective I would encourage us to — and one of the things that I brought in my perspective of a case study at a district scale — preservation operates not only on the object of the building, but also very effectively at the scale of a district. And I think it's a tool that historic preservation has really leveraged in building out arguments for non-use value, public good from an economic investment perspective, public dollars and what the benefits of those investments are when you draw a boundary around a place that matters today for tomorrow.

So I think what you're suggesting is team building. There is not one approach to practice that can meet these challenges in a singular way. I think it's sort of interdisciplinary and to that point, when you get interdisciplinary about practice you have to reestablish vocabulary, shared vocabulary at the beginning. So the fact that we're talking about what retrofit means and what it does, its use value, is fundamental to identifying how to do this work.

And then from a more technical perspective, there's the types of measurements involved in . . . I'm sorry that Andrew [Potts] is not here because I think the sort of legal side of balancing equations of how you enter into these contracts of performance where we're talking about qualities as opposed to quantifiable ways of saying "We are doing better. We are improving. There is a measurable impact, et cetera."

I would encourage us to think in a lot of ways about impact beyond the sort of singular material use of a building or a brick for that matter, but also then within the sort of social function of the district scale of preservation opportunities and retrofit practices.

JAIN: I believe I'm next in line so I'll just go. That was really good. I mean, I feel like we all have such diverse contributions and as Daniel said, we haven't read each other's papers — but it's kind of interesting to hear where everybody is coming from.

Just to me, you know, the whole retrofit conversation at least as it connects to climate and energy, it's really technically focused I think. It always has been when I was working and even, you know, when you read the kind of histories of technical features, climate-related energy features in buildings.

And I think from listening to all of you, you know, one of the things and in current discourse, you know, the move from "LEED" to "WELL" building standards and things like that . . . here is a social cultural and behavioral dimension to it that is equally if not more important, right?

But I still think that the field or this whole kind of conversation around energy and climate is very forward-looking. At least in my contribution in this issue, you know, something that I think was revealed to me — after a deeper dive into the historical record and this retrospective look is that even the construction of those paradigms that we may see as aspirational or, you know, something that we train people to now do, are themselves so socially and culturally framed that they were not hard technical facts, right?

I mean, Daniel's work, Jiat Hwee Chang's work, and so many others' recent work, you know, has really kind of, I think, brought that to the fore. And talking about I think, Kai, your conversation about repair, retrofit — really kind of insightful in my preservation career has been the fact that even retrofits are so episodic. They are so ephemeral in kind of everything else. We may think of them as, you know, radical, but over time even they kind of have a life. So they kind of follow the continuous story that we're talking about . . .

This whole kind of push about making buildings more resilient, more adaptable — I mean I feel like we list them — again goes back to the human that uses them. We are more adaptable and resilient sometimes than I think we give credit to each other, the people who occupy these buildings and their ability to change with [them] — and I'm talking about things like comfort or, you know, water usage or anything, right, anything difficult things that we sometimes think we have to do. I mean, already people are quite resilient in different parts of the world. So I think that part is also something we should probably take into account.

SIRY: Yeah, I'm writing down as fast as I can. There are so many things I'd like to respond to in what people are saying. But I guess my paper was focused on the Portland Building, which was a Michael Graves post-modernist building in Portland, Oregon. It was a public building in the early 1980s, and it's recently just finished a major transformation.

Three or four points that I think tie from what I was doing to the broader discussion. One is this question of definition of retrofit versus restoration versus reconstruction. There's a great deal of intellectual struggle surrounding appropriate terminology for what is done with a building when there is a major change in its energy systems or its material fabric.

From the point of view of what I was struggling with with the Portland Building, that was never resolved: What would be the appropriate term, what are the appropriate categories, to what degree is a retrofit becoming a reconstruction and is transformative rather than just preservational. Virtually everyone involved with that process I think was struggling with appropriate definitional balance.

The other point that I think relates to what Priya was just saying is that in the case of the Portland Building, it was an office building, but the whole culture of office work changed greatly from the late 1970s, early 1980s to now. So there is an evolution of usage and behavior in different building types that I think as far as I'm hearing connects with what other people are saying, just as there are changes in material systems and ways of valuing and thinking about energy systems.

The biggest problem that I ran into is that—and I think this relates maybe to if I'm following this correctly Yat Shun's paper and Priya's paper is that if you look at one building and try to think about its history from its origins to its transformations, then there are so many different discourses involved in the making of the building.

There's an architectural attitude, but there's also a technical literature that's coming from the side of mechanical engineering. And there's also a client-based contribution to the discussion. It's very hard to recover all those archival records. It's really hard in my experience to understand the dialogue between mechanical engineers and architects.

I mean, there are beautiful architectural archives like at the University of Pennsylvania and Columbia University and places like that. But my dream is that somehow the archive of the mechanical engineers and the other team members who are involved with the creation of these buildings and the retrofitting of these buildings somehow comes back into accessibility, and that dialogue isn't lost and it can be reconstructed and those team members can be users and occupants over time. So to me, there are big challenges in the recoverability of archivally based information for doing energy studies and retrofit that involves energy issues.

AIDOO: There was a moment I'd say in the '90s and definitely in the early 2000s in which history of science and technology was really having its day in architectural history. And we certainly have the remnants of that, and there are people like Carla Yanni and others who kind of still kind of champion that line of intersection and there was certainly some amazing scholarship that came out of that moment.

But I would agree with you, Joseph, and I think, Priya, you mentioned this kind of almost forgetting that happens because of the episodic nature of these actions. They don't—there's a disconnect between that moment in even architectural history, let alone the moments in architectural practice, and there isn't a kind of active strain of recovery of those inquiries even, let alone the actual dialogues, as you put it, Joseph, that they're engaging with.

And so to some extent, I think that can be attributed to the fact that preservation and conservation as fields or disciplines I guess we could say have a pretty decentralized knowledge base. And so you have organizations like APT, Association for Preservation Technology; you've got several conservation organizations across the world, and not—you know, we don't have to the same degree a really centralized—and I think this is a good thing [laughs] I mean, in ways—a centralized, like an international association for people who study this, right?

But what that also means is that there is even more of an impetus on those of us engaging in these inquiries, whether they're case studies or more engrossing examinations, to identify and integrate these different discourses into narratives that are of use to people trying to kind of engage in these recovery practices.

And so in the last half-hour of our conversation in the course of your comments, if you can share with us what strategies you've been employing to kind of make those connections and those reconnections. And I'll leave it there because I believe we've got some more people in the stack now. Susan.

BARBER: Sorry, I think we had a few above.

ROSS: Yeah, I'm not next. I am fourth or fifth.

AIDOO: Oh! My apologies.

BARBER: That's okay. It's an imperfect system. I think Yat Shun is next after Joseph.

KEI: I will keep it very quick. I love Priya's comment about humans are more resilient than you think. I'm writing — I'm studying a pavilion design by Alison and Peter Smithson expanded to a townhouse in London. It's a 7.5 million pound townhouse. There's no heat in that expansion and it's just a single slab concrete box, but it's being maintained because It's an Alison and Peter Smithson thing and very wealthy family can live in that non-heated environment if they choose to do so. So I think there is a lot of this type of disjunction here that we can explore.

And I think going back to Fallon's question about the audience and this relationship of history and science and architecture, I'm sure, Daniel, you know, that my colleague Barnabas [Calder] is writing this rewriting of history of energy. And I think what we find interesting in teaching architectural history through this framework of energy is actually like high school students are very well-equipped with physics and laws of energy and all this basic science, and in my generation we have forgotten about those and we approach those in grad school and make things very complicated.

But when we actually start to have this kind of conversation with them in the first year of study, it's actually a lot easier just because they remember what is an alloy compared to a metal and all these things that somehow as practitioner architects we put aside.

But I think going back to your question, it's whether this is — whether we can keep this going or we will have to revisit it in another generation that is another question.

KAI: Yeah, okay. I want to respond to a few things I guess. But in terms of what Priya said about humans being more resilient than we think, that really resonated for me, too. And I think it fits with Fallon's question as well, or suggestion, which is I think it's valuable to look at other parallel cultural histories that are kind of well outside architecture.

So just as an example, in a different project that I've been working on, I've been looking at seventeenth-century orangeries, so like kind of proto-greenhouses for cultivating citrus fruit in Germany. And it kind of comes out as this hinge moment between — so there's an architectural dimension but it's drawing a lot on literature and kind of iconography to — as a hinge between the kind of classical humanist idea of climatic hegemony I think you could say of the Roman — of Rome being the climatic center of Europe and of the worlds north of the Alps being somehow barbaric. Quite literally, Tacitus, the Senator historian wrote the *Germania,* foundational text for German nationalism — a really interesting text in which he kind of of argues for a coherent idea of these German tribes based on their climate. And because he says that "Why would anyone ever live here?" so since no one would ever willingly move here, they must have—they must be from here. *[laughs]* And that's his analysis of—that's central to his analysis of Germany as a nation.

And so this idea of a kind of inhospitable territory being the same nations such that [they] then purvey their cold airs throughout the global south and purvey an idea of climatized air that's cooler and valorize coolness. That reversal is really interesting. And that shows up more in literature, history, in texts.

So I think that these parallel cultural histories, I think that that's a valuable place to look at the way that these things are—you know, it's not a great word—but constructed, right? I think that really clearly shows the way that climatic ideas are deeply cultural and contingent and historical.

And so, yeah, I think it speaks to what—to again what Priya was saying about resilience because you see very clearly that these norms are cultural and also bodily, right? There are these shared dimensions of those histories. So, yeah. Now I'm kind of trying to advocate for literature or texts, yeah.

AIDOO: That's okay. We appreciate that.

ROSS: I think I might be next. I just want to quickly say that as soon as you started talking about greenhouses, Kai, that I was remembering one of my favorite books from when I studied architecture, which was *The Glasshouse* by John Hix, about the history of the greenhouse. They've come out with a newer edition since, but it is all about that sort of early climate control frenzy. You must have come across it, or you will.

However, I wanted to respond to Joseph's comment about the archives and missing mechanical engineers and link that with the question around strategies. You mentioned APT, Fallon. I have been very active in APT partly through their Technical Committee on Sustainable Preservation ever since it was created in 2003 or so. One of the things that we long worried about was that we didn't have any mechanical engineer members. We really needed, in preservation and sustainability in particular, to have mechanical engineers who were interested in the history of buildings.

This is important from the point of view of telling the histories of buildings, but it is also important because I think one of the things that's been happening with sustainable design as it gets more interesting is that architects, according to Hattie Hartman, who edits the sustainability part of the *Architects' Journal* in the UK, are trying to reclaim architecture from the mechanical engineers. She argues that the structure and fabric and uses of buildings can do what the systems had been doing, and that this is an interesting new development in sustainability. So if you think about it conceptually in terms of retrofits as opposed to within new design, that could also mean having a disregard for systems and just sort of envisioning all this ductwork, as so much scrap. This is potentially an interesting area of historical inquiry and connecting that with the professionals who would be able to support that would be important.

And then I also want to make the connection to the strategies. For me and through my entire career being part of networks like APT have been incredibly important, partly because they're very multidisciplinary, surprisingly so. People tend to think it is all architects or all engineers. There are also people in landscape, in planning, in materials science, and of course engineers. Even just having an association where engineers and architects talk in the same committees that is actually not that common. My awareness of the emergence of different aspects of the discipline have come a lot through being part of an association like that.

So I would encourage that we make sure that we have exchanges happening, you know. Valuing the other that is present in associations that don't have a strict disciplinary focus.

JAIN: I think I'm next. And Susan, I'm glad. I think what I was going to say segues well with what you just said. One of the things that I think you, Fallon, or Daniel, both you and Fallon asked about in the document you sent us was about the marginalized I think aspect of our history, our archives. And I don't think . . . they are marginalized in the sense that—but one of the things that I feel and something that I focused on in my paper, going back on Susan—we have focused on kind of architectural archives, so we sometimes miss the engineers and kind of their archives and their contribution to the project.

But even beyond that, I feel like the manufacturers— especially . . . the people who make things that we put into the buildings, their histories, for example. In this case I was looking at the air-conditioning manufacturers and the technologies that they were providing that would then be employed by architects and engineers. So in a lot of ways, the decisions that we make down the road are already predetermined for us up the line. And I feel like those—maybe delving into those archives and bringing them into the fore of architectural history research would be really good.

And of course, you know, there have been . . . papers on insulation history. I think Daniel, you looked at "Thermopane" and insulated glazing. And, you know, there are those things coming. But I mean, APT has a building heritage technology library which has great catalogues from so many manufacturers, and they're amazing. I mean, I would love to do something like that for India, because I feel like it would be so instructive to look at that and what—how these are getting marketed to the Indian consumer.

But a while back I remember pouring through those to see how these manufacturers were talking about repair for their own products. Were they even thinking about how the things that they were manufacturing and marketing? Were they including information about repair and maintenance of those in their documents?

Anyhow, I feel like they set the stage for us. So focusing on them as the drivers for a lot of architectural production that happens can be really instructive as historians to us.

MORRIS: Priya, it's interesting to think of the various professional role-playing that is required to tackle the future and the past simultaneously in all of these different modalities. I think we, from being sort of an architectural historian or a practitioner or a planner, [take on] the aspect of storytelling in all of these cases, whether it's a sort of retroactive storytelling of mining the archive or project records, or consultancy with all of these different participants in processes to do this work together. And, when there is no central figure as far as leadership is concerned or who is the steward from a disciplinary perspective of this work—I think that's where we're kind of looking to various types or organizations globally but also necessarily locally. That really is where you are able to operate outside of industry in some ways, which is what you're talking about, whether it's from a perspective of being a manufacturer, being a sort of service provider as part of the green industry circular economy type of framework. If we're trying to all consider operating outside of that in order to advance this way of considering—

A bit of a non sequitur. Future anterior, I learned in high school Latin as the thing that will have been, and I think that it's a really important framework for preservation practices and those who are doing this work now . . . engaging climate scientists. That which will have been, we will understand, you know, the history of the recent past. But I think the depth of historical distance or historical depth-of-field is also really essential to continuing to operate in the now, bringing that immediate or past along in order to project a more balanced future is the sort of responsibility . . .

My question is from an operative need to do this work together, where does the leadership come from? Who? Is it the architect? It became the engineer when we were talking about building performance, reclaiming these processes and systems. Does it become a sort of a, you know, social scientists . . . There are cultural activists who demand for preservation activities to happen when other things are changing too fast and pushing back against, you know, development in cities.

So I wonder where — you know, is it at the same time carbon pricing will make retrofitting happen, period. So there is this need to kind of — are we in the middle of now both the sort of past and the future at the present all working together. How we organize to do what is, I think, an essential part of the question, as essential as, you know, what is a retrofit and how do we kind of continue to do that in our present day. Whether it's a building or a societal shift in a functional sense, I think we've got to figure out how to work together to do that.

AIDOO: Laying down tall tasks for us. Kai, I believe you are next. Am I correct? Yes. And then Francesco.

WOOLNER-PRATT: Sorry, me? Is that what you said?

AIDOO: If you don't want to, that's fine. I just — I'm trying to follow the stack here.

KAI: Okay. Yeah, I guess just to respond to — I think I just forgot that I had an earlier stack. *[laughs]* To respond to Jessica, yeah. I think that question of the present, future, past is so crucial and so key. And I think for me, something that came out in this project is the value of remembering other pasts. That sounds like very simple, but I think it's also kind of somehow important when there are such strong —

I mean, I think this is exactly what Daniel Barber is doing, right? — such strong historiography is already in place, and to undo those or to remember other pasts. I think that's the best way to say what I'm trying to get at, that there are other things to remember, and that tracing especially kind of moments of bifurcation I think is really interesting. Because you see ways in which things that we are looking to do now are not — not only not new, but were only abandoned in the past few centuries.

For example — I mean, that's obviously the time scale that I'm interested in is the early modern period as I've already said. But for — so just as one example in my case, the geothermal wells for conditioning the air — to me that's always been a contemporary thing, but you know, when you look at Renaissance garden history, the grotto, all of these very elaborate pneumatic devices that were produced in antiquity and then kind of reengaged in the early modern period. These are very sophisticated technologies.

And I don't know if you can draw a clear line between a Renaissance grotto, especially with the sophisticated pneumatics, and something like a kind of contemporary geo-thermal well at this gas station. And I think remembering those continuities, whether that's through maybe more of a technical history, but also through garden history I think you have to kind of move across disciplines because these things are remembered in different ways in different fields.

But I think tracing those connections makes it so that the future is more proximate. I think imagining different futures can be very historically rooted, kind of in canonical history. And I think that's—to me that's something that's very valuable because it kind of puts things on other terms. It's not so speculative in that case, right? It's a recuperation. And I think there's so much of that to recuperate. As we all know. But I think that is an important framework for me for thinking about that past, present, future conjunction. It's kind of recollecting other pasts as a way of moving forward.

CIANFARANI: I think it's my turn. And just to come back to Kai's point: the importance of remembering other pasts. That this is especially important for scholars that are really focused on, again, public housing and mass housing and how public and mass housing evolved through different decades.

I think that one topic that is emerging through this discussion is the importance of generating new archives, of creating new archives from the mapping, the understanding, the surveys . . .

Because all this transformation, this spontaneous transformation can really help us understand also the different needs of—in terms of energy of those communities through the decades. I imagine, for example, in the survey of post-war mass housing projects in Italy, complex cities are characterized by a very, very low, low, low maintenance. And all that spontaneous transformation, all that spontaneous adaptation, all that adaptation that were focused mainly also on improving, on improving the energy performance of these buildings from the perspective of by the initiative of the community, it's important to map. Because all this information really helped build also an understanding of how the buildings perform.

And in that case, again coming back also to the importance of having teams that understand this transformation, the importance of architects, preservationists, designers to team together with the mechanical engineers and other figures that really help us to understand this transformation, especially from the energy point of view.

KAI: So can I just quickly say I think a better way of saying what I was trying to say is that I think other disciplines—I think there's an archive in other disciplines.

KEI: I just want to add to the other history in thinking about different people of different cultures' attitudes towards history. So I'm originally from Hong Kong, and the colonial legacy is so much well-loved there. Two years ago they were restoring a 19th century prison where they used brick that was sent from Lancaster to Hong Kong as a part of colonial economic policy — to force us to buy the material from the UK. And in order to restore it last year they went back to that factory and purchased the same brick again.

And this is kind of bringing the elephant in the room in preservation: authenticity, right? Where does the question of authenticity play when we are -- like it was so important for so long, but where do we place this question in all this discussion, I guess? Yeah.

AIDOO: Thank you so much for bringing up the "A" word of authenticity here that we have somehow avoided at least explicitly this entire conversation. And then there's the "I" word of "integrity," which is the other kind of elephant in the room that looms very large, particularly in the US context when it comes to these practices, especially because of the way in which they do dovetail with these cultural histories and these economic histories and these different infrastructures that are already in place that either these team — whether they're led by architects or engineers — are reentangling themselves in or disentangling themselves from.

And, you know, I think that what's going to happen shortly — this is the US context — is misremembering of the history of building in Texas — from the kind of manufacturers of the systems and the regulators of the built environment to the, you know, far less considered trade associations and unions even (because, you know, I mean Texas doesn't have unions).

But there are organizations of individuals and companies that engage in and that are invested in the maintenance of a particular way of building and a way of living that will — can be upended by a new discourse on retrofit or the revival of some preexisting kind of discourse of our fields.

And I think there's an opportunity for us all to be not so much kind of zeroed in on what's happening and going to happen with that in Texas, but in all of these places and crises around the world to be engaged in that practice of organizing the conversation, as Jessica was alluding to. That can be engaged in curating the knowledge, perhaps even not allowing people to forget — from whence the bricks came, let's say, or who's arts and craft tradition is being revived in the process of kind of reenacting a particular energy hegemony of the now.

So we are now kind of five minutes before time, and we don't want to take up much more of your time. I know that we initially said that we'd give you all an opportunity to kind of give some closing / concluding remarks, but with five minutes left there's not enough time for you all to do that.

We invite you all to share with via email, any kind of concluding thoughts that you may have, especially as you kind of allow this all to sit and marinate a bit. And I particularly invite you to share with us any references. I know that there were some things that were thrown out in the course of this conversation. But if there is something that comes to mind as part of this conversation at least in your head that you would like us to sort of reference, we can certainly do so in our footnotes and citations, and we want to do that. Daniel.

BARBER: I'll just jump in for a second maybe to just really thank everyone for your time this morning/afternoon/evening. And really appreciate the dynamic of the discussion.

I think what in some ways, for better or worse, we framed as a kind of exploration of some of the challenges and research of this kind of emerging nexus or this increasingly important nexus. I'm coming away from this conversation really with more of a sense of the kind of opportunities and kind of excitement about the future research that all of you will be producing and of course many others around some of these same discussions.

I guess I just want to commend us collectively for opening up a really broad and dynamic set of questions and discussions. And also just to thank you all and if I can, Fallon, on our behalf for your contributions and your work. We know this has been a year like no other, right? And so of course our schedule is not what we imagined it to be and so many other caveats. But just really amazing dedication to the project and we really appreciate everybody's hard work in bringing it all together. It's really been a great experience from my end, from our end. And to have a chance to do this. You know, hopefully we'll find more opportunities to bring this group and maybe some others together to think through some of these ideas in the future.

Fallon, I don't know. Do you have any other—

AIDOO: No. I think that's all. Thank you so much.

MORRIS: I'm used to using a Webex where I can kind of clap hands silently and let everybody know I approve. *[laughter]* It's a pleasure to meet you all.

[Thanks and goodbyes]

[Background conversations]

[END OF RECORDING]

Book Review
Susan M. Ross

Perceptions of Sustainability in Heritage Studies

Marie-Theres Albert, Editor
Berlin: De Gruyter, 2015

Going Beyond: Perceptions of Sustainability in Heritage Studies No. 2

Marie-Theres Albert, Francesco Bandarin, Ana Pereira Roders, Editors
Berlin: Springer 2017

It has been argued that urban retrofitting for decarbonization may paradoxically have a role in propagating a global repair paradigm, whose constant devaluation of the built environment better serves capitalist models of redevelopment than sustainability.[1] Sourcing new materials through mining and harvesting to meet retrofit standards of the West can also be related to the destruction of natural and cultural heritage in the global South. To be meaningful, concepts of sustainability and related goals must address such contradictions and gaps.[2] In 2015 and 2017, two consecutive volumes of the DeGruyter–Springer Heritage Studies series were dedicated to linking perceptions of sustainability in Europe and well beyond. This review responds to these two edited volumes, to help understand how the international focus on sustainability in heritage studies is providing insights into broader ambitions for sustaining the historic environment. Pivotal policy developments that inform this discourse are important to understand, so the review begins with a look at this context.

With the United Nations' 2015 launch of the *2030 Agenda for Sustainable Development,* seventeen wide-ranging sustainable development goals (SDGs) were defined for the entire world.[3] Bridging the pillars of society, economy and ecology, the goals range from eliminating poverty and hunger, to providing affordable and clean energy, clean water and sanitation for all, to protecting all forms of life on land and below water.[4] The so-called developed countries are called upon to repair global problems they have generated through unsustainable development, with their over-consumption and resource inequity constituting global imbalances. Assessing how well retrofitting the built environment meets the United Nations' goals of sustainable development (SD) can thus be a globally responsible way of formulating associated objectives and metrics.

For those focused on the sustainability of buildings and their uses, systems and materials, connections are evident to SD goals for more efficient and equitable use of resources and perhaps also reducing impact on land and water.[5] The reuse

Future Anterior
Volume XVIII, Number 1
Summer 2021

and repair of the built environment has, however not until recently, been recognized as essential to social and cultural sustainability, except as part of conserving the historic cities, settlements and landscapes of value to multiple peoples. SDG no. 11, to "create sustainable cities and communities," is a point of reference for this shift to address protection of both cultural and natural heritage. Building rehabilitation, however, and specifically the discourse on retrofitting for decarbonization and energy efficiency, mainly falls under ecological and economic sustainability. On the other hand, addressing gaps in social and cultural sustainability is important in advancing the integration of urban, landscape and cultural heritage into sustainability paradigms, and localizing the goals in diverse challenging contexts. Arguably these advances in integrating sustainability theory and policy in planning for historic environments are now useful to examine to expand the aims of retrofitting, to address, among its other goals, the objectives of social inclusion, peace and reciprocal respect between diverse cultures, and recognizing Indigenous and human rights.

There is some deserved skepticism about the capacity of those pursuing these SDGs to enact real change within a world that has so little capacity to resolve long-term conflicts.[6] Nonetheless, it is now broadly recognized that there is a need for the conservation of the built environment to become more integrated within the global SD project through sustainable preservation practices. The official discourse of how heritage conservation relates to sustainability has expanded continuously in the last decade, with two key policies marking this growth: the 2011 UNESCO *Recommendations on the Historic Urban Landscape* (HUL), and the 2015 *Policy on the Integration of a Sustainable Development Perspective into the Processes of the World Heritage Convention*. Both of these guidelines reflect a growing conversation about environmental, social, cultural, and economic sustainability in the World Heritage context. World Heritage Convention instruments and activities, as creations of the United Nations, are required to reflect and adapt to the shifting contexts and challenges embedded in other UN-fostered global agreements, notably the UN 2015–2030 SDGs, but also the UN *Sendai Framework for Disaster Risk Reduction* (2015) and the UN *Declaration on the Rights of Indigenous Peoples* (2007).[7] Although World Heritage is a catalyst, part of this global exchange is helping reframe the overall meanings of heritage, the historic environment and conservation.

Emerging within heritage studies, as well as heritage management and planning, studies in World Heritage are now the focus of a number of academic programs and vehicles for exchange, in humanities and social sciences contexts of scholarship and training that are distinct from historic preservation or architectural conservation. The Brandenburg Technical University (BTU) at Cottbuss-Senftenberg in Germany has one such program, and has hosted international meetings to address UN approaches. Its theory, policy, research, and practice-oriented symposia and workshops on heritage and sustainability are documented in the two volumes from the Heritage Studies Series, the first published by DeGruyter in 2015, the second by Springer in 2017.

Marie-Theres Albert, the lead editor for both above-mentioned volumes, is Chair of Intercultural Studies at BTU Cottbuss-Senftenberg and former Chair of Graduate Studies in World Heritage. As she explains in the very useful introduction to the 2015 volume, related workshops were partly intended to provide exposure for young researchers, including by publishing selected papers. The two volumes published closely together reflect an assessment that addressing the gaps between SD discourse in different parts of the world has become increasingly critical. On the one hand, there is recognition that UN policies are only starting points, and the work of integration and localization must move beyond World Heritage sites. On the other hand, too many ideas about sustainability or SD have been proposed by rich countries that have had access to, or used up, most resources. The second volume was therefore based on a larger workshop intended to broaden the perspectives beyond the limits of European ideas on the integration of sustainable development in heritage work. The voices that help illustrate concerns and advances from around the world include those from Argentina, India, Indonesia, Iran, Saudi Arabia, South Africa, Vietnam, and Zambia. If North America was only represented by a US Parks context in the first volume, the second book adds perspectives from Tribes and First Nations, which are expanded by Indigenous perspectives from South America and Africa.

Furthermore, with over forty chapters by nearly fifty authors, the two books together compile a widely varied selection of disciplinary viewpoints, from geography, planning and urban design; and from sociology, geology and information studies; to traditional knowledge keeping, anthropology, and Indigenous studies. As is usual in heritage studies, architecture and other disciplines of built heritage are in the minority of represented perspectives. Authors include not only academics but also many representatives of agencies active at different levels in governance and advocacy, while practitioners tend to be more in heritage planning and management than architectural or engineering practice.

Both books share a similar structure. Each starts with an overview, including helpful brief summaries of each part and chapter. They then provide a combined historical and political review of the context, including relevant principal UN policy documents. This is followed by a series of chapters on the ways that existing paradigms are being challenged or expanded, and then related to theoretical or disciplinary considerations. Throughout both volumes, these initial sections devote a lot of attention to positioning heritage — tangible and intangible — in relation to culture, and to defining cultural and or social sustainability, and how this relates to aspects of sustainable development. While at times this can seem like a theoretical exercise mainly of interest to scholars and policy makers, an underlying message that emerges is how political both heritage and sustainability have become, as public issues that need hard work to reflect diverse and disparate realities of individuals and groups.[8] Finally, more pragmatic questions are addressed through case studies that explore new tools and strategies and their implementation. The 2017 volume expands the exploration of diverse contexts, with a longer focus on Indigenous heritage, and includes two sections more focused on implementation or practice. Given the diversity and scope of the books, this review provides insights from selected chapters, making connections to the thematic "retrofit" issue.

A limited number of examples in the first volume reference built heritage per se. The chapter by Giovanni Boccardi stands out for its pragmatic call for breaking down boundaries between heritage and the broader building stock and urban environment as part of an approach of adapting to — and not only mitigating against — changing social and environmental contexts, in order to embrace new objectives and priorities while nurturing continuity. The HUL approach has been particularly helpful for shifting the emphasis away from official heritage to see all built fabric, designed and vernacular, as a resource. The second volume includes more concrete examples of how new ideas, paradigms and practices can impact on material heritage. Importantly however, both books firmly anchor discussion of architectural heritage in a broader concept of urban heritage, and connected urban conservation strategies. They also make significant connections to cultural landscape approaches and to planning for historic settlements. These shifts in scale from building or site to city and region are very important to comprehend the political potential of the discourse.

Attention to intangible heritage is also key to this expanded view, with understanding that the continuity in patterns of use is meaningful, not just in a single site, but in terms of entire economies, moving for example from agriculture to tourism. Existing built fabric is seen as much more than spaces, forms, materials and details that can be manipulated to meet the objectives of environmental and economic sustainability. While looking beyond individual buildings and projects also highlights the role of historic public space as a context for social sustainability, broader landscape or planning approaches also help reframe strategies for adaptation both physical and social resilience. Urban historic districts and neighborhoods, with mixed uses and infrastructure that have already been adapted over time, are a resource for urban resilience. Resilience seen like this is to be addressed as much through careful design and construction, as appropriate materials, adapted use and integrated planning.[9]

A number of themes emerge that provide a useful counterpoint to the usual concerns of sustainable retrofits of energy and resource efficiency, or decarbonization. This includes recognizing resource scarcity as a problem of injustice; reporting on post disaster reconstruction that engages affected communities; modeling seismic retrofits that reflect understandings of local materials and building capacity; planning for culturally sensitive adaptations to climate change; testing newer tools like Heritage Impact Assessments (HIA) as processes for engaging and communication between experts and stakeholders.[10] The broader scale at which built heritage is conceptualized in this series is important in understanding the importance given to HIA, which is most useful in contexts of infill and development in a landscape context.

The expanded Indigenous perspectives amplify the importance of sustainability strategies that consider intangible heritage and cultural landscape approaches. Perhaps most helpful in bridging social, cultural and ecological sustainability for architectural heritage is Claudia Lozano's exploration of the role of the Andean landscape as home, site, climate and material source for multiple Indigenous, colonial and International groups. Diverse strategies for sustainable development need to recognize and be informed by emotional and ethical dimensions of Indigenous approaches to taking responsibility for the way they have used what the planet has provided.[11]

Strategies for the built environment are also identified in chapters that focus more on social and cultural sustainability to address development pressures, such as the impacts of mass tourism on historic landscapes and settlements, including from major infrastructure, highway and bridge construction. This includes designing criteria for culturally appropriate accommodation and services; recognizing the importance of local government-led heritage planning and grassroots led projects for redevelopment; or addressing capacity gaps in skills in building materials repair workshops from school level up. In every case, the examples — from contexts as diverse as Mecca in Saudi Arabia, Shanghai in China, and Mpophomeni in South Africa — help reframe urban development in valued places as distinct human development struggles, concerned with aspects of spirituality, local identity, or social cohesion.[12]

Despite the expansive nature of the books, some omitted themes of critical importance to note might include how changing climates challenge our understandings of heritage's past and future; how to better engage with nonhuman perspectives on material heritages; and, possibly not the least, the sustainability of the ideas and processes of World Heritage itself. Furthermore, although the expansion beyond architecture is refreshing, with much of the world's built-environment legacy comprising of twentieth-century modernist urban planning, engineering and construction methods, perspectives from heritage planning in modern cities challenge any focus on protecting traditional settlements from modernization. The urban/rural divide is a construct that denies their interrelationship, especially when the cities and rural areas are continents apart. Furthermore, in this urban planet, grappling with increased density is an ongoing concern that a heritage assessment of twentieth-century planning systems and forms can help understand. The urban heritage and sustainability discourse has however been addressed in other equally ambitious publications.[13] Otherwise, given the rich cultural diversity embedded in the contents, the limited number of images seems a shame. The thematically organized reference lists provide very useful resources for tracking the policy developments of the last decade. Both books are also available as e-books, which makes them useful for teaching.

Neither of these volumes is intended to provide a coherent single view, but rather reveal multiple viewpoints. In that sense the two parts of *Perceptions of Sustainability in Heritage Studies* serve as very effective guides to multiple concerns that should reframe our objectives for retrofitting buildings as part of the larger built environment. In planning repair and reuse, greater consideration is needed of: reducing immediate and longer terms impacts of resource extraction on ecosystems and peoples; enabling sustainable uses and protecting biocultural diversity and depleting resources, while managing scarcity and inequity of access; ensuring that we are considering culturally-aware adaptation to climate change as much as mitigation of our impacts; and fostering both social and physical resilience as risk preparedness for climate-related and other potential disasters. Most critically, those promoting the retrofit of the built environment should also look at how our projects can help empower those whose lands have been taken, whose voices have been silenced, whose traditions are being erased, and whose poverty is not helped by developments exclusively planned by others. These are tall orders for any single project, which is why a broader approach to retrofitting is needed.

Works like these that are more part of heritage management and planning studies provide important theoretical context but also explain the usefulness of broader tools like mapping and HIAs, and as such, more strategic approaches to conserving the built environment.

Biography

Susan Ross is an architect licensed in Quebec, a former senior conservation architect in the Canadian government, and now associate professor at the School of Indigenous and Canadian Studies at Carleton University, with cross appointment to the Azrieli School of Architecture and Urbanism. Her publications include: the special issue on Heritage and Waste Values of the *Journal of Cultural Heritage Management and Sustainable Development* (2020), which she co-edited with Victoria Angel; articles published in the *Journal of Architectural Conservation, The Historic Environment: Policy and Practice, APT Bulletin, IA,* and *Docomomo International*; as well as book chapters on urban water reservoirs, modern wood conservation, and 1930s apartment buildings. She is also co-chair of the National Roundtable on Heritage Education, and a member of the College of Fellows of the Association for Preservation Technology.

Notes

[1] Sarah Knuth, "Cities and Planetary Repair: The Problem with Climate Retrofitting," *Environment and Planning A* 51, no. 2 (2019): 487–504, https://doi.org/10.1177/0308518X18793973.

[2] Marie-Theres Albert, ed., *Perceptions of Sustainability in Heritage Studies* (Berlin: De Gruyter, 2015), 17.

[3] United Nations, 2015, *Transforming our World: The 2030 Agenda for Sustainable Development,* https://sdgs.un.org/2030agenda.

[4] See, for example, Sustainable Development Goals nos. 1, 2, 6, 7, 11, 14, and 15 in United Nations, 2015.

[5] Sustainable Development Goals nos. 8, 14, and 15.

[6] William Logan, "Heritage, Sustainable Development and the Achievement of Peace and Security in our World: Ambitions and Constraints," in *World Heritage and Sustainable Development: New Directions in World Heritage Management,* ed. Peter Billie Larsen and William Logan (New York/Abingdon: Routledge, 2018), 148.

[7] UNESCO/World Heritage State Parties, 2015, *Policy for the integration of sustainable development perspectives into the processes of the World Heritage Convention,* https://whc.unesco.org/en/sustainabledevelopment/.

[8] Samantha Lutz and Gertraud Koch, "Sustainability, Sustainable Development, and Culture: Diverging Concepts and Practices in European Heritage Work," in *Going Beyond: Perceptions of Sustainability in Heritage Studies 2,* ed. Marie-Theres Albert, Francesco Bandarin, Ana Pereira Roders (Berlin: Springer 2017), 73.

[9] Matthias Ripp and Andrew H. Lukat, "From Obstacle to Resource: How Built Cultural Heritage Can Contribute to Resilient Cities," in Albert et al., eds., *Going Beyond,* 104.

[10] See Marie-Theres Albert, "Mission and Vision of Sustainability Discourses in Heritage Studies," in Albert, ed., *Perceptions of Sustainability,* 11–20; Simone Sandholz, "Shaken Cityscapes: Tangible and Intangible Urban Heritage in Kathmandu, Nepal and Yogyakarta, Indonesia," 161–74; Mohammad Ravankhah et al., "Integration of Cultural Heritage into Disaster Risk Management: Challenges and Opportunities for Increased Disaster Resilience," 307–22; Ripp and Lukat, "From Obstacle to Resource," 99–114, in Albert et al., eds., *Going Beyond*; and Michael Kloos, "Heritage Impact Assessments as a Tool to Open Up Perspectives for Sustainability: Three Case Studies," in Albert, ed., *Perceptions of Sustainability,* 215–27.

[11] Claudia Lozano, "Feeling Responsible for the Good Life on Earth: The Construction of Social Spaces and Sustainability in the Andes" in Albert et al., eds., *Going Beyond,* 203.

[12] See Sara Anas Serafi and Kalliopi Fouseki, "Heritage Conservation and Sustainable Development in Sacred Places: Towards a New Approach," in Albert et al., eds., *Going Beyond,* 115–32; Ron van Oers, "Cultural Heritage Management and Sustainability," in Albert, ed., *Perceptions of Sustainability,* 189–202 ; and Debbie Whelan, "Aspects of Social Imperative: The Sustainable Historic Environment in the Developing World," in *Going Beyond,* Albert et al., *Going Beyond,* 175–88.

[13] See, for example, Sophia Labadi and William Logan, eds., *Urban Heritage, Development: International Frameworks, National and Local Governance* (New York: Routledge, 2015).

Book Review
Douglas R. Appler

Case Studies in Retrofitting Suburbia: Urban Design Strategies for Urgent Challenges

June Williamson and Ellen Dunham-Jones
John Wiley & Sons, Inc., 2021

June Williamson and Ellen Dunham-Jones have been advocates for reimagining suburbia at least since the 2009 publication of their first co-authored book, *Retrofitting Suburbia*. That book quickly became a standard in the field of urban design because it so clearly addressed a glaring need. It documented how existing suburban form could be made more urban, more sustainable, and more vital. *Retrofitting Suburbia* enjoyed a revision in 2011, and the book presently under review, *Case Studies in Retrofitting Suburbia,* represents a logical continuation of those earlier works. As Williamson and Dunham-Jones indicate in their introduction, it is meant to be a sequel, not a revision. At this point, the case no longer needs to be exhaustively made that the suburban landscape presents challenges that can be addressed through more thoughtful urban design. But things do change, even in suburbia. This book is a successful effort to respond to those changes, and it puts a finer point on the issues facing suburbia today.

The first of the book's two chapters is devoted to identifying the most significant design challenges that the authors see as facing suburbia. The second chapter includes thirty-two case studies that approach at least one of the challenges introduced in the first chapter, though most of the case studies address two or more. The case studies are typically five to six pages in length, and are richly illustrated with color photographs, renderings, and maps. The ample footnotes include sources and supplementary information that students and other researchers will appreciate.

The six challenges presented by the authors help to situate the book within various planning and design discourses, while also serving as an organizational device. The challenges featured are: disrupt automobile dependence; improve public health; support an aging population; leverage social capital for equity; compete for jobs; and add water and energy resilience. While the challenges themselves are not necessarily new, in many ways they manifest themselves differently in the suburbia of 2021 than they did in the suburbia of the late twentieth century, or even suburbia at the time of their first publication in 2009. Disrupting automobile dependence has long been a goal of New Urbanists and public health advocates, for example, but no one writing in 2009 was thinking about the consequences of

Future Anterior
Volume XVIII, Number 1
Summer 2021

ride-sharing apps, and driverless cars were even more experimental than they are today. Other forces that have influenced the changes required of suburbia since this series first began include the rising purchasing power and changing lifestyle preferences of the Millennial workforce, the consequences of the Great Recession (though the first waves of that event did shape the 2011 revision), greater awareness of the relationship between racial inequality and the built environment, and the increasingly obvious pressures of climate change.

The case studies that the authors use to explore how suburbia can be retrofitted in response to these challenges are geographically diverse, with Georgia, California, Texas, and the DC Metro area receiving similar levels of attention. The Upper Midwest, Southern New England, seven other states, and the Province of Quebec are also represented.

The case studies range in scale from less than an acre in East Greenwich, Rhode Island, to a four-mile stretch of the Rockville Pike in Montgomery County, Maryland. Without getting into the specifics of the case studies, for which one should certainly buy a copy of the book, they highlight the redevelopments, re-inhabitations, and re-greenings (the authors' terms) of a variety of existing suburban forms.

From an instructional perspective, the book will be very useful. The case studies are current, the indexing system used makes it a simple process to see why the given case studies are being highlighted, as well as to find other, related cases. Students will have no trouble determining which of the book's case studies align with their interests.

From a preservationist's perspective, the idea of thirty-two case studies promising to significantly alter suburban landscapes identified as functionally obsolete may provoke a certain amount of heartburn. What one generation judges to be without value is what the next fights most valiantly to save or re-create (see generally: small-town Main Streets; dense, walkable urban neighborhoods; Victorian residential architecture; electric streetcars, etc.). It is always worthwhile to proceed with caution when making permanent interventions in the built environment. Despite its many well-known faults, suburbia contains many historically and architecturally significant sites. How could it not? It has been the dominant urban form in the United States and Canada for at least fifty years and was a major cultural driver for decades before that. Several of the case studies do include properties that have been formally recognized as historic, and that received the requisite level of consideration as a result. The Eero Saarinen and Hideo Sasaki–designed Bell Labs campus in Holmdel, New Jersey, is one example, and the Mies van der Rohe–designed gas station in Verdun, Quebec (the subject of Kai Woolner-Pratt's essay in this issue of Future Anterior), is another. With that said, the pieces of suburbia contained within this volume do not generally appear to have a great deal of preservation value in the traditional sense. Most of the case studies examine strip malls, parking lots, big-box stores, street intersections, and even stormwater facilities. These sites are not likely to appear on any organization's "most threatened" list, even if some are more than fifty years old.

Although most of the case studies represent unfamiliar territory for preservationists, the work profiled often achieves goals that are at least "preservation adjacent." This is one of the reasons why this book would be of benefit to many in the preservation community. Turning a former Cleveland, Ohio, Big Lots store into a community recreation center, for example, keeps building materials out of the landfill and helps to promote physical activity. In Peachtree Corners, in Gwinnett County, Georgia, the development of a new walkable town center, a new bike trail network, and the introduction of apartments inside an aging five-hundred-acre office park helped to keep existing facilities from becoming vacant and created recreational amenities that could be enjoyed by both workers and residents within the former office park. The One Hundred Oaks Mall in Nashville, Tennessee, was converted to Vanderbilt Health at One Hundred Oaks—retaining the late 1960s-era shopping mall's footprint, but with the different clinical groups inserted in the former retail spaces. This, again, kept the old mall's building materials out of the landfill and met a community need—something preservationists do on a regular basis. Cultivating a "something other than total clearance" mindset among public officials, developers, and local residents can only encourage a more thoughtful relationship with the existing built environment. From a slightly less altruistic perspective this may also make arguments about the environmental benefits of rehabilitation, or walkability, or the value of making history visible, more palatable when preservationists advocate for the protection and reuse of threatened historic sites.

In short, Case Studies in Retrofitting Suburbia is a successful, useful, and timely book. It brings the authors' interests into the present with salient observations about the challenges facing the suburbs, and it provides ideas for how to address those issues. It creates a bridge to the preservation community by highlighting successful examples of how the nonhistoric suburban environment might be treated when guided by many of the same principles that typically drive preservation projects. It should be a welcome addition to the library of urban designers, planners, preservationists, students, and faculty seeking to engage with the existing suburban environment.

Biography

Douglas Appler is Associate Professor, Chair, and Director of Graduate Studies in the Department of Historic Preservation at the University of Kentucky. Appler's research explores innovation in the treatment of historic resources through public policy, with an emphasis on the actions of local government. Appler holds a PhD in City and Regional Planning from Cornell University, a Master's in Urban and Regional Planning from Virginia Tech, and a Bachelor of Arts in History and Political Science, also from Virginia Tech. He is a former practicing city planner and is a member of the American Institute of Certified Planners (AICP).

Carolina I

Carolina III

Carolina IV

Camuy II

Guayama I

Guayama II

Biography
David Hartt creates work that unpacks the social, cultural, and economic complexities of his various subjects. He explores how historic ideas and ideals persist or transform over time. Hartt's work is included in the collections of the Museum of Modern Art, New York; The Studio Museum in Harlem, New York; Whitney Museum of American Art, New York; Art Institute of Chicago; Museum of Contemporary Art, Chicago; The J. Paul Getty Museum, Los Angeles; the Museum of Contemporary Photography, Chicago; Henry Art Gallery, Seattle; Nasher Museum of Art, Durham, NC; National Gallery of Canada, Ottawa; and Stedelijk Museum, Amsterdam, among others. Born in Montréal in 1967, Hartt lives and works in Philadelphia where he is Assistant Professor in the Department of Fine Arts at the University of Pennsylvania.

Acknowledgments
The production of this work was funded by the Graham Foundation for Advanced Studies in the Fine Arts with additional generous support from Oakville Galleries. All images courtesy of the artist, Corbett vs. Dempsey, David Nolan Gallery, New York, and Galerie Thomas Schulte.

Submission Guidelines

Future Anterior is a peer reviewed (refereed) journal that approaches the field of historic preservation from a position of critical inquiry. A comparatively recent field of professional study, preservation often escapes direct academic challenges of its motives, goals, forms of practice and results. Future Anterior seeks contributions that ask these difficult questions from philosophical, theoretical, and critical perspectives.

Articles should be no more than 4,000 words (excluding footnotes), with up to seven illustrations. It is the responsibility of the author to secure permissions for image use and pay any reproduction fees. A brief abstract (200 words) and author biography (around 100 words), and a list of numbered image captions with credits must accompany the text. Acceptance or rejection of submissions is at the discretion of the Editorial Staff. Please do not send original materials, as submissions will not be returned.

Formatting Text: All text files should be saved as Microsoft Word or RTF format. Text and citations must be formatted in accordance with the *Chicago Manual of Style,* 15th Edition. All articles must be submitted in English, and spelling should follow American convention.

Formatting Illustrations: Images should be sent as TIFF files with a resolution of at least 300 dpi at 8" by 9" print size. Figures should be numbered clearly in the text, after the paragraph in which they are referenced. Image captions and credits must be included with submissions.

Checklist of documents required for submission:

__ Abstract (200 words)
__ Manuscript (4000 words)
__ Illustrations (7)
__ Captions for Illustrations
__ Illustration Copyright information
__ Author biography (100 words)

All submissions must be submitted electronically, via email to Future.Anterior.Journal@gmail.com

Questions about submissions can be sent to the above email address or mailed to:

Jorge Otero-Pailos
Editor, *Future Anterior*
GSAPP
400 Avery Hall
1172 Amsterdam Ave
Columbia University
New York, NY 10027

https://www.arch.columbia.edu/future-anterior

SUBSCRIBE TO FUTURE ANTERIOR

Future Anterior is published twice per year, in summer and winter. Prepayment is required.

PRINT EDITION
Subscription Rates:
- Individuals: $32.50
- Institutions: $75.50
- Outside the U.S.: add $5.00 for each year's subscription.

To subscribe to the print edition of *Future Anterior,* please visit the University of Minnesota Press website at http://www.upress.umn.edu or complete and submit this form with your payment.

DIGITAL EDITION
Institutions may subscribe to the digital edition of *Future Anterior* through JSTOR at http://jstor.org.

PAYMENT | Two convenient ways to pay:

☐ Check enclosed, made payable to University of Minnesota Press. (Checks must be drawn on a U.S. bank in U.S. funds.)

☐ Mastercard / VISA (please circle):

No. _____ Exp. Date _____

Signature _____

ADDRESS | Mail my subscription to:

Name _____

Address _____

_____

Daytime phone _____

E-mail address _____

Mail orders to:
Journals Department
University of Minnesota
    Press
111 Third Avenue South,
Suite 290
Minneapolis, MN 55401-
    2520

Fax subscription orders to:
612-627-1980

Back issues may be ordered from the University of Minnesota Press website at http://www.upress.umn.edu/.

Become a *Future Anterior* Sponsor

Future Anterior is funded by grants and distributed in the spirit of making knowledge available to everyone. Donations are critical to helping us accomplish this mission. If you would like to become a sponsor, please fill out this page and mail it, with a check payable to Columbia University, to:

Future Anterior
Graduate School of Architecture, Planning, and Preservation
400 Avery Hall
1172 Amsterdam Avenue
Columbia University
New York, NY 10027

Or contribute by credit card online at:
https://arch.givenow.columbia.edu/#

All sponsors will be recognized in each issue of *Future Anterior* and receive a one-year subscription to the journal.

Please check the appropriate sponsorship level:

Individual Sponsor: ❑ begins at $100/year
Institutional Sponsor: ❑ begins at $500/year
Patron: ❑ begins at $1000/year

Name*: _____

Address: _____

_____

City: _____

State: _____   Zip: _____

Country: _____

Institution/Office: _____

E-mail:_____
*please provide your name exactly as you would like it to appear in print

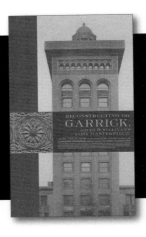
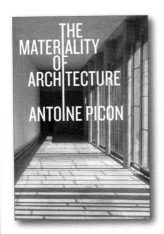